Written in Stone
A MODERN HISTORY OF CURLING

BRIAN CHICK

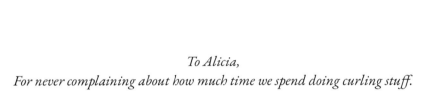

To Alicia,
For never complaining about how much time we spend doing curling stuff.

CONTENTS

ACKNOWLEDGMENTS

I'd like to thank everybody who made this project possible. My parents for starting me in this sport, and for stressing the importance of grammar. My wife, who has seemingly endless patience for hanging out at curling clubs and cold arenas. My editors Al, George, and Mom for making sure I cross all my Ts and dot my lowercase Js. Jim Waite for opening all sorts of doors in this sport for young coaches and aspiring curlers. All the people who helped me track down some of the interview subjects.

Finally, and especially, a sincere thank you to all 48 of the people interviewed for this book. Thank you for taking the time, sharing your stories, and lending your voice to this project.

Al Hackner	Ian Tetley	Mark Nichols
Amy Nixon	Jan Betker	Mike Harris
Ben Hebert	Jeff Stoughton	Mike McEwen
Brad Gushue	Jenn Hanna	Paul Boutilier
Brad Jacobs	Jill Officer	Paul Savage
Cathy Overton-Clapham	Joan McCusker	Paul Webster
Chad McMullan	John Epping	Rachel Homan
Chelsea Carey	John Morris	Randy Ferbey
Cheryl Bernard	Kaitlyn Lawes	Reid Carruthers
Colleen Jones	Kelley Law	Richard Hart
Craig Savill	Kerry Burtnyk	Rick Lang
Don Bartlett	Kevin Albrecht	Scott Pfeifer
Earle Morris	Kevin Koe	Shannon Kleibrink
George Karrys	Kevin Martin	Sherry Middaugh
Gerry Geurts	Lisa Weagle	Warren Hansen
Glenn Howard	Lori Olson-Johns	Wayne Middaugh

FOREWORD
BY REID CARRUTHERS

I love curling; some might say too much. A friend of mine decided that I was a little too passionate for the sport for his liking. I guess that might be why he has since left the game and why I have soldiered on. It's probably why I left my job as teacher to pursue the sport full-time. It's why I'm more motivated than ever to play at the highest level, despite the fact that I've already won a Brier, a World Championship, and a Mixed Doubles Canadian Championship. What can I say? I love this sport.

I've heard it referred to as a cult. Once you start curling, and you drink that Kool-Aid, you're hooked, and it takes over your life. I don't think it's a cult, but it's certainly a lifestyle, a not-so-secret society, a borderline addiction. Maybe we should go to support group meetings. "My name is Reid Carruthers and I curl out of Winnipeg, Manitoba. I'm a card-carrying member of the 'I love curling' team."

I am truly honoured to introduce this book for my good friend Brian Chick. Just so you know, Brian would be the leader, or at least a high-ranking official, of the aforementioned cult. Let's just say he'd be a captain of the team, and a proud member of our support group.

I met Brian at the Trillium Curling Camp in Kitchener-Waterloo, Ont., in the summer of 2012. I had heard amazing things about the camp courtesy of my good friend Kaitlyn Lawes. Jim Waite ran the camp, and was responsible for rooming arrangements for the instructors. To be honest, I really didn't know what I was in for when I found out I'd be rooming with Mr. Chick. I think I'd met him once briefly, and recalled that he had something to do with Johnny "The Hammer" Chow, but that was about it. One adult beverage later and we were best friends.

Over the course of three Trillium camps, and the first three editions of my own version, Camp Carruthers in Winnipeg, I have been privileged to witness Brian in his element, teaching curling. He is a great player, but an even better coach. Anyone that is willing to sacrifice a portion of their precious summer months to teach curling is a friend of mine, and I believe Brian would be a friend regardless.

When Brian mentioned to me that he had planned to write a book about curling, I was very intrigued. Part of the reason I love curling is because of the stories. I have been very fortunate to be part of some successful curling teams and play with some of the legends of the sport: Jeff Stoughton, Jon Mead, Steve Gould, Mark Nichols, and now some guy named Mike McEwen. Each guy I've played with or against has a thousand stories of a shot, a game, a fight, a party, a bonspiel. Some of my fondest memories were of the times off the ice hearing about the "good old days" from some of the game's greats.

And that's what makes this book so enjoyable. It's like you've been invited to the table with dozens of the biggest names in the sport; to have a cold one, and listen to first-person accounts of Briers, Scotties, Olympics, Slams and more. The game has changed over the years and "Written in Stone" helps explain how, mainly through the voices of the players who were there, myself included.

So grab a drink, and pull up a chair. You're about to hear a lot of good stories from some curling legends.

Curlingly,
Reid Carruthers

INTRODUCTION

I started curling in the early 1980s. That is to say... as a preschooler. I pushed my first chunks of granite around the Dalewood Golf and Curling Club in Port Hope, Ont., before I made it to kindergarten. As the youngest of four children in a very active family, curling was just one of the ways we passed the time, but as the years went on it became a bigger and bigger part of my life as hockey, basketball, and baseball fell by the wayside.

As I entered my teenage years, Russ Howard, Jeff Stoughton, and Kevin Martin were at the top of the game, while players like Al Hackner and Ed Werenich were still revered as recent champions. Even though my family had moved to upstate New York by this time, we'd still watch the Labatt Brier and the McCain's TSN Skins game thanks to recorded broadcasts sent down on VHS tapes.

When I was in high school, Wayne Middaugh was cementing himself as one of the greatest shooters of all time, and my team did whatever we could to emulate him. We competed at three U.S. Junior National Championships before most of us turned 18, and then we all moved our separate ways for university. I headed back north, to study journalism at Toronto's Ryerson University.

7

Prior to graduating high school, I had attended the Trillium Curling Camp in Peterborough, Ont. Top coaches from across Canada and around the world came to teach 96 campers what it takes to be a top-tier curler. My first coach at camp was Keith Wendorf, then the national coach for Germany, and now a recently retired bigwig for the World Curling Federation. The minute my parents picked me up at the end of the week, I begged them to let me return the following year, and Bob and Ann (both active curlers, coaches, and all-around awesome folks) were happy to oblige.

The next year, camp director Jim Waite had just returned from the 1998 Olympic Winter Games in Nagano, Japan where he had been the head coach for the Canadian men's team. The camp had moved to Guelph, Ont., and the first edition of Jim's annual Olympic slideshow (yes, I think there were still actual slides at that point) was a hit, and suddenly a huge inspiration to the assembled campers and staff.

The next year I was too old to be a camper at Trillium, but I was accepted back as an "assistant," the coaches-in-training who also act as the camp counsellors. I was assigned to work with Kirsten Harmark (who later became Kirsten Wall, and went on to play with Sherry Middaugh at two Scotties Tournament of Hearts, and with Jennifer Jones as an alternate at the 2014 Olympics) and Atina Ford (who had just returned from Nagano as the alternate for Canada's gold-medal women's team). Atina passed around her gold medal, the first of many I've been privileged to hold.

While I wouldn't have said so at the time, holding that medal was probably the seed that eventually grew into a lifelong career in curling. Guidance from Jim Waite, Keith Wendorf, and other members of the Trillium family helped nurture the passion and provide opportunities to grow in the sport. Meanwhile, I was picked up by a curling team in Toronto, and toured the province, learning the men's game.

It's almost 20 years later and I still coach at Trillium and similar camps across Canada and around the world. In the last decade, I've instructed at camps in

Germany, taught courses in Latvia, coached a team to a Swiss championship, worked on the Olympic broadcasts in Russia, and coached at world championships in Spain, Denmark, South Korea and oddly, again, Latvia. In the year and a half it took to write this book, I also made another trip to Korea, having acted as the media attaché for the Canadian Wheelchair Curling Team for the 2018 Paralympic Games.

In the meantime, I've also worked with/for Curling Canada, the World Curling Federation, Curl Atlantic, the Ontario Curling Association/CurlON, Hot Shots Curling Camps, Northern Ontario Curling Association, the Grand Slam of Curling, CurlingZone, The Curling News, Rock Solid Productions, Rocks & Rings, and too many curling clubs to count. All the while, I was still a moderately competitive player, too! I reached a few provincial championships, played on the cash tour, and still play a couple of nights a week at the Royals in Toronto, while working full-time at the Toronto Cricket, Skating, and Curling Club.

Over the years, I've been extremely lucky to meet Olympians, Canadian champions, Grand Slam teams, and top-level coaches. I've had the benefit of hearing their stories, either in formal presentations, coaching seminars or, usually, over a few beers at the local curling rink.

I asked them to help document the modern history of our sport in Canada...

CHAPTER 1:
THE EIGHTIES

When tackling history, one needs a place to start. For lack of a better choice, we'll pick this story up at the 1985 Labatt Brier in Moncton, New Brunswick. The Brier had, until 1979, been sponsored by a tobacco company. The new sponsor, Labatt Breweries, didn't exactly catapult the sport into an image of athletic perfection. It was still strictly played by amateurs; guys with day jobs who were also really good at the game.

Although I was only four years old at the time, the 1985 Brier featured the first curling highlight I'd ever remember. It was seared into my brain, thanks to Doug Maxwell's "ABCs of Curling" video. By the time I was ten or eleven, I'd seen that video dozens of times. My parents were both coaches so they were frequently involved with curling club open houses and instructional events, where that grainy VHS tape played on repeat.

After Mr. Maxwell had described the stones, the sweeping, and the strategy, he shows one of the greatest shots ever thrown, which, at the time of the video, was relatively new.

But first, let's set the scene...

AL HACKNER (Two-time Brier and World champion): We were used to some of the teams but not all them, and as the week progressed, it was hit and miss. We were playing well, then playing not well. And we finished the round robin at 7-4. But then the this other guy named Pat Ryan... he was 11-0! So, the rest of the field was all heavily bunched up at 6-5, so we had to win all these tiebreakers before we played Eugene Hritzuk. We won a tough game against him, and that set us up the final game against the undefeated Ryan...They were in control all game, the way they controlled all week, up until the last end.

RICK LANG (Two-time Brier and World champion): The Brier ice was always dead straight and we'd get rocks from a local club. Everything was prone to something like what Pat Ryan came up with... like, "Let's just get the hammer in the first end and peel out." And he shows up to that Brier and pulls it off. He doesn't leave any rocks in play. We'd throw guard after guard, and they'd just peel, peel, peel. Fans would show up for the first five ends, and after five ends, there would be a mad rush to the Brier Patch. It was incredible, we'd sit there and watch. If there were 6,000 people, all of a sudden, 5,000 would get up and leave for the Patch. I would have left myself. It was dead boring, awful to watch.

There were fans of that game. They'd say "That's skill, you're pitching a no-hitter. Can you believe what they're doing?" We were the opposite though, maybe because we didn't have that skill to do it, but we were saying "This is just bullshit." It was disinteresting to us. It was terrible.

We get to the 10th end, down two. One deuce, one steal, and we win the Brier! What the heck? We had a good chuckle about it, because it seemed so hopeless at the time.

It may have seemed especially hopeless because The Ryan Express, as they were known, hadn't given up a steal all week. Meanwhile, the Ice Man, Al Hackner needed some rocks in play to generate two points... which was also rare against Ryan's Alberta squad.

AL HACKNER: We got a miss on the guard early in the end, and I think we tried to go around it, and when they hit they rolled to the back twelve, and then we tried to go around the guard again, and end up - I think we came short on that one. It stopped slightly in front of the house and then they tried to get rid of the guard again. I think they missed it.

RICK LANG: The end develops and we actually get a corner guard. They missed two shots. And our eyes got wide and we were suddenly saying "Holy smokes, we got a chance here!" But there was zero curl in the ice, so generating a deuce, even with guards, was still difficult.

AL HACKNER: So we actually had two missed guards in the end I believe... You know, everybody said that I made a pretty good shot with my last one, but my first one was pretty good too... I split that guard into the house to lie first and third.

RICK LANG: So Al actually had to make the split on his first one, which was a hell of a shot... especially in those days, given the conditions.

Hackner's first shot split Lang's guard into the edge of the 12-foot ring while the shooter rolled into the top 12. Alberta's Pat Ryan opts to play the hit off the outside rock and roll behind the remaining guard. He makes it nearly perfectly.

CBC announcer Don Duguid shouts "What a curling shot! He's got his hands in the air because I think he realized he just won the Canadian championship because Al Hackner cannot get at that rock to make the double!"

EARLE MORRIS (Three-time Brier participant, two-time Canadian champion coach): The thing that stuck out in my mind was that Pat Ryan was absolutely convinced he'd won it. Arms up in the air.

AL HACKNER: I didn't see him do that until I saw the film after. What I did see was this woman reporter run out onto the sheet and she's following him at that point. Pat Ryan was walking down the ice, he's almost to the hogline, she's at the middle of the rink, in the middle of the ice right down the middle and she's running down the ice, taking photographs. She's walking down the ice! What is that reporter doing on the ice? She's walking all over my line. She's tracking junk all down that line.

IAN TETLEY (Three-time Brier and World champion): First thing was, I was screaming! If you watch the video, there's a woman - a photographer - who thought the game was over and ran out on the ice, so I was screaming at her to get off the ice because the game wasn't over.

You kinda thought the game *was* over, but then you get down to the hack and you see Ricky motioning "How much can you see?" and we show him an inch or whatever.

AL HACKNER: But from where we stood, we can see an inch of it. An inch, we had an inch and that was too much. We had to hit like half an inch. So, it was sticking out enough to make the shot. I mean the ice was running pretty straight, which made it easier to read. We just put the broom down and tried not to hit the guard.

EARLE MORRIS: Ryan was a very confident player, and that's how he expressed himself. I don't think people were upset with him for doing that, but I remember thinking at the time, "Boy, you'd better be right, because you're going to feel pretty badly if Hackner makes this amazing shot."

Ryan's hit had rolled an inch too far. A sliver of it was poking out behind the guard, and Hackner could see just enough to attempt a thin double, which he needed to stick for two points.

The piece of rock showing was so thin that the CBC analysts originally thought Hackner was throwing the runback double because he couldn't see enough.

RICK LANG: When the situation presented itself, he was just as focused and as calm, and probably slowed things down. The game became slow for him. We always had lots of time to think, but he always used that process... he was absolutely calm. He was thinking this could be made.

AL HACKNER: No sweeping. All by itself.

And then the rocks stop, and there are two left the rings, and we got our two to tie. ▶[1]

RICK LANG: And then Al pulls off that shot, and it was honestly one of the biggest roars I've ever heard. It's like the people were waiting for something to cheer for. They were bored out of their minds, I'm sure, the whole week!

AL HACKNER: What had been a pretty quiet arena for most of the game, because there wasn't a whole lot going on because of no free guards, and the ice was pretty straight and Ryan's team was hitting pretty good. It was actually some action and the arena just erupted!

EARLE MORRIS: And he did make it, and it brought the house down.

AL HACKNER: Those kinds of shots are made all the time now, but with a lot better conditions. The rocks, the ice, the sweeping are all so much better. But even now, if that shot is made in that circumstance, to win the Brier, it would be spectacular... so much on the line. And of course that wasn't even to win, we still had to steal the extra end.

What people don't tend to recall about this shot is that it was just to force an extra end. Keeping in mind that Alberta hadn't allowed a steal all week, it was still an uphill battle for Northern Ontario.

RICK LANG: Then, the tension in that building for the extra end. You could cut it with a knife. We weren't tense at all, because we're thinking we were on borrowed time already. It was a bonus, we were playing with house money.

---

[1]When you see this icon, it means you can find video of the event on YouTube, and the footnote tells you what to search to find it. This one is "1985 Brier Final" - and is found directly at: http://www.youtube.com/watch?v=rccq3ql2l1o (start at 2:20:00)

EARLE MORRIS: When you're Ryan, you go, "Holy crap, we were going to win this, but we just gave up two." Now, you don't want to think about it, but now it slips into your head that there's a possibility that they can steal, and win the extra end. I think it makes you a bit more vulnerable.

AL HACKNER: So I guess we got couple of misses out of the front end. And we actually had some rocks in play so when I go to throw my last one, we were actually lying one in the back eight, behind the guard, which is pretty unusual. I mean it's a Pat Ryan team! And we're actually drawing to lie two, with a guard.

RICK LANG: On our last shot, we were debating what to throw. Al said, "He's gotta draw. We can't put a rock where he can hit it. Even if we don't improve our situation, he's gotta draw." Not that he couldn't draw, but given the circumstances, it was the shot he was more likely to miss.

AL HACKNER: We force Pat Ryan a little wide to draw and we got a miss out of him, and he only missed it by an inch.

IAN TETLEY: If you watch at the hogline, they were dusting it, because it looked good! It went an inch or two deep. We were walking in anticipating the moment, and it comes to rest. I just see Ricky give it the cheer, and go racing for the other guys. I ended up jumping over the shot-rock... Ricky starts asking me, did you touch it? Because they were still looking at it.

His last rock, if it curls and inch or two, they're probably champions.

WARREN HANSEN (Director of Event Operations, Canadian Curling Association/Curling Canada): And in the end we had to measure. And that's the one thing that people probably never fully realize without saying... that it went to an extra end and there was a measure required to determine that Hackner actually had won.

AL HACKNER: Coming back from the 1985 Brier... and that was when Labatt used to hand out all the beer you wanted to the players. One team shows up at the airport with this garbage can all taped up and they want to bring it on the plane with them. And what was it? It was all beer, full of ice. They had, I don't know, like a hundred beers in this huge garbage can, all iced up, and they were going to bring it on the plane with them.

I guess security caught them and they wouldn't allow it. So now this garbage can is sitting in the middle of the lobby, before you go through security. And now they take the tape off, and the lid off, and the curlers are all standing around there, and everybody started grabbing beers, and opening them up and drinking. Then, curling fans would come by and they'd grab one. It turned into a little mini party there right in the middle of this airport lobby. Every other curler and all the fans were trying to leave... suddenly it turned into a party. Everybody drinking beer out of this thing.

To their credit, the security people just stood there, back to the wall, and they just watched it all go. They didn't try to stop anybody, charge anybody. Because they knew within half an hour or an hour, we'll all be gone anyway. So, this is what happened. They let just impromptu party happen in the airport lobby. And it is pretty wild that curlers could get away with this.

You want to know names? That was the Eugene Hritzuk (Saskatchewan) team. They did that. It was pretty cool.

HOW I MET RICK LANG

I think I met Rick for the first time in 2009. National Development Coach Paul Webster had asked if I could help with some video stuff at the Grand Slam's World Cup of Curling event at the Hershey Centre in Mississauga, Ont.

Years later, as I was doing more work with Curling Canada as Team Leader, I found a few more occasions to talk to Rick and pick his brain. At one point in 2014 there was a plan for me to shadow him on a trip to the World Championship in China... but unfortunately that fell through.

Instead we'd chat at Briers and Slams, and in 2017, we were teamed up as coaches at the Amethyst Curling Camp in Sudbury, Ont. I'd worked at several camps each year for nearly two decades, and don't recall learning as much from any of my other colleagues.

I like to think Rick learned a bit from me, too. I showed him a training game called "Distraction Curling." The rules are simple... you can do whatever you want to distract the opposing player while he or she throws. No touching, no impeding their vision or slide path. Otherwise, go crazy.

It's a fun exercise to develop concentration and mental routines during one's delivery.

Somehow what Rick took away from our week at camp together was the one major principle of Distraction Curling. He seems to think that it's a staple of my coaching philosophy... probably because I yelled it at our campers a few times.

"Sportsmanship be damned!!"

As early as 1982, the International Curling Federation (now called the World Curling Federation) was lobbying the International Olympic Committee to include curling in the Olympics. In the 1984-1985 season, it was announced that curling would appear in the 1988 Olympics in Calgary, but only as a demonstration sport.

The Canadian Curling Association (now Curling Canada) needed to select a team.

WARREN HANSEN: It was it was kind of a difficult situation because we had been fighting to change a lot of things, if the sport was ever going to become Olympic. I mean, we started working and stuff back in the late 70s. In the 1980 Brier, we introduced on-ice officials for the first time, which was another absolute brouhaha. But certainly realizing that if the thing was ever going to be recognized at the level with other Olympic sports, there had to be game control. Curling had to be officiated. We did do statistics at the 1980 Brier as well. Based on the same approach, there had to be records and things that just simply, for the most part, didn't exist. So it went that far back.

So when we got into the process of getting athletes in the Olympics it was sort of the same thing. Can we continue with the processes that have been going on here forever, which were sort of more or less just completely by chance? Or do we have to start to try to formulate something to make this sport look more like other sports that are Olympic? So that was sort of the beginning of the whole process.

The CCA came up with a Trials process where certain teams could qualify intact based on performances in the 1986 and 1987 seasons. The remaining participants would be invited to selection camps and placed on "all-star" teams.

IAN TETLEY: I think it was September of 1986 at Mississauga Golf and Country Club. You had to go through fitness testing, and psychological analysis, and then you had to go out on the ice and make shots. They paired us up with different people, and Pat [Perroud] and I got paired with Russ and Glenn Howard for some of the scrimmage games. If they didn't win the Brier

18

that year, there was a pretty good likelihood that we could have been playing with them for those put-together teams.

PAUL SAVAGE (1983 Brier and World champion): The CCA thought that they could build a good curling team. The guys who had played the game their whole lives knew that wasn't the case.

RANDY FERBEY (Six-time Brier champion): They didn't understand the dynamics of it, so that's what they tried to do. They potentially looked at building an all-star team from across Canada that would that would rival these other great teams that played together... almost like an experiment, you know? I mean they do that in other countries, they'll put together the four best curlers. You know, to this day, they still do that in a lot of countries but we've just got too much depth in Canada that it's not realistic.

COLLEEN JONES (Six time Scotties champion): I guess what was controversial was that they chose the team so I didn't have any say in that. And also you had to do drills. So you went to several different camps where you were tested on your hitting ability, your drawing ability. They had a sports psychologist interview you. So all that stuff was ahead of its time probably.

WARREN HANSEN: The whole camps set-up, more than anything else, it was an information-gathering exercise. Because at that stage of the game, nobody knew anything about the players as far as what their athletic abilities were. What were their mental abilities with regard to the sport? Nothing. So to a very large degree a lot of what was being done there was a gathering of information.

RICK LANG: We'd formed a new team. We had a new front end who didn't have any international experience, but it was still our team. We were informed that Al and I were invited to the camp, and our front end was invited, but it was going to be more of a try-out for them. When we argued that maybe we could just be invited straight in, instead of having to tryout, we were told

"No, because of this new team, you all have to try out." But they also said, "But you and Al are going to get in." But the front end was going to depend on how they performed at the try-out camp.

Al was really adamant that this was going to be our team for the year. He said, "We can't go into a Trials with two strangers. I'm just not doing it."

KERRY BURTNYK (Two-time Brier Champion): Hackner was part of it as well. We all felt that inviting one or two of us and not inviting all four really didn't make any sense because curling is a team sport... so we felt strongly enough. Well, I mean, we didn't organize anything, we just felt strongly enough that rather than go and try and be part of an experiment... if they didn't want our whole team to be there, then we were not going to participate.

RICK LANG: I remember really rueing that decision at the time... Al's decision to not participate. Just because I thought it was going to be darn exciting and it was the Olympics. Even if it was just a Trials spot, I wanted to be there. We were still very much in our prime, and thought we could compete with anybody in that day.

But Al said it, and I was really loyal to Al. I wasn't going to go off and leave my skip to go play with somebody else. That would have ruined our team. I didn't have much of a choice. So we made the decision not to participate in this tryout camp.

GLENN HOWARD (Four-time world champion): I hated the fact that my two teammates at the time couldn't go because, like you know, it's a four-person team and yet they picked Russ and me. So yeah, in that respect it was bizarre. Really, really weird. But on the same token you had your chance of maybe going to the Olympics.

COLLEEN JONES: The same thing was happening on the women's side where teams were split up. I wound up getting a team with Kim Dolan from Prince Edward Island and she was traditionally a skip... and she became my lead? So yeah they jumbled up the women's team but we knew the rules. We knew what they were trying to do. They were trying to create some "super teams" in a time when no one was thinking of cross-border curling.

AL HACKNER: There was some all-star team that they'd selected. There was some grumbling about other players and why this person made it, why that person made it... all that stuff was going on. When I heard all that, I was glad I didn't take part in it.

GLENN HOWARD: Of course, we win the Brier, win the Worlds in '87 and obviously, because we won, it was decided that team should go instead of the make-up team. So we were then chosen for one of the spots... Kirk Ziola, maybe, and somebody else [Mark Olson] filled in for us on the made-up team. The Trials were literally, if I'm not mistaken, a week, or two weeks, right after our World Championship. So we win the Worlds in early April and then a week or two later we went to the Trials.

IAN TETLEY: Ed Lukowich's team stayed the same because they won the '86 Brier. Howard's team stayed the same. With all the kerfuffle that went on with Eddie [Werenich] and his team, they left his team together. They told Eddie he had to lose weight if he wanted to go to this combine thing. I was on one of the two throw-together teams.

WARREN HANSEN: This is an interesting story... the Werenich team. So all three members of that team had qualified without question, except one... Ed, because he hadn't taken the whole thing seriously in any way, shape, or form. I mean, he came in there and it was a joke to some degree to him. And so at the end of the day, the situation was an interesting one because all three members of the team had had qualified clearly, but he hadn't.

There was the feeling of some that, "If the Werenich team didn't go intact, then the other three guys wouldn't go." And the other side discussion was, "Well if that was the case, they shouldn't have come here, because they knew what the deal was coming into this, and if that wasn't what they were prepared to do then they shouldn't have entered."

So it went around, and around, and around. And then there was one of the executive people on the committee, one of the presidents came up with an idea that besides Ed Werenich, two other men had failed to pass the physical fitness requirement, the 5 percent of the evaluation item... which was Paul Savage and Randy Ferbey. So this individual thought, "Well you know, maybe we could justify it, if we were to have all three of these people meet the physical requirement before they would be acceptable to go into the Trials, we could justify keeping the Werenich team together. In the end, there were two of us... and I will say I was one of them, who were profoundly against that whole process taking place in the manner in which it did. And I warned that there would be huge fallout from this whole thing.

PAUL SAVAGE : So, I phone [CCA's] Garry DeBlonde in Ottawa, and he says, "I've got some good news and some bad news. The good news is that you guys are invited to the Trials. The bad news is that you, Eddie Werenich, and Randy Ferbey are going to have a fitness requirement." That's when he told me that we had to lose 22 pounds... Randy too. And we had to improve our level of fitness and be able to do so many sit-ups. So that's how we got the news... and away we went from there. Shit hit the fan. It was quite an interesting time.

AL HACKNER: Yeah, both Ed and Savage, they had to go on a diet ,which, you know, I thought that was rather silly. Those guys have been like that all their lives, so they're obviously tremendous curlers at that normal weight for them. To make them lose weight was just all about superficial looks, it had nothing to do with their curling. So I thought that was really silly.

PAUL SAVAGE: The Fitness Institute is a fabulous facility in Toronto, on the 44th floor of the Royal Trust tower. I was down there five days a week, working out. Eddie just stopped eating. He starved himself.

RICHARD HART (1998 Olympic silver-medallist, 2007 Brier and World champion): Eddie got on with the program, but he claims it really affected his game for a couple of years. He dropped 20 or 30 pounds and it affected his draw weight, it affected his slide. He said it was detrimental to his performance.

PAUL SAVAGE: I think he put himself in a very difficult situation. Definitely losing all that weight, he was weak. I think it had more to do with him being undernourished. He basically starved himself for six weeks. It had to have affected his balance, and his touch.

Ed Werenich's career and Olympic Trials saga is expertly covered in Jean Sonmor's book, "Burned by the Rock.[2]" His frequent battles with the CCA, and specifically Warren Hansen, are covered in great detail, as is the famous story of "Marina."

PAUL SAVAGE: We were playing in North Bay, Ont. in a bonspiel, and they always had strippers at the club. This very attractive young lady sat down at our table after the game, and we collected some money from all the guys, and got her to come back to the hotel for a private show, with 20 or so guys from the bonspiel.

So I thought, we've got an extra ticket to Calgary for the Trials, we're allowed to bring a coach. We've never been interested in having a coach, so I half-jokingly said to this girl, her name was Marina, "Do you want to come to Calgary to the Olympic Trials, and be our coach?" and she said, "I'd love to come to Calgary and be your coach." So we got her contact information, and the next day we're driving back to Toronto, and John Kawaja, who was madly in love at the time, said, "Guys, this isn't going to work out for me. I can't do this." Then Harry [Neil Harrison] said, "I don't think this is a good idea." Eddie and I were like "Come on, this is going to be a riot!" We let it drop.

Two days before we leave for Calgary, Eddie gets a phone call. "This is Marina! Am I still coming to Calgary?" But Eddie had to give her the news. It would have been hilarious though, to show up at the rink with this 23-year-old, gorgeous young lady, and introduce her as our coach.

---

[2] "Burned by the Rock: Inside the World of Men's Championship Curling" by Jean Sonmor; Macmillan Canada, 1991

In Sonmor's book, Werenich says "I wish we had the balls to go through with that." As it happened, they took a friend, Steve Clement, who paid his own way to "coach," and the CCA wasn't happy about even that. I'm not sure how they would have reacted to Marina.

WARREN HANSEN: The camps were something that could have been of great value, I felt, going forward. It certainly could have been refined, could have been developed to be a far more sophisticated process, and could actually have been something that could have been used to match and develop teams in the future. However, because of what took place with the whole weight thing, everybody was afraid to touch it with a 100-foot pole... and so it was buried.

KERRY BURTNYK: But I think the whole process proved that we were exactly right, because the teams that they did put together - the all-star teams - all finished at the bottom. And the teams that went there as teams all finished at the top.

But you know, some chose to participate. "Well I'll try it anyway as an individual." One of my ex-teammates had gone as an individual and afterwards he basically told me that it was kind of a disaster in terms of his chances to try and compete. You can't just throw four guys together that haven't played together and expect to get results against the best teams in the world.

In the end, once all the teams were selected and invited, the Labatt National Curling Trials took place in Calgary in April of 1987. Ed Lukowich beat Pat Ryan for the right to represent the men. Ed Werenich's team, intact, lost the semifinal to Lukowich. Linda Moore defeated Connie Laliberte for the women's right to wear the Maple Leaf.

PAUL SAVAGE: The one thing I remember was when we lost the semifinal to Ed Lukowich, you could see the board of directors of the Canadian Curling Association leaving the building with big smiles on their faces. The last thing they wanted was for us [Team Werenich] to win and represent Canada at the Olympic Games.

In some ways, I don't blame them. They were working so hard to get curling into the Olympics, and the knock on curling was whether it was really a sport, and if we were really athletes. Eddie and I didn't look like athletes. We were back-end players, so our contribution was skill and touch. Neil and John were in good shape. They looked athletic, they were great brushers. But yeah, the CCA was pretty happy.

In February of 1988, Moore would bring home a gold medal for Canada, while Lukowich claimed the men's bronze in Calgary. Although it was still a demonstration sport, curling was back in the Olympics for the first time since 1924.

HOW I MET WARREN HANSEN

Over my years with Curling Canada (formerly the Canadian Curling Association), I've had the pleasure of working at many of the *Season of Champions* events including Briers, Worlds, Continental Cups, etc. As Curling Canada's Director of Event Operations, Warren was at all of them. I didn't have many occasions to interact with him personally, but he was always running around, ushering players, guests, and broadcasters one way or another. In the odd quiet moments, he'd handicap the event and let you know what to look for in the coming games.

One such prediction came at the 2014 Tim Hortons Brier in Kamloops, B.C. John Morris and Jim Cotter were representing the hosts in the final against Alberta's Kevin Koe squad, who had essentially already announced they were disbanding after the season..

Warren turned to me and said, "No matter who wins this game, I'm going to bet that John Morris is skipping Team Canada at the Brier next year."

And he was right. Even though Koe won, he formed a new team for the next four-year Olympic cycle. Morris was recruited to fill in, and skipped the squad to the 2015 Brier championship... even though it was Pat Simmons who covered the button to win the final.

PAUL SAVAGE: People always say to me, "Too bad you're not playing now because there's a lot more money." Well that's not really true. In the '80s, there were car spiels. We won two in the '70s and one in the '80s. If you look at the value of those four cars, that's a bigger prize than they're playing for now in the Grand Slams. We also won a 'spiel in Calgary where first prize was $60,000. I think that was 1987. If you tack on inflation, that's probably $200,000 now. We were winning about $100,000 a year in the '80s. That was a lot of tax-free fun!

RICK LANG: In the '80s, people talk about the fun we had, but we were pretty dedicated to our mission. We wanted to win as bad as anybody wants to win now. We had to make every bit as much of a sacrifice.

I remember so many times, coming back on Monday morning. Flying in and going right to work. And then Thursday at 4 p.m. you're back on a plane and heading out again. You still had to get your job done!. You really had to be committed just as much in those days. We weren't as dedicated as athletes. I'll be the first to admit that. The game has come a long way in that way. But everything we sacrificed or gave up was just as much as they do now.

AL HACKNER: I heard Glenn Howard say last year [2017] that he had a very reduced schedule. He only played in six spiels. That was our normal season. We'd play six 'spiels and every now and then, we'd throw a seventh one in there if we wanted to play a bit more. We would start mid-October and we'd play our six 'spiels and then the different playdown levels and so on, and maybe one more at the end of the year kind of thing. And that was our season.

We thought that was lots, because we all had jobs, we all had to work and that's what all we could squeeze out of it. I mean the people that are doing all that curling now... wow, I don't know how they do it. You know, they've got to be not working or all have jobs that are super flexible and allow them all that time off.

RANDY FERBEY: You could say, before the Slams came along, we had to pick and choose where we wanted to fly to. Today they don't have a choice. That's the biggest difference. They've got no choice. They have to go where the Slam events are planned... Back in the '80s and '90s, we'd pick where we want to go. I mean, there were some good money events, other certain events we liked... well, then that's where we would go.

But a lot of times our schedule was dictated by how far we wanted to go. If there was a bonspiel, say Saskatoon for ten grand, and there was a bonspiel in

Toronto for twelve grand, we'd go to the one in Saskatoon, because it would cost a bit less to get there. That was the biggest difference.

JEFF STOUGHTON (Three-time Brier champion, two-time World Champion): There were already a lot of big bonspiels at the time. Even at the [Winnipeg] Granite, they had a Thanksgiving weekend bonspiel that was already $15,000 first prize... I think I won it in 1988, or maybe '89. That was pretty darn good prize money, especially back then. And the entry fees were only $700 or $800.

There were a ton of competitive teams. You felt like you really had to play your best to beat any of the teams you were playing, especially in Manitoba. There were a lot of good teams. Garry DeBlonde, Burtnyk, Vic Peters, Mike Riley... and a bunch more I'm going to forget. It just seemed to be never-ending quality.

Thunder Bay had a couple of big bonspiels every year, and a lot of the Manitoba teams would go there. It was a busy flight.

KEVIN MARTIN (Four-time Brier champion, 2010 Olympic gold medallist, 2002 Olympic silver medallist): Alberta was extremely difficult because Lukowich was still in his prime, Pat Ryan was in his prime. Dan Petryk was in his prime, and there was just an extreme amount of depth in Alberta. And of course, in the mid '80s there wasn't a World Curling Tour. It hadn't been invented yet. There was no players association. There was no Grand Slam of Curling.

So the season really was from Thanksgiving weekend until you either won or lost at the provincial playdowns. So generally, you played from Thanksgiving to sometime in early January and that was pretty much the season.

AL HACKNER: That's true, I know when we used to go to spiels, there were six spiels and they were just about money. You go there and you always say you want to play and compete and get better but the end of the rainbow was the money that you won. If we wanted to have a little fun while we were at it, just money lost. Who cares? But now, these days, with the Order of Merit points, where you stand in it as the season goes on, and at the end of the year, there's all kinds of Olympic funding and so on. Now every game that you play at any one of these 'spiels is really as important as anything else you play. You can't go out there with your head a little ballooned up from a night of revelry, or whatever, it's too costly. It's too expensive to party in that way, a lot of the teams just don't and it's all about work. You go, you play and then you get your rest and then you get some sleep and then you go play again and there's no time for fun.

JEFF STOUGHTON: There were some epic times. You had a lot of fun with your competitors and everyone else who was around. That's probably changed quite a bit, with the Olympics. Teams have more sponsorship, more responsibility, and more expectations. Back then, you were responsible to yourself, your team, and whoever was at home... your family and so on. But now, there's sponsorships, TV, and everything that goes into it. You really need to be at your best.

I asked Hackner if he was implying that, in their prime, his team might have enjoyed the odd adult beverage, and played a game or two under less than ideal performance states... you know, shitfaced.

AL HACKNER: Yeah. I might have stepped on the ice that way once or twice, but I was maybe fortunate with my head and my body in that I was still able to play pretty good. So we all set a team rule. There was no curfew, you can do whatever you want. Just play good the next day. And if you didn't play good, then we'll have a little chat.

Meanwhile, in Ontario, Russ Howard and Ed Werenich/Paul Savage were battling for supremacy. Savage went to the Brier in 1988, while Howard returned in 1989.

PAUL SAVAGE: Russ was always a challenge, not just because he was skillful, but he had his idiosyncrasies that could be annoying at times. He was defending World champion, won it in '87. We beat him in the Ontario final in '88, which was a big thrill. He won the [Ontario] Tankard one year, and beat Eddie in the final, and me in the semifinal, the year they went on to win the Worlds, and I had my last rock pulled by a hogline official in the ninth end. We had control of the game, there was no Free Guard Zone rule, I had a solid hitting team... and bang, my last rock in the ninth gets pulled.

The replay on TV, I still have it... there was no way that rock should have been pulled. That's another shitty memory of playing Russ. But that wasn't his fault.

IAN TETLEY: It was quite bitter. There were times I can remember when Russ would stand behind Eddie and Kawaja and mutter "Tick! Tick!" I don't know if he wanted to, or if his inner emotions were just coming out loud. I remember Kawaja turning around and screaming at him a couple of times.

PAUL SAVAGE: When he [Howard] first won the Tankard playing out of Penetang-Midland, he did it with three local guys [brother Glenn Howard, Tim Belcourt, and Kent Carstairs], which was really hard to do... to build a team that could win Ontario from guys in a small town. In Toronto, you've got a huge number of curlers to draw from. When Russ won with that team, it opened all sorts of opportunities for him, and that's how he was able to recruit Peter Corner and Wayne Middaugh, and build that team. And that was a goddamn awfully good curling team.

He had a hugely successful career. If you didn't like playing against him, it was because he was really, really good. And I'll leave it at that.

HOW I MET GLENN HOWARD

The first time I met Glenn Howard was at the 2007 Ontario Provincials in Sarnia. I was playing with Damian Villard out of Renfrew, and we had fluked our way through a zone and a region, losing only one game at each, despite having never played a game together.

Our group of misfits - Damian had long, shaggy dreadlocks, and insisted our team wear bright neon-green jackets - had the great pleasure of playing Team Howard (along with Rich Hart, Brent Laing, and Craig Savill) in our first game.

We decided to go right after them, thinking "Go big or go home." Glenn pops four on us in the first end.

They're sitting another mitt-full in the second end, sitting behind a wall of granite, and there are no angles in to remove his stones, two of which are sitting frozen on the top button.

I'm throwing third, and with my second shot I throw a wide in-turn draw that swoops around the guard to sit frozen, on his two already frozen rocks.

As I'm sliding through the house towards Damian, Glenn looks at me and says, "That might be the nicest shot I've ever seen to force a steal of two."

One of the greatest curlers of all time just gave me one of the greatest backhanded compliments of all time. I was thrilled.

Remember that guy from the beginning of the story, Pat Ryan? He finished off the decade with back-to-back Brier wins. One over Saskatchewan's Eugene Hritzuk, and the next over Rick Folk, the 1980 Brier winner from Saskatchewan, who was now representing of British Columbia.

The Ryan Express (now featuring Randy Ferbey at third in place of Gord Trenchie from the 1985 team) hadn't changed their model. Hit everything, up and down the ice. In 1988, Ryan didn't lose a game, but had to score three in the 10th end of the final to beat Hritzuk. He managed to do so without needing to throw the hammer, after Hritzuk's last shot stopped about halfway down the sheet.

The following year against Folk, Ryan won the final 3-2... the lowest score ever in a Brier final. Of note, that was also the year Russ Howard lost his voice mid-week and opted to use walkie-talkies to communicate, stating that there was no rule against it.

The CCA acted quickly and voted to change the rule mid-tournament, which was a first.

That wasn't the only rule change coming...

CHAPTER 2:
THE NINETIES

Although many of the big names interviewed for this book got started in the 1980s, most of them made their marks in the decades that followed. While Ryan, Hackner, Howard, and Werenich were still part of the top tier, younger teams featuring Kevin Martin, Jeff Stoughton, and Wayne Middaugh would become the cream of the crop in the 1990s.

Meanwhile on the women's side, there was a team in Saskatchewan who was about to spend the decade dominating women's curling.

But for now, let's pick up where we left off...

WAYNE MIDDAUGH: It actually all got started back in 1983. Back then in schoolboys and juniors, you used to get billeted at people's houses, and sure enough Pete [Corner] and I were playing at the schoolboys in Midland, Ont., and we were billeted at Russ Howard's house. At that time, Russ had only been to one Brier, but to meet somebody like that when you're maybe 15 years old playing in Ontario Schoolboys was pretty awesome. It was quite a treat.

And after that, we just kept in touch. Not like it is today, this was before cell phones. A few years later, he was playing in the Brier final in Kitchener, Ont., and remember I sending him a message. I'm not even sure how I got it to him.... I must have left it at his hotel or something... I just said, "Russ, good luck in the final. I'm cheering for you!" The next year, 1987, we're playing in the junior final, and sure enough a message shows up at my hotel from Russ Howard. "Wayne, good luck in the final." It was kinda cool to get that.

GLENN HOWARD: Pete and Wayne came up to what might have been... a little junior bonspiel and I'm going to say they might have been 13 or 14 years old. I'm going to say a bantam spiel. Whatever it was, it was in Midland and Russ actually billeted them. So the two of them stayed at his house while they were in the area.

That's when Russ got to know, and I got to meet, Pete Corner and Wayne Middaugh. Lo and behold, you remember them, and keep an eye on them. Russ and I watched them curl, growing up, and I remember us saying, "Oh my God these two kids are unbelievable... they're going to be something."

WAYNE MIDDAUGH: Our first year out of juniors, we made it all the way to the men's provincials, which was a big deal. You had to go through club, zones, and regional playdowns. That was back in the day when Eddie was there, Savage was there, Russ was there. There were a lot of big names players around, and we talked to him [Russ] a bit more.

GLENN HOWARD: When did Russ sort of decide he'd had enough? He was actually thinking of packing in curling, if you can believe it, in probably '88 or '89. It was a couple of years after that, and it was when word got out that we sort of disbanded the team, Wayne called Russ and said, "Hey, you remember me?"

WAYNE MIDDAUGH: Then in 1989 right after the Brier... I was actually helping Shorty [Jenkins] do the ice at the World Juniors, and Russ was there doing a speaking engagement, and we got talking again, and he said "Do you want to play a 'spiel?" So I said, " Sure! Get your brother, I'll get Pete" and we went and played a 'spiel together... and lo and behold every 'spiel for the next five years.

GLENN HOWARD: And he said, in Wayne's words, "You know, Pete and I are just coming out of juniors, we want to get into the men's ranks. We want to play with you and your brother. We want to learn. We want to play front end and we want to learn as much as we possibly can. We'll win a World Championship or two, but I'll be honest with you... after that I'm going out on my own." In true Wayne Middaugh fashion.

RICK LANG: We played them in the '91 Brier. I was skipping Northern Ontario for the second time, it was kind of after my time with Al. We're playing in Hamilton, and it's the battle of Ontario. And we beat them, on national television - TSN. And I got in the van after, and my team was a bit younger, and maybe not that knowledgeable about the game. They said "Holy smokes, you're pretty happy about that." and I said "Happy? We just beat the best team in the world, and maybe one of the best teams of all time." And they go, "Nooo..." and I said "Yeah, you know who's on that team? And what they've done lately. And how they've dominated?"

We played really well, I was on top of the world, and my team didn't even appreciate what we'd just done. Look at what they turned into... Russ was great. Glenn won the Worlds skipping. Wayne won the Worlds skipping. Corner had a good Brier run as a skip.

In 1991-1992, Russ Howard and team won $100,450 according to The Curling News Gold Trail list. The second-place team was Al Hackner, nearly $25,000 behind. The Howard brothers, with Middaugh and Corner, lost the Brier final in 1992, won the Brier and the Worlds in 1993, and lost the Brier final again in 1994.

RICHARD HART: They had one fantastic year, when they lost something like five games. That in itself, I don't think anybody else has done that. It was something crazy like that. I played juniors against Pete and Wayne. To see them come out of juniors and be on this World Championship team, it was kind of a motivator for us. Mike [Harris] and I started thinking like, that's the next step for us.

WAYNE MIDDAUGH: Everybody has been on those runs in their life. Ferbey had runs like that. Brad Gushue had runs like that. They've all had runs like that, when every cash event you enter, it was just a matter if you won the final or not. We got on a roll like that that lasted for a bunch of years.

On the Brier side, we only went to a few... three I guess... but as far as the tour went, we'd have stretches where we made six finals in a row, and we won four of them. It was crazy. We had something like 30-game winning streaks... it was crazy how many games we were winning.

MIKE HARRIS (1998 Olympic silver medallist, CBC/Sportsnet analyst): The best team of all time for me was Russ, Glenn, Wayne Middaugh, and Peter Corner. I'd put them up against any team of any era. In their prime, relative to the rest of the world, obviously. They're the most talented team.

WAYNE MIDDAUGH: All the years I curled with Glenn, especially when we played with Russ, Glenn and I would fight on the ice all the time. We'd be toe-to-toe with each other, just screaming at each other. We'd get off the ice, and we wouldn't talk to each other. We'd go our separate ways, and I'd head out to whatever bar was in town, no matter where we were... Portage, Saskatoon, whatever... and usually around 1 a.m., I'd look around and on the other side of the bar, there's Glenn Howard. And we'd laugh at each other, buy each other a drink, and let bygones be bygones. This happened all the time... like 10 different times.

GLENN HOWARD: I tended to look at the game a little differently than Wayne did. He knew the game very well but he would get a little frustrated with Russ and then with me, being third. I was the go-between, for the front end and the back end. And he'd get frustrated, "Why'd you let your brother do that?" He left it all on his sleeve, he didn't leave anything secret. I'd tell him everything's fine, he'd swear at me, and then we get a little at loggerheads. And he'd disagree with me, or I disagreed with him, and we have a little sort of a moment on the ice.

But ultimately, we'd all go off somewhere and at the end of the night, it could be 1:30 in the morning, I look across wherever the hell we are, and there's Wayne in the corner. I go over, and we'd hug it out, have a few drinks and everybody's all perfect again. And literally that happened *many* times.

RICK LANG: That team was as talented as any team that's ever played the game. I definitely recognized that early on. I didn't know that they'd last as long as they did, or be as good as they ended up being. But at that time, I just thought they were already the best shooting team in the world.

The 1991 Brier turned out to be a tipping point for something else; something the Ryan Express and friends had already started in the 1980s.

JEFF STOUGHTON: I was part of a 1991 Brier game where Kevin Martin scored a deuce in the first end, and he threw it through in the second end. They didn't want any rocks in play. They knew they were that good, and they could just run us out. And of course it was a TV game on TSN. So that was really the killer game. I think it was a 3-2 final? Maybe 2-1... I think we scored one more point in there somewhere.

KEVIN MARTIN: I think one of the big games that changed things was the game when we played Stoughton in the '91 Brier because we got a deuce in the first end and we threw the rock through in the second. It's true! And we peeled the whole game. We won a 3-2 or 2-1. Boring as boring could be.

DON BARTLETT (Two-time Brier winner with Kevin Martin, 2002 Olympic silver medallist): That was back in the time before the Free Guard Zone rule. We just blasted everything. In the last round-robin game, we're playing Stoughton. If we win, we can finish first... if Saskatchewan loses.

Of course the crowd is booing us. But you know, there weren't very many teams that could peel for nine ends. We were one of them. Pat Ryan's team could do it back it the day.

It was 3-2, with six blank ends.

MIKE HARRIS: A change was necessary. Pat Ryan changed the game. They could just hit everything. Even when Eddie won the Brier with Kawaja, Tetley, and Pat Perroud... they'd get two and hit out. They'd win 3-1. All the best hitting teams were the ones that were winning.

RANDY FERBEY (Six-time Brier winner, twice with Pat Ryan): You know people say that we initiated the Free Guard Zone rule... we figured out a way to to win the game, or to be at the top of our game by being the best team ever to play the game up until that point, and I think we accomplished it. So it was kind of flattering to see them change the rules because of us. You know I really believe it was because of us. A lot of people would agree.

DON BARTLETT: I remember talking with Don Walchuk and Ferbey. They would get together for the coin flip, and stand beside each other. And then they'd win this coin toss, and they'd go to each other "Ballgame!" That's how important the coin toss was back then.

KEVIN MARTIN: We needed the change for sure because the players were getting better, getting ridiculously good. So if you didn't have hammer to start the game... in order to lose you would have to miss two peels an entire game. But if you've only missed one, that only nullifies the hammer.

JOAN McCUSKER (Three-time World champion, 1998 Olympic gold medallist): In those days we were the lean green, hitting machine. We'd count two and peel. But it was a skill! I know people make fun of that, especially people from Ontario. It was hard to peel all game, with inconsistent rocks and inconsistent ice conditions. To figure out how to peel was a badge of honour.

RICK LANG: We were always a draw team, maybe because we couldn't hit. We were playing in a Brier one time, maybe our first, and were so bad at peeling. Our friends were sitting in the front row, and brought out some oranges and put them on the boards, and said "See if you can peel these!" That's how bad we were.

We loved the draw game. Al hated hitting. He was bored to tears with it. He'd check out. He'd say, "I don't even want to be out here. The ice is dead straight. The guys are just going to hit everything. Let's go somewhere else. We'll have more fun."

Considering people were upset about the lack of offence as early as the mid-1980s (and probably before), rumblings from the powers-that-be were that a new rule was going to be instituted. A bonspiel in Moncton, N.B., was one of the biggest - both in terms of profile and money - and it showcased the first version what was later to evolve into the Free Guard Zone. The Moncton 100 bonspiel in 1990 featured a new caveat, inspired by Russ Howard, that lead rocks couldn't be removed.

GLENN HOWARD: Basically how it started, was that for years, the two of us would go out and throw rocks together. We'd practise, and we played a lot of one-on-one. And when you do that you don't hold a broom, you just throw the shot. We'd decide we're playing four or five ends, then he'd get up three and he'd peel everything. And the next time, I'd get up and I'd peel everything. And he goes, "Jesus Christ, this is boring! Okay, just for just an idea. The first four rocks of every end, no matter where they are in play you can't remove them."

As the rule evolved for competitive play, protected rocks were limited to those in front of the house. The Free Guard Zone, as it became known, only applied to guards, and only for the first four shots, when it was finally instituted. The WCF had already decided that a Free Guard Zone rule would be in play for the 1992 Olympics in Albertville, France, and the following World Championships, meanwhile some Canadian associations were still debating the rule, with many variations also being considered.

WARREN HANSEN: So they [provincial associations] were very vocal. Huge discussions. I remember, particularly, Alberta was absolutely dead against any kind of adjustment, to introducing two-rock, three-rock rule, or anything.

And so there was a lot of dispute and a lot of discussion and the four-rock rule was kind of brought in by the WCF against Canada's wishes and it happened very suddenly.

And by my memory, the decision to bring in the three-rock rule was a discussion of compromise by the provinces, particularly led by Alberta, who didn't want anything. So the three-rock rule was introduced as the lesser evil of the four-rock rule.

GEORGE KARRYS (1998 Olympic silver medallist, Owner/Publisher of The Curling News): I should haul out the 1992 position paper, drafted by NACA [Northern Alberta Curling Association]. It's about six or seven pages, and clearly presents the argument that the Free Guard Zone is a disaster, and that close, low-scoring games are the best kind of curling... both to play and to watch. I kid you not. I have it, and it's a piece of work.

JEFF STOUGHTON: I think Manitoba wanted it, but if you went to Saskatchewan, Alberta, B.C. ... probably not as much. They liked to run it up and down, they were really good at hitting.

SHERRY MIDDAUGH (Five-time Ontario Scotties champion, Saskatchewan Scotties champion): Ontario always bragged that they had the best ice. "We've got Shorty, we've got the best ice conditions. We're 'drink, draw, win' and you guys [the west] are 'hit, sleep, lose.'"

RICK LANG: I remember having a conversation at a Brier in the '80s when it was going to be voted on. And the Saskatchewan Curling Association group asked if they could meet with us, and they were lobbying to *not* have the rule. That year [1989], at the Brier in Saskatoon, the scores were all 3-2 and 2-1, and they didn't know what they were running into by inviting us to this session. They were trying to garner our support and convince us that it was going to change the game, or ruin the game... They thought it was going to be an advantage to Wrench and Howard and those guys, and of course they're for it because they [Werenich and Howard] can't hit. And we were like bulls in a china shop going, "Are you kidding us? The sooner the better, bring in the rule! We need it so bad, the game needs it so bad."

JOAN McCUSKER: I hated it. I hated it when they first introduced it. Our first Worlds in 1993, of course, was four-rock rule. So we won [the Scotties] in Brandon by hitting everything in sight. And everyone said, "Oh, that team from the prairies is going to lose the Worlds because they don't know how to draw." We said that too! We don't know how to draw! We were scared. So we practise like crazy... and I think we had about six weeks between Canadians and the Worlds. We had to play Dordi Nordby [1991 World champion from Norway] in our first game, and we were beating her 8-2. We had our fifth-end break and everybody's like, "I don't think that's enough points!"

IAN TETLEY: I ended up going to play with Paul Savage in 1991, and slowly found my way with that Moncton Rule. I had to learn to draw a bit better.

Although they were slightly different in regards to which stones were protected and where, the terms "Moncton Rule" and "Free Guard Zone" were used somewhat interchangeably for several years.

MIKE HARRIS: I think it was Paul Savage who said, "The Free Guard Zone shortened some careers and lengthened others." There were teams who quit. Lyle Muyers from Saskatchewan, they all just quit. Guys like Paul, Eddie, Russ, and Glenn - their careers blossomed.

PAUL SAVAGE: One of the advantages we had, when we were playing teams from Alberta and Manitoba, was their front-end players. These big strong guys who could sweep like hell and throw bullets. Our front end, Neil [Harrison] and John [Kawaja], had great touch. Harry [Harrison] would throw a corner guard, and if they whiffed it, he'd make the come-around and away we went. That's the way we played... but that's the way we practised too. We never threw a take-out in practice.

KEVIN MARTIN: Rick Folk, I believe, was really, really against it... but otherwise not many. I think most people realized a little bit that more rocks in play was a good thing. At the time, I wasn't a big fan. I was a kid and probably a little bit more kind of in the middle somewhere. I didn't really know the game that well. I was only 24 years old. Looking back, it was certainly a good thing.

JEFF STOUGHTON: We used to call it the "Saskatchewan Head Fake." We'd have a guard up, and their skip would indicate they want a draw in the house. The whole team would shake him off, and they'd go up and peel the guard. And we were always like "Awww! I thought they were going to draw!"

I don't remember people fighting it too much, because we wanted it. Kerry Burtnyk was very aggressive, so a lot of the teams who came after him were kind of used to it and liked it that way.

KERRY BURTNYK: I know at some point there there was the controversy while Canada switched to three-rock rule, and the Worlds was at the four-rock rule and you know, there was a period there where I guess we were trying to feel out which one was going to be the better rule, or who was going to win the argument. I think that was a little bit secondary to the fact that we actually changed from the old rules to any kind of free guard zone!

PAUL SAVAGE: The three-guard rule still let them get out of trouble pretty easily, so CCA eventually had to go to the four-rock rule. The skill level of their front ends - they realized right away that the guys who were going to play on a competitive curling team had to be able to play that game. They had to throw hack-weight takeouts around a guard. So they had to change... and now, the front ends are all good finesse curlers.

Following the selection camp fiasco prior to the 1988 Olympic Games, the CCA decided that the winner of the Brier and Scotties in 1991 would represent

Canada in Albertville, France, where curling would again be a demonstration sport at the Winter Olympics.

WARREN HANSEN: What happened in '92 was a result of probably a lot of backlash from '88.

I mean we were led to believe that the manner in how we put on that whole demonstration in '88 was going to impact whether or not the sport became full-medal going into '92 or '94. So we put a huge emphasis on the presentation in Calgary and as a result, we did a very good job in that aspect of it. Curling, as a demonstration sport, ended up getting a way higher profile in the Calgary Olympics, compared to things such as bobsled, luge, or cross-country skiing.

So the IOC was not happy with that. Mark Hodler of the IOC had made a statement that this was never going to happen again. And actually as a result of that whole thing, it was announced shortly after 1988 in Calgary, that following the '92 Games in Albertville there would never be any more demonstration sports.

They did not want demonstration sports to be overshadowing the Olympic medal sports. So we knew going in '92 that this was the last demonstration, which was also made pretty clear to us. While curling was going to be a demonstration sport in Albertville, it wasn't going to have any bearing on anything - whether curling ever became a medal sport or didn't.

So the discussions went around and around again, following '88. A number of people changed... Garry DeBlonde left in 1990. I stepped back from it, and as usual, everybody throws up their hands and says they will just send the Brier and Scotties winners to the Olympics. Because a demonstration in Albertville, it was a non-event anyway.

COLLEEN JONES: That was controversial. Nobody likes that. I mean, so many people complained about the process for the Trials for 1988. And then along came the next Olympics and it was just based on who won that year's

Scotties and Brier. No one liked that. Like it was just... that didn't seem like the process.

You had to win your provincials; there was a lot of pressure there. We were at that Scotties trying... we knew it was an all-or-nothing at one event.

RICK LANG: I was playing in my eighth or ninth Brier in 1991, and Kevin Martin is playing his first. He and his team showed up, but we never saw them. I didn't meet Kevin Martin other than when we played them. There was a social room and a lounge at the arena where everybody would hang out before the game, and we never saw them there either.

It dawned on me around Day Four... Who the hell is this Kevin Martin kid? We haven't even seen the guy. Why are they not with us? Why are they not part of the Brier? Well, they had a plan to not do that. They weren't going to mix and mingle with the opposition and tell jokes. They weren't there to make new friends, that wasn't their gig. I remember thinking, "Oh, this is different," and of course, they go and win it.

MIKE HARRIS: Kevin Martin won the Brier in 1991, and he had no idea that would come with an Olympic berth. Apparently, his coach knew. But Kevin was in the post-game media scrum after the final... and people were asking him, he had no clue. What are you talking about?

KEVIN MARTIN: I did not know that. Jules [Owchar] was my coach then, and of course he was for a long time. He thought, because I was so young, he thought it might add too much pressure; knowing that the final game actually had an Olympic berth on the line. So he just didn't tell me!

He thought, after the game, if we lost it's no big deal... like nothing. But if we won, then he'd take a minute, you know pull me aside, and say "Hey, by the way, we're off to Albertville for the Olympics, so you can expect the questions from the media." But it didn't work that way.

At the Brier, especially back then, there are huge media benches and as soon as the game was over, you shook hands with the other team and they pulled you into a scrum. There was no time to discuss anything with Jules. So my first time realizing we're going to the Olympic Games in '92 was within the media scrum... so that's a pretty unique situation.

It would have added a lot of pressure. If all of a sudden... you know, trying to go to a World Championship is great, but now you're trying to make it to the Olympic Games. That's a different world. All of a sudden the amount of pressure is exponential. And I didn't even know. So that was great.

I think Jules is the best coach in curling history and he proved it, definitely proved it, that time because I was like, almost 24 at the time. Twenty-four. You know, you hit me with that right before the final, or the day before the final... I don't know. I'm not sure how I would respond at that age. Yeah, but I think he made a great decision.

COLLEEN JONES: I remember Don Duguid and I were doing the play by play in Albertville [for CBC] when it was still a demonstration sport in '92. And you know they only came to curling when skiing was a fogged out. So we got on a couple of times, Don and I, but not a lot though.

RICHARD HART: We just took our Brier winner and sent him. It was a three- or four-game round robin, then a playoff. It was a really strange event. It almost killed curling in the Olympics.

Maybe because it was 25 years ago, or maybe because it was a "non-event" (as Warren Hansen put it), or maybe simply because we didn't have 24-hour network and cable coverage like we do now, but a lot of my interview subjects didn't have specific memories regarding the 1992 Olympics.

The format was strange. Two pools of four teams played a round robin, in which Kevin Martin went 3-0, and Julie Sutton (later Skinner) did the same on the women's side. Both teams lost their semifinal, although only Sutton (with her sister Jodie Sutton, Melissa Soligo, Karri Willms and Elaine Dagg-Jackson) was able to rebound for the bronze-medal victory.

Martin lost his bronze-medal game to the USA's Tim Somerville. Kevin Park showed up late for the game and Don Bartlett was missing, attending to his pregnant wife. A strange event, indeed. Dan Petryk rounded out the team.

Thanks to the miracle of the internet, you can watch some of these games on YouTube. A few things strike me about a game you can find between Martin and Switzerland's Urs Dick. ▶[3]

First, the ice seemed impossibly slow. Two of the four sheets were literally unusable. A problem with refrigeration had turned them into slush. In "Burned by the Rock," Martin says, "The conditions were unplayable... I had the high individual percentage at 74. At the Brier the poorest team's average would be higher." Players are throwing massive hit weight to reach the far end.

DON BARTLETT: I guess it was a problem with the brine or something. The funny thing about that was, Kevin taught the icemaker guy from France... like, they wanted to have their own icemaker, because it was their Olympics and everything. So that year or the year before, Kevin taught him how to make ice. So he was fresh, he was green, he didn't know very much. So now there's two sheets we could play for the rest of the event. The other two are basically water. We only have two sheets. So they had to make it a shorter round-robin and everything was backwards. It was fast on the edges and slow in the middle. You'd take negative ice all over the place.

Kevin knew how to fix this, because he was an icemaker. He was familiar with everything. Well, of course, they're not going to allow a competitor to change the conditions, right?

The next thing I noticed was, Kevin Martin had a full head of hair and a killer mouth-hat. That was a serious duster. It was a moustache for the ages.

---

[3] Olympische Spiele Albertville 1992 - http://www.youtube.com/watch?v=qHNI7L6ZM7M

And finally, the thing that strikes me the most was that Kevin Martin was still using a corn broom.

At this point, corn wasn't entirely extinct, but it was certainly on its way out. Martin seemed to be one of the last holdouts, at least at that level. His famous corn broom also made an appearance following his 1991 Brier win, in the World Championship final in Winnipeg vs. Scotland's David Smith.

KEVIN MARTIN: Breaking out of the corn broom in those days, from the mid '80s when the push brooms kind of started until the early '90s... bringing out corn, if you were down, because the ice was so straight, was the only way you're going to ever get around a guard. Everybody would just peel, there was no way to get a guard. Many, many, many teams would bring in corn. That was just kind of standard back then.

PAUL SAVAGE: The Scottish skip called him out on a live mic. "Canadian cheating bastards!"

KEVIN MARTIN: That was no problem at all. But yeah, that was pretty commonplace in Canada. Maybe it wasn't in Scotland at the time.

PAUL SAVAGE: Don Chevrier said it on the air, "This is no way to win a World Championship," after Kevin brought out the "emergency broom." We knew from a player on his team years later... it wasn't just a dirty broom, it was a doctored dirty broom.

A doctored broom would imply that perhaps the corn was soaked in a sticky substance - say, a clear soda pop, such as 7UP or Sprite. The resulting pounding on the ice releases some of that sticky substance on the ice surface and is nearly impossible to sweep up.

In "Burned by the Rock" Martin denies this charge, and "laughs at the uproar." He says "Everybody who knows curling knows I wasn't cheating." He also notes that the controversy was great for corn broom sales at his curling equipment business.

DON BARTLETT: People claim that Kevin dipped it in 7UP or it baked it, or whatever. It was never any of that. It's just the broom that he was using at the time... it was dark green and sometimes the chaff that came off was sticking to the ice. Most teams didn't know how to sweep against straw that was on the ice. We were one of the last teams to use it.

KEVIN MARTIN: I don't know about Scotland. But it was certainly commonplace in Canada. The other team would obviously bring corn brooms and bang them around a little bit to get some extra swing in the ice.

PAUL SAVAGE: I think Kevin saw the evil of his ways at some point, because he got a huge amount of criticism. And then he evolved as one of the greatest to ever play the game.

HOW I MET KEVIN MARTIN

In 2003, I was promoted from Assistant to Coach at the Trillium Curling Camp. Now that I was responsible for the lessons my groups would receive, I tried really hard to develop new materials that weren't the same old PowerPoint presentations everyone was using at the time. I wanted to come up with at least one new, cool, thing each year.

So in September of 2005, I went to the Shorty Jenkins Classic in Brockville, Ont., to shoot some video. I remember interviewing Mark Dacey, Mike Harris, and Kevin Martin about things such as Mental Preparation, Team Dynamics, and other topics we might cover at camp.

Kevin was really chatty and ended up taking the majority of the screen time in the finished video about team dynamics. He said "You don't need to get along, and you don't need to fight. But you have to understand each other."

A year later, he'd form his new team with John Morris, Marc Kennedy, and Ben Hebert, and I'm sure his team dynamics theories were put to the test, both leading up to and following their 2010 gold-medal run in Vancouver.

While all of this was going on, there was a team forming in Saskatchewan that would define women's curling for the decade. With all due respect to Julie Sutton, who won the Scott Tournament of Hearts in 1991 (it was renamed the "Scotties" in 2007) and an Olympic "demonstration medal" in 1992, or to Connie Laliberte who won her second and third national titles in 1992 and 1995, or to the Ontario teams skipped by Alison Goring or Marilyn Bodogh who won in 1990 and 1996 respectively...

Without question, the most dominant team of the 1990s was Sandra Schmirler, Jan Betker, Joan McCusker, and Marcia Gudereit. (For the record, Sandra Schmirler was Sandra Peterson for much of that time, and Joan was an

Inglis, and Marcia was a Schiml when the team got together. For the purposes of this story, we'll stick to the most famous versions of their names).

The Regina foursome appeared in the Scott Tournament of Hearts seven times, winning three. Each time, they went on to capture the women's World Championship.

SHERRY MIDDAUGH: Sandra lived about a half hour away from my hometown. I don't know if she's a role model because we curled against each other... But that she attained what she did made it seem realistic. She was a mother, they all had careers, so it actually seemed doable for pretty much anybody.

She was a little bit older. We lost the provincial final to her in '93. They went on to win the Worlds. We beat her in the provincial final in '96. But I can tell you that we hated playing them because they were so good.

CHERYL BERNARD (2010 Olympic silver medallist, four-time Alberta champion): They just never, ever quit. They never thought that the shot wasn't there. I remember being afraid to play them. They'd never go away, the lead was never safe.

JAN BETKER (Three-time World champion, 1998 Olympic gold medallist): I don't know, maybe that's part of being from Saskatchewan; it's like we always think we're the underdog. I think we always sort of felt, you know, we never really curled against anyone thinking that we were going to walk away with anything.

We always knew that we were going to be in for a fight. So it really served us well I think.

COLLEEN JONES: I think everybody takes a page from the best. So we definitely tried to study her, and the way the team worked. I mean they had such great chemistry. And their style of game. I mean they they are a terrific, balanced team, maybe with a heavier hand toward defence more than offence.

So we watched a lot of tape. I watched a lot of tape of Sandra from all of their Scotties wins, and the Worlds.

SHERRY MIDDAUGH: They played together for so long, and they were friends. They could probably say things to each other that most teams couldn't. Women get tears flowing, and she's PMSing, and so on. They have to be careful. Sandra and Jan would get into it [each other's faces] a little bit, and you don't see that much in women's curling.

JAN BETKER: We just had a ball. We were lucky of course that it clicked and whatnot, but you know we couldn't wait to get to the rink because we love to spend time together. We had such a great time.

SHANNON KLEIBRINK (2006 Olympic bronze medallist): You'd always go to a 'spiel and you look at the draw. If you saw Sandra's name, or their team, you were trying to figure out where you would meet them... then hope that they dropped out before you actually had to play them because they were just the powerhouse team of that era.

JILL OFFICER (2014 Olympic gold medallist, six-time Scotties champion, two-time World champion): I think that they were all really good friends, and they had a lot of fun together, and a lot of laughs together. When you put that much time and effort into curling, you've gotta enjoy it, and have some fun with it. They certainly had fun with it. They liked to joke around.

COLLEEN JONES: I was at one of their Worlds in Bern when they won. It was just really interesting to me to watch Sandra's decisions and her demeanour on the ice, and the way the team interacted, and I think that helped shape our team a lot. Watching Sandra's team, they were definitely an inspiration. After we won in '99, I remember having a long phone conversation with Sandra just about how to get ready for the Worlds and how to prepare, and she was most generous in her comments.

JOAN McCUSKER: Back in the day, no one could make a living on curling. No one. If you were Team Canada, you might get someone to pay for your flights or your entry fees, and then you'd get to keep anything you won. If you were able to win, that's in your pocket. But there weren't big sponsorships like there are now.

We knew it was a choice. A choice that we had to support with a real job, and our families had to be on board, and we needed to be having fun. We were all taking time off from our real jobs... my real job was as a teacher... so this had to be fun.

So we were crazy. The stuff, the laughter that happened with this team. When we would get together, it was a fun-fest, a girls weekend that started as soon as everybody got to the airport.

GEORGE KARRYS: All the off-ice stuff is what you think about. The ability to gel... and a huge sense of humour. One or two of them were pranksters, I'm thinking Marcia. They were all jokesters.

One victim of the pranks was a young Jennifer Jones. Still in juniors at the time, Jones and her team were in Bern, Switzerland for a big women's bonspiel. Schmirler's team was also playing in the event.

JILL OFFICER: I would have been 19. We were there for a week, and saw Sandra's team for about half that time.

JOAN McCUSKER: They're the junior team from Canada. We have no idea who they are, but they probably know who we are because we were Team Canada. We decided that we should introduce these girls to Bern, because we loved Bern. We loved that bonspiel [International Bernese Ladies Cup], the Swiss chocolate and all that.

JILL OFFICER: We had just arrived in Bern, sitting in our hotel room. The phone rang and Jen [Jennifer Jones] answered, and of course, I can only hear half of the conversation. Jen keeps saying "I speak English! I speak English!" and this person is clearly speaking German to her on the other end of the line.

JOAN McCUSKER: Jan can do a great Swiss German accent. And we wanted to invite them to dinner. So Jan calls their room and pretends to be the hotel staff. And Jennifer totally bit.

JILL OFFICER: Then, Jen says all she heard was laughter and Sandra comes on the phone. Apparently Jan Betker had been the one speaking German, and they were just pranking us.

JOAN McCUSKER: We were just cackling in the background. But that was a harmless one. We did a lot of stuff like that to a lot of teams.

JILL OFFICER: Turns out they were actually just calling to invite us out for dinner, which was really nice of them.

I just remember showing up in Bern and they just took us under their wing. They wanted to make sure we were safe, that we knew where we were going.

JAN BETKER: Sandra and I always joke that we would have played together until the end of time, so it wouldn't have surprised me.... You know, you can't predict what's going to happen but certainly we know the friendships wouldn't have changed, and the reasons we were playing were the friendships more than anything. And of course if we're successful, that always helps too. But if we wouldn't have been having fun, we would have packed it in I'm sure.

JEFF STOUGHTON: We both won the Worlds the same year, or within a year, I guess. And the next year, we're all going up to this big bonspiel in Nipawin, Sask. We were going to fly from Winnipeg to Saskatoon and drive up together from there. But I screwed up our flight times, and we ended up getting in really late. And then we had to drive.

They ended up shuffling the whole draw for us. Teams were already done two games and we hadn't even played yet. So Sandra's team had to play at 9 p.m. when we got there, and again at 8 a.m. So they gave me the gears for a long time about that ... for a *long* time.

CATHY OVERTON-CLAPHAM (Five-time Scotties champion, 2008 World champion): It was fun to be around them. They were are a lot of fun... They got along so well, they enjoyed each other.

I'll never forget a time when we were in the Saskatoon 'spiel and we had just beaten them to qualify. And I was always taking my curling bag everywhere. People were losing stuff so I took it everywhere I went. So I'd always kind of put it by the door where we're leaving, so I could grab it on the way out. So I was going to leave, and my bag was gone. I was freaking out all over the club.

JOAN McCUSKER: It'd be impulsive. We'd be sitting at the Nutana Curling Club late at night, and think, we should hide somebody's curling bag.

CATHY OVERTON-CLAPHAM: Anyway they had it piled up in the women's washroom in the back corner.

JOAN McCUSKER: We'd wake up the next morning and think, "I wonder if they found their bags?" That wasn't that smart. Why did we do that?

Even after three World championships, Team Schmirler's legacy wasn't complete. In 1997, 10 men's teams and 10 women's teams played off in Brandon, Man., for the right to represent Canada at the 1998 Olympics in Nagano, Japan. This time curling would be a full medal sport.

JOAN McCUSKER: We'd just lost the Scotties in Calgary in '95. It had been announced that curling would be a full medal sport, and that spring, they were working on the process to qualify. I was invited to be one of the players to be part of the group to help decide that.

But also, I had just quit the team. I felt very strongly that I wanted to have another child and that I needed a break. And I had a two year-old at home. It was time to step back. So I had just quit the team.

So we go to this meeting, and there were representatives from all over the country. It was really good as far as hashing things out, about how this was going to work. They talked about what was important to the players, bonspiels, international experience, and so on...

GEORGE KARRYS: In the case of our team [Team Mike Harris], it was the Olympic drive that brought us back together. We were split up. I don't remember which guy called me, but he said, "We're back together!" I was not invited back. I wasn't to consider it. We were back. Like, "You are coming with us." They'd announced how you were going to qualify for the Olympics.

That's when we heard about the Trials, which was to be expected. But the road to the Trials was through these cashspiel qualifiers. And if there was anything we'd won, it was a lot of cashspiels. So that brought our team back together after two years off.

JOAN McCUSKER: The committee decided that the first spot in the Trials would go to the winner of a playoff between the '94 and '95 Canadian champions. So when that was announced, I had to go back to my team and say, "I know I just quit... but I kinda think I earned this one." I wanted that crack!

So in December of 1995, we played a best-of-three series against Connie Laliberte's team. We were a five-man team, because I was pregnant with baby number two, and it turned out Jan was pregnant as well.

But we played that series and won, so we had nearly two years until the Trials. We all took a break over that two years, we all had little kids. We needed that break. So in January of 1997, we got back together, all four of us.

We were going into playdowns as a warm-up for the Trials, and ended up winning the Scotties... and Sandra was pregnant. She was pregnant for the Scotties, for the Worlds... and then has a planned C-section two months before the Olympic Trials.

SHANNON KLEIBRINK: Initially, at that point we were just really excited that curling had made the Olympics and I can't remember exactly what the qualification process was back then. I think you just had to win a single 'spiel, and that got you into the Olympic Trials. So, much different than it is in the modern day way that you have to qualify. It sort of opened things up to teams that didn't maybe play as much as others. I believe we won the Autumn Gold in Calgary, which is the first 'spiel of the year. That qualified us for the Trials.

SHERRY MIDDAUGH: My first Olympic Trials was Brandon in 1997. That process was different. To qualify, you had to win a spiel. Some of those were huge, I don't even know how many teams they let in to those spiels... like 48 teams?

IAN TETLEY: Mike [Harris] and his team were probably one of the best bad-ice teams ever. They always used to win the Ottawa 'spiel [the Welton Beauchamp], and it was always on notoriously bad ice. You're playing at six different clubs, and the conditions were terrible, but they always seemed to waltz right through it.

GEORGE KARRYS: It makes me wonder if some of that could be chalked up to being artists, not technicians. Mike was definitely an artist. Richie has a natural feed, and he's a lefty. I've always had a good pretty textbook in-turn, but I don't know what I do to make an out-turn. Collin [Mitchell] always asked me, "How do you do that?!" when I threw an out-turn. Collin was more technical, but we had three guys who were heavily into the arts.

RICHARD HART: When I talk to people from that era, a lot of them still joke how the Olympics ruined curling. It was a clear line, right from that [1996] Welton Beauchamp qualifier... it was an Olympic Trials qualifier, but still one of the last "old time" events where there was some great competition, but also a good party. That year, people went to the bar looking for the party and it wasn't there. We ended up winning it, which qualified us for the Trials in Brandon, but that was the start of it.

JEFF STOUGHTON: The Beauchamp 'spiel in Ottawa was one of the best 'spiels running. All the big teams would go. They had buck-a-beer night, they'd have karaoke and live bands another night. We left the Ottawa Curling Club at 2 a.m., and they'd lock the door behind you. But if you were in, you could stay in. We got back the next morning at 8:30 because we were playing at nine a.m., and people were still on the dance floor.

WAYNE MIDDAUGH: Things were different back then. I immediately think of the Ottawa 'spiel, the Welton Beauchamp. Did you ever play in that one? That was one where'd you'd just try to survive until the playoffs, and then you'd try to sober up for that and try to win three in a row.

SHERRY MIDDAUGH: We won the Welton Beauchamp so we got our spot. We were already entered in another qualifier in Halifax, and I think we lost out in three straight. We were done in less than three days, but we stayed for six... just waiting for teams to get knocked out so they could come drink with us at the Liquor Dome [a legendary Halifax nightclub].

I didn't mind that process!

You weren't points-driven. You didn't have the stress of three years, going hard for points all the time. You didn't have that mentality. I didn't mind those regional events because you could pick and choose. If the maritime teams didn't want to go to B.C., you didn't have to. It wasn't feasible for some of those teams. Most teams didn't have the big sponsorships at that point.

RICHARD HART: Everybody had those Olympic dreams, and they all thought they needed to start acting like Olympians and having a different approach. You can literally mark the date on the calendar.

I played in the Welton Beauchamp once in 2000. I was 19. It was my second major men's bonspiel, but the first really big one. Like in 1995 and 1996, it was still a qualifier for the Olympic Trials. Everybody said the party wasn't what it used to be... and if that's true, I wish I had been around a few years earlier, because it was still one heck of a party.

Three distinct memories of that weekend stand out. First, we played 1992 Brier champion Vic Peters in our first game. He'd also lost the Brier final in 1997. At the time, he was hands-down the most famous curler I'd ever played against. I did face John Morris twice in juniors, but he wouldn't be really famous for a few more years.

The second memory is of the late, great Clarence "Shorty" Jenkins. Known for being a pioneer of curling ice, he was lying down on a couch, watching a hockey game during the party, and the club was packed. He asked me to save his couch while he got up to visit the men's room. And yes, he was wearing his famous pink cowboy hat.

The most vivid recollection from that night is that of Wayne Middaugh and Glenn Howard wrestling in a hallway. These were two of my curling heroes, now on different teams, rolling around on the floor, laughing their heads off as they grappled. Wayne told me, "Glenn and I have been friends a long, long, time. Whether we were playing together or not, we're always got along together and had some crazy times together. He had probably just beaten me at that 'spiel, and I was taking exception to it. That's the curling I grew up with."

It was a special event... and I only made it to one.

Anyway... 20 teams qualified for the 1997 Trials in Brandon, Manitoba through events across the country. The men's side was stacked with big names like Howard, Werenich, Burtnyk, Stoughton, and Martin. The ladies, meanwhile, featured just as many names including Schmirler, Laliberte, Kleibrink, Scheirich (later Middaugh), and Kelley Law, who would make her mark four years later.

JAN BETKER: I get that the media would portray us as favourites but from our perspective, Sandra had just had a baby in the middle of September that year. And so we hadn't played in hardly anything leading up to those Trials. So we, if anything, felt underprepared.

KELLEY LAW (2002 Olympic Bronze Medallist, 2000 Scotties & World champion): We were maybe a little bit young in the fact that we didn't really know the magnitude, I don't think? We didn't feel it. Although we were right in there. And it could have gone any way, I think.

RICHARD HART: We [Team Mike Harris] clearly weren't the favourite. I think if you asked any curling fan at the time, it was a 10-team field, and they might have ranked us between seventh and 10th. That being said, we would have ranked ourselves higher. We had beaten those teams before, we had a pretty successful record versus people like Russ Howard and Ed Werenich. They would have been ranked higher, but we knew we had a chance. We didn't count ourselves out. We weren't going for the fun of it.

GLENN HOWARD: They [Team Harris] weren't even on the radar, not because of a lack of talent, but because of all the talent that was there. They weren't a consistent team that was at the top of the heap all the time. They could beat anybody any given day and they proved that. But you never thought that they could sustain it over a week and win the Trials. And lo and behold, they were the best team there.

JAN BETKER: So that's kind of crazy when you're preparing for the Olympic Trials. So we were going in there thinking, "Let's just give it our best shot, and see what happens. Because, you know, we haven't been playing that much." I mean, Sandra had her baby there! "Let's just go see what happens. Let the chips fall where they may."

JOAN McCUSKER: For that whole week, Sandra was in one room with her husband, and her eight-week old baby, breastfeeding and trying to keep the peace, while the other three of us were in another room going "How are we going to make it through this week?" Sandra had just started throwing again. We just didn't know what we were going to get out of her. Not that we were worried about who we were as a team, but was her body ready for curling? We felt like we were underdogs.

IAN TETLEY: We [Team Middaugh] were one of the favourites going in. We liked to play a really aggressive game, especially in the first half. The ice was definitely not conducive to that kind of play. The four-foot path would get right up to speed, but outside of that it was always a struggle to guess what the speed was. We didn't know how to adapt our game, and consequently we ended up going 3-6 or something, walking away going, "What the hell just happened?"

WAYNE MIDDAUGH: In 1998, there was some pushback against the CCA about how they were leading the game. Werenich was playing that year and they were still on him for his appearance and his shape, because he didn't look like an Olympian. They still had officials on the hogline pulling rocks, and most of the time, if you saw the video later, they were wrong. That was one of the hard things that year.

Some teams got together and decided they weren't going to do what the officials say. "If they pull a rock, we're going to leave it on." And other teams didn't get in on that. There was a lot going on behind the scenes.

IAN TETLEY: We got focused on some of the wrong things. The very first day, we were talking to Werenich's team in the bar and kinda make this agreement that the hogline officials are always wrong, so why do we listen to them? So Eddie agrees, and says we'll ignore them if you guys will. But then we're playing them in the first or second game. In the seventh end Graeme [McCarrel] makes a fantastic shot, but gets called on a hogline violation, and they pull it off. Eddie says, "Look, you got us in trouble and Kawaja wasn't privy to that conversation." So Wayne got his nose out of joint and it was just like, "Aw fuck."

WAYNE MIDDAUGH: 1998 was the year where Mike and Rich, and Collin and George just got on a roll, and things started going their way. They played really well.

JEFF STOUGHTON: It was phenomenal. They played a game where they didn't expect to lose. They put a ton of rocks in play. It wasn't a traditional strategy. When we played them, they were three up... and kept the pedal to the metal. Most teams would pull it back a bit. But when you're playing that well, and they were that week, you can get away with it.

A bit of a surprise to some curling fans, because hey... "Who is Mike Harris?" They were the best that week, no doubt about it.

GEORGE KARRYS: We weren't surprised. For every moment we could have been irritated by it, we also knew it was a blessing in disguise. We knew there wasn't a lot of pressure on us, and people might be underestimating us a bit. We really paid attention to the draw. We had Kerry Burtnyk first, and we really wanted to win that one. Then we had Howard, and Stoughton. So we focused on the first game... actually, the first three. We thought, we've played these guys. We've beaten these guys in cash events before. We know what we're capable of, we wanted to shock some people.

JOAN McCUSKER: Our week was... all cliches aside... trying to stay in the moment. What can we do now? How do we get through this end? Can we get through this game? Okay. We did that. Who do we have next? Oh crap... It's Anne Merklinger [two-time Scotties runner-up]. Oh crap... somebody else really good. Every game was somebody good. We were never looking ahead, we were surviving.

JAN BETKER: I think we finished in first and then waited for I think it was Shannon and Kelley Law maybe?

KELLEY LAW: Sandra's team definitely had the upper hand. They were solid from top to bottom and very conservative. My style at the time was a lot different. I played probably more of a risky game. We played the semi against Shannon Kleibrink, and that probably came down a couple bad calls on my part. We were still young.

In the final, Schmirler and Co. played Shannon Kleibrink, and were in a tight battle until the seventh end, when Sandra made an amazing in-off takeout to score three and take control of the game.

JAN BETKER: That's the only shot we had. There was no discussion. That was it. So yeah, in that respect there wasn't any, "Should I play it? Should I not play it?" There was no discussion. So when Sandra went to throw it I think Joan and Marcy just said, "You know what? Give it your best shot. What have we got to lose at this point."

Clearly, everything... it just was perfect. I mean the physics of making that shot. You could throw it a hundred times and maybe never make it exactly perfect again. ▶ [4]

SHANNON KLEIBRINK: We didn't even see it coming. They called it, and I knew, out of her hand, that we were in big trouble. She rose to those moments when there was a big game on the line.

JEFF STOUGHTON: Sandra definitely had that knack for coming up with a big shot at the right time, and clearly they knew when they had to take some chances.

You knew she was going make it.

JAN BETKER: After that craziness, I distinctly remember all the girls were just excited. We got together and they were completely overwhelmed by the emotion of the situation. And I just said, "Okay guys, let's just refocus. We have three more ends to play. Let's just dial it back."

So I have an image of Sandra, even just after that, going to the back to collect herself. Take a few deep breaths to try and slow everything down because your heart's pounding. Yeah, it was a little bit difficult to be the voice of reason most of the time, on that team.

---

[4] 1997 Olympics Trials: Sandra Schmirler Amazing Shot -
http://www.youtube.com/watch?v=cM67XJS7yM8

SHANNON KLEIBRINK: I don't think it was meant to be for us. At that time, they were definitely the number one team in the world, and the team that really should have gone to represent Canada.

MIKE HARRIS: After we won the Trials, we all got piped out together, got our jackets, we were on the podium with Sandra. And we said, "You're going to get mentioned a lot around us," and she looked confused. She said, "What are you talking about?" I told her she should get used to hearing, "Who the hell are those guys with Sandra Schmirler?"

HOW I MET MIKE HARRIS

I met Mike in 2005 at the Shorty Jenkins Classic in Brockville, Ont. A year or so later, we were both in Calgary at the Kingsmith Junior Camp run by Paul Webster at the Glencoe Club. A couple years after that, I remember playing him (with John Epping) at the OCA Challenge Round in Marmora, Ont.

Over time, we'd cross paths more and more, but in 2015 we started seeing each other weekly. I started working at the Toronto Cricket, Skating, and Curling Club where Mike was a member. We each skipped a team in the Monday Night Men's league, and would chat regularly about the status of certain teams, his adventures coaching in Scotland, or my trips abroad with the juniors.

He was a slam-dunk choice for my first interview, not only because of our rapport, but also because of his experience as a player, coach, and broadcaster. We met around the corner from the Cricket Club and knocked off a few plates of chicken wings (and maybe a couple of beers) as we chatted.

PAUL SAVAGE: When they won, they asked within an hour if I wanted to go to Japan with them. I said, "You guys are nuts. You gotta take someone who can actually play! I'm not that person anymore." They insisted. I was going to be their alternate player and their coach. So I told them I'd go, as long as they let me play one game so I can qualify for a medal.

JOAN McCUSKER: It was a crazy time in my life. I told my sisters at the time, "I don't ever need to do this again." Sure, our families celebrated a bit, but immediately your schedule became so crazy, and other people were relying on you, you had to be certain places. It would be great if you were single, and didn't have a job, or didn't have children.

It was fun to say, "Oh my God! I'm an Olympian!" It was exciting, but it was scary. We were the first ones. There was no path. The Canadian Curling Association was learning with us.

CHERYL BERNARD: On their way to the Olympics, Sandra's team came through Calgary. They were looking for a practise game, and we played them. My claim to fame was that we beat them. They were the Olympic team and we beat them in a practise game at the Calgary club.

MIKE HARRIS: To be frank, the curling itself was awesome. The march in the Opening Ceremonies, meeting the other athletes. All fantastic. But it was an absolute shitshow dealing with the Canadian Olympic Committee. Dealing with the Canadian Olympic Committee was one of the least enjoyable things I've ever done. Going through staging, getting uniforms, going through the whole process, all the bullshit... Everybody's got their hands on everything.

PAUL SAVAGE: We met in Calgary after the Olympic Trials in Brandon. We met with the CCA and the COC, and they talked to us about the Olympics, and doping, and all that. And the two front end-girls, Joan and Marcia, said "Guys, let's all get tattoos on our butts!" And I'm thinking, that's fine for you guys, but I'm too old for that. But they're going to get tattoos on their butts.

So I'm in Toronto a couple weeks later, and I see tattoo shop on Queen Street East, and I think "Fuck it." I went in and I got a tattoo... I got a curling rock and the Olympic rings tattooed on my ass.

JOAN McCUSKER: We never agreed to tattoos. Marcia and me, we said "We're Crayola marker girls. We'll draw on some circles... but no tattoos!"

PAUL SAVAGE: So I show up in Calgary, for the staging, where you get all your stuff. We meet the girls in the room where you get all your equipment and uniforms and all that. I say, "So, let's see those tattoos!" Not a single person got a tattoo. I was the only one.

Then somebody mentioned it at the press briefing in Osaka [Japan] and they asked if they could take a picture of it. Later on, we're at the ceremony where they're introducing the flagbearer for Team Canada, and [newspaper columnist] Christie Blatchford says, "Paul Savage, your ass is on the front page of the Toronto Sun!"

JOAN McCUSKER: I never, ever, said I'd get a tattoo. I knew that I'd get old and sag. The Olympic rings would become ovals!

JAN BETKER: I'm pretty sure things are a lot more streamlined these days. But back then we had a lot of logistical things that seemed like we were taking care of ourselves. You know, our outfits didn't fit properly or curling outfits. We were trying to coordinate a lot of that, and we were trying to coordinate travel for our families, and to organize practises, and try to figure out a media plan and all this kind of stuff.

All this stuff that normally, in a curling season, you don't even have to consider. And so quite a lot of it, frankly, fell on Sandra's shoulders. So we would get together for practises and spend a lot of the time just talking about paperwork and logistical things rather than actually practising... so it's kind of a less than ideal preparation.

MIKE HARRIS: We're not used to that as curlers. We do everything ourselves. We'd gone through staging, fitting, and all that. But when we got to Japan, none of us got even half of our gear. No jackets, no boots. Everybody else got theirs... all the administrators, and bureaucrats, they all got theirs. But as an athlete, I didn't get my stuff. We went to the opening banquet in suits, ties, and running shoes.

So I go in for the 19th time, to try to get our gear. And I say to the girl behind the desk, "I know this is not specifically your fault. But you're about to get an earful." So I blasted her for 15 minutes about what a joke it was that they couldn't get their shit together. We'd been promised things four different times! I'm about to march in the opening ceremonies, and I don't have boots!

The Schmirler girls nicknamed me "Fuji." As in Mount Fuji, because I was blowing my top.

JOAN McCUSKER: We were scared going there. There's so much expectation. And when you get there, you just want to curl. But there's so much hurry up and wait. You have to go here and do this, or go to that reception.

GEORGE KARRYS: We were able to throw some rocks at the Karuizawa Curling Club, a little two sheeter, while the Olympic ice was being made. We had a couple Battle of the Sexes games with the women. They won.

RICHARD HART: It was an amazing experience that you think about often, like all the time. It was a life-changing event. Being a part of it all, meeting all the other athletes, and being accepted as part of the larger Canadian team. NHL hockey players were legitimately interested in the Canadian curling team. Some of them travelled an hour and half outside of Nagano to where our venue was... some of the hockey players made the trip to check it out. It was pretty cool.

GEORGE KARRYS: We were playing the games in our own little curling bubble in Karuizawa, away from Nagano. It almost didn't feel Olympic because we were so far removed.

JAN BETKER: The pressure can be oppressive, and even during the event, even when we'd already had games under under our belts, I remember playing a game against Japan and I just... I just, all of a sudden... I just lost it. Like I had all these negative thoughts going through my head, you know, "I'm so struggling," and my emotions were right on my sleeve. And I went to the bathroom at fifth-end break and I just broke into tears. Looking back on it, I think, "What the heck was that?"

It was just the pressure of being in a situation of feeling that you had to perform your best. And when I wasn't performing, it felt terrible. So it was a very stressful, stressful week for sure.

PAUL SAVAGE: I played the first two ends against Germany, then I had to fake an illness. Of course, it was the only game that didn't get televised because of the Ross Rebagliati drug scandal. It dominated TV for those few days.

Rebagliati was a Canadian snowboarder who won a gold medal in Nagano, but tested positive for THC, the principal psychoactive chemical found in marijuana. At first, he was disqualified and his medal was taken away, but the decision was reversed, largely on the argument that marijuana was not actually on the banned substance list. It was big news.

Both Canadian curling teams finished the round robin in first place with a 6-1 record. In the semis, the men beat the USA and the women beat Great Britain. Both teams were guaranteed a medal.

JAN BETKER: We struggled in that semifinal game. Oh my goodness, it was horrible. The ice was different, so frosty, there was no curl. It was just one of those struggle games... where nothing seems to go your way.

When Sandra went to throw her last shot, Joan and Marcia were saying, "I think it might be a bit keener but we don't really know." You know, one of those. And then when they dropped off about halfway down I thought, "Oh, no way." You know you get that sinking feeling bubbling in your stomach.

And we knew that on the adjacent sheet, the other favourite Sweden had just lost. So it was then I was thinking, I had a flash in my mind, "Oh my God, we've got to play Sweden for the bronze."

But yeah, it just dug in. I can't explain it. It did look like it was heavy and it just stopped.

JOAN McCUSKER: We won by *this* much, and I was terrible. I thought I had lost it for us. I know there's all this pressure on Canada to win a gold, but I tell you when you win that semi in the last end, by half an inch, the pressure is off at least for a bit. You're guaranteed a medal. That semifinal is so scary. You might come out with nothing.

So the highlight of my Olympic experience was getting through that semifinal without losing. And I remember bringing the girls in after the game for a hug, and they all went to pull away, but I said, "No, can we stay here for a second? I'm not in a good space, a good headspace. I thought I lost that for us."

Once we got through that, I thought this is all going to turn out.

I think every team that's won a national championship can look back through the week and say, "We got a few breaks along the way." Or you're not going to win. That's pretty much a given. So that was that was our break.

GEORGE KARRYS: Mike was sick in the semifinal and shot 90 percent. We killed the States. The team joke for years was if Mike had a cold, or he was feeling ill, he wouldn't miss. We were almost feeling invincible going into an Olympic final with him looking as white as a ghost. We had no reason to expect otherwise.

MIKE HARRIS: I was pretty sick for the semi, and we still drilled the U.S. The final was at 5 p.m., and I was still in bed at 3:00 p.m. I was sweating right through my jacket and two shirts.

Mike had viral pneumonia and was running a fever of 103°F. Jan Betker had also been affected earlier in the week. After shooting 92 percent in the semi, he followed it up with a 25 percent effort in the final against Switzerland.

MIKE HARRIS: I could have maybe used our fifth man. But I really wanted to play. I felt bad for my team. I let them down. I was terrible.

PAUL SAVAGE: I went out at the fifth-end break. Mike was sitting on the backboards looking downtrodden. The other three guys were out by the hogline. I went out for our five-minute break, and tried to convince Mike that it wasn't over. Trying to tell him that the Swiss guys already think it's won, and that they could tank. He didn't hear a word I said.

GEORGE KARRYS: I think it'll always sting. It still stings. It feels like a ripoff. We didn't lose because we played badly. We didn't lose a tight game that was great for television. We didn't lose because of wonky ice conditions. We lost because one of our players basically couldn't throw... Not to pin it all on him, because it affected all of us horrendously. It wasn't just Mike. He was the catalyst, but we just went downhill from there. We were under-equipped, unprepared to deal with that.

PAUL SAVAGE: I never really even thought about that [playing]. It would have been up to Richard, Collin, and George to suggest a change. The logical change would have been for me to throw lead rocks and call the game, and let Rich throw skip's stones.

And you never know, we were only down 6-1 at the time, and the other three guys were playing great. They were the best team there all week. We only lost one game all week, to Norway, because the Norwegian skip was God for a game. Other than that, we just dominated every game.

MIKE HARRIS: I just feel like we had a bad day, we lost. It sucks.

But if you're not willing to put yourself in the position to fail publicly, you're not playing the game. It's a privilege to be there. But yeah, you might lose. If you're not willing to put yourself in that position, then don't play!

The teams now would have a better understanding of how to deal with that. You'd have a plan, you'd have doctors, and fitness people. In Nagano, we had the five of us. Now you'd have a whole entourage.

CCA learned from it. We learned from it. Everybody would do things a lot different these days.

Schmirler's foursome would make quick work of Denmark in the final, earning Canada the first gold medal in women's curling.

JAN BETKER: A lot goes through your mind when you're up on that podium and a lot of it, for us, was just, "Oh, what a struggle!" You know it's not easy to get there and so you reflect on so many things. You know, Sandra giving birth two months before our Olympic Trials, and getting through that, and just all the all the things that you have to overcome, and all the times where you really have to draw on that inner strength, or whatever you call it... gumption, to pull yourself through.

And to do it with your best friends is just gravy. I mean that's just the most amazing feeling you can feel.

The Saskatchewan foursome was named "Team of the Year" by the Canadian Press, and appeared on the cover of the New York Times. They were inducted to the Canadian Curling Hall of Fame in 1999.

JEFF STOUGHTON: I don't think we realized how big the Olympics was. Being overseas, we didn't get to see a lot of it because it was all in the night time at home. You wanted them to do well, but back then... it didn't have that Canadiana feel to it, like it does now.

CHERYL BERNARD: It really wasn't until the '98 games, of course with Sandra, when it finally hit me that you could get to the Olympics curling. That's what really set me off to pursuing it further.

Tragically, the team's great run was cut short. In 1999, shortly after the birth of her second daughter, Sandra Schmirler was diagnosed with a rare form of cancer, which brought with it an endless string of medical complications.

She died in her sleep, on March 2, 2000, at the age of 36.

IAN TETLEY: She was just a bubbly, outgoing, vivacious person. You always felt like you could strike up a conversation with her at anytime. Even her husband, Shannon [English], he personified that as well.

JEFF STOUGHTON: The enjoyment of the game for them was just outstanding. Their understanding of what it takes to play, and win, and do everything like that. It was fun to be a part of that time.

MIKE HARRIS: After three World championships and a gold medal, the legend of Sandra becomes the question of how much more they could have won. Are they the best team ever? You can never say, but they're certainly always mentioned in the conversation. Their record at the Worlds and the Olympics was a perfect four-for-four, so what else can you say?

JAN BETKER: It was tough. You know obviously we were more like sisters than than just teammates. It was, for sure, more than just your average team. We'd done so much together and we were such good friends.

When Sandra died, we had no idea how big of an impact it would have on people, but we really felt just the pain of everyone. Everybody was so sad.

I remember the day I heard about her death. I was in living in residence at Ryerson University's Pitman Hall, and my roommate mentioned she had passed. I had never met Sandra, but I shed some tears anyway. My roommate (who clearly wasn't a curler) was quite confused as to why I was so emotional. I tried to explain, but I'm sure I didn't do her justice. I just knew that the curling world had lost a bright star, and to this day, I have still never heard a bad thing said about her... except that sometimes she was a bit mischievous. I like to think we would have gotten along.

On the day of her funeral, Brier games, which were being held in Saskatoon, were delayed, and TSN and CBC both carried the funeral live, which was broadcast in the arena.

Brian McCusker, husband of Joan, gave the eulogy. According to a CBC article at the time, he said, "If Sandra is watching, and I'm sure she is, she would be saying, 'C'mon McCusker, get this thing over with. The Brier is on and I don't want to miss the first draw.'"

HOW I MET JAN BETKER

I've never met Jan Betker. I've never spoken to Jan Betker. I cheated.

While in the process of writing this book, I reached out to dozens of curlers from all eras over the course of 14 months. While I was in Korea for the Paralympics, I listened to a podcast featuring an interview with Jan, whom I hadn't asked yet.

I realized that the *2 Girls and a Game* hosts had just performed the exact same interview that I would have. So to spare Jan having to answer the same questions and tell the same stories, I just asked the *2 Girls*, podcasters Lori Eddy and Mary Chilvers, if I could borrow some of her answers and put them in the book (with proper credit of course).

So any Jan Betker stories originally appeared on the *2 Girls and a Game* podcast, and if you're a curling fan, you should already be listening to it.

With one official Olympic cycle in the books, and the death of one of the sport's biggest stars, it appeared that the new millenium would bring with it some major changes to the landscape. And as the 2000s kicked off, major changes were indeed on the way.

CHAPTER 3:
THE 2000s - THE BOYCOTT

The period from 2001 to 2004 was one of the most bitter in the history of competitive men's curling. A group of top teams including Kevin Martin, Jeff Stoughton, Glenn Howard, Kerry Burtnyk, and Wayne Middaugh (among many others) decided to help form a new Grand Slam event series, which meant that they wouldn't be playing in the CCA's Brier, or the related playdowns.

Not everyone chose to join the cause, for a variety of reasons. Some were geographical, some were financial, but while 18 of the top teams were headlining the the Grand Slam events, Edmonton's Randy Ferbey and Russ Howard (recently relocated to New Brunswick) stayed on board with the CCA and were the main draws at the Brier.

KEVIN MARTIN: There are only two people involved in the first conversation and that was myself, and a guy by the name of Kevin Albrecht, who is the head of IMG Canada at that time. Well, I just had the idea. We were very successful doing those events in West Edmonton Mall and Sask Place in Saskatoon. So the kind of template of running a cash event in an arena, on television, was started. We knew that it would work. Well, okay, now what are you going to do to get this going?

KEVIN ALBRECHT: I told him that I thought I could help the WCPA [World Curling Players Association] but I would need their full support. We were talking about changing decades and decades of tradition that was not favourable to the elite athletes in the sport. I knew it would be a long and difficult process but if the players were willing to try, then so was I.

CHAD McMULLAN: I was working for the World Curling Tour when it was Arnold Asham, Ed Lukowich, Ray Turnbull, and Jim Furgale from 8 Ender [a curling broom manufacturer]. I was working for them, right out of school, it was a part-time job, so I worked with Asham [another curling equipment company] as well, to make it a full-time job.

KEVIN ALBRECHT: I raised the funds that allowed for the purchase of the World Curling Tour from a group of four individuals – Arnold Asham, Jim Furgale, Ray Turnbull, and Ed Lukowich. It wasn't the easiest deal to get done. It took months and months due to their internal debates... I then negotiated a national broadcast agreement with CTV Sportsnet - yes, CTV owned it back then - and convinced Doug Beeforth, Sportsnet's president, that their new sports network should show WCT events from curling clubs. Yes, we started in curling clubs with sometimes less than 100 people there cheering the curlers on.

CHAD McMULLAN: When Sportsnet was coming to be, and needed content, that's when IMG became involved. Those guys basically sold to IMG. I was still in Winnipeg, and we do our thing for a couple of years.

KEVIN ALBRECHT: These were not easy years as the WCPA was in a very public battle with the CCA and we constantly felt the negative effects of that battle in the media. A lot of companies said they wouldn't get involved until the dispute was settled. We sustained significant losses in those early years. Weak TV ratings and lack of sponsor interest was such a factor due to the WCPA/CCA fallout.

WARREN HANSEN: I can remember we [CCA] had a meeting in Calgary, that was January of 2001, with Kevin Martin, and Karen Purdy, who was representing the women... And in that discussion, we unveiled to them the plan that we were going to start in 2002. These two new events, the Canada Cup and the Continental Cup. We were still in the process of formulating how those things were going to fall into place. So progress was being made.

Everybody seemed to be onside with where we were trying to move things, and then we were blindsided in April of 2001, when the announcement of the Grand Slam and the whole boycott thing was started by Kevin Albrecht.

KEVIN ALBRECHT: We continued to move forward and developed the Grand Slam of Curling for the 2001-02 season. We felt we should focus on the four major events of the WCT. The public and the sponsors needed strong brands to associate with.

CHAD McMULLAN: Then IMG decides that we need to put this push on to really build our brand. That's when the "boycott" began... we did everything we could to not call it a boycott.

It was a decision for these players to play in something different...

JEFF STOUGHTON: I never boycotted anything! I chose to play in a different event. I don't know why people call it a boycott. We chose to play in the Slams, rather than the Brier. We didn't boycott anything. I don't know what you're talking about.

CHAD McMULLAN: At the time, I was the executive director of the World Curling Tour, but IMG was basically paying my salary. It was pretty cloudy. There was the World Curling Players' Association, who were a bunch of guys who were pretty much calling the shots over something that really wasn't worth that much. So we were trying to make it into something.

Part of it was trying to build the tour, and have a functioning tour. And the other part was trying to get more out of the Canadian Curling Association. More sponsorship ability at the Brier.

GEORGE KARRYS: I was the first consultant for IMG for curling, when they launched all this. I was brought on by Randy Paul and Kevin Albrecht to basically be the conduit to the athletes, to tell the curlers who IMG was, why it's a great thing that they're creating, and to tell them why exclusivity was needed. It wasn't on the books right from the beginning. Albrecht realized we needed something to stand apart, to attract big sponsors, and make the property sing.

RICHARD HART: For me, this was never presented as a boycott of the Brier. When our decisions were made, it was about promoting a new series. No one went to the CCA with demands saying, "We want this," or, "You have to do this." IMG came to us and said "We want to form a curling series, we think there's something to this, we love the sport. *But...* we need exclusivity."

They had to be able to say, "The only place a curling fan can watch Kevin Martin, Jeff Stoughton, Wayne Middaugh, Kerry Burtnyk, [2000 Brier winner] Greg McAuley, and Glenn Howard - to a lesser extent - is at our events. It's not forever, but we need this to get this thing off the ground. We need you all to agree to this." That was the pitch.

CHAD McMULLAN: One of the biggest things was trying to get an aligned schedule through the year. All the provinces ran their playdowns whenever they wanted, so we couldn't run any tour events in January, February, March... there was always some playdown event in the big provinces. So part of it was getting the CCA to tell the provinces they had to do it on certain weekends, to free up more time for other events.

KEVIN MARTIN: Playdowns took all of spring because the provincials took four weeks in different provinces, and regionals would take two or three weeks in different provinces. There is no room to fit in any bonspiel. It was all blocked.

So what are we going to do to get this going? The Grand Slam of Curling idea was brought up. Kevin [Albrecht] secured a title sponsor and television... but they needed to have the security of 18 of the top 20 teams and to do that. They had to sign off not playing in playdowns because playdowns blocked everything. So 18 of the top 20 teams had to sign off and it was a lot of work. Because people had to trust in something that didn't exist.

GLENN HOWARD: And we just felt things had to change, and they had to change from the Canadian Curling Association, and start at the top. They had to make some changes. I went to seven Briers with my brother, and I'd come home with a bill of, two, three, four thousand dollars. And yet you know the organizing committees were putting a million bucks in their pocket and the CCA are putting money in their pocket, and we're going, "What's wrong with this picture?"

WAYNE MIDDAUGH: I had played in enough Briers. I was fortunate I got to go at a young age, and we went in '91, '92, '93, and '94. In Regina in 1992, everything was sold out all the time and it was great, and it was fun... For Ontario, there was the North-South party, and the club hosting party, and some other things... and it was always a great time. But you saw what else was going on, and all the tickets being sold. There was all this going on, but at the end of the day, it usually cost us money to go.

In 1993, we won the Brier and we go to the Worlds in Switzerland. I think it cost our team $13,000 to go to the World championship in 1993. I was thinking, "This isn't right!"

KEVIN MARTIN: I was trying to run a business. Briers were were detrimental to your financial well-being. It's great to play in Briers, but they're killing us at home... especially if you win! You've got to take another couple of weeks off for Worlds. That's a real financial disaster! You're gone almost a whole month, but who's paying the bills?

RICHARD HART: It was hard. I had never been to a Brier, I grew up wanting to go to a Brier. And now, we're going to boycott the Brier. You're already thinking you may never go, and now you're going to take this stance?

JEFF STOUGHTON: There was never any doubt in our team's minds that it was the right thing to do. We'd been to Briers and to Worlds, and things were changing. Players were getting more recognizable, and it was time to ensure the growth of the sport. It's not just the events, it was about the players as well.

There were some upset people about whether teams were playing, or not playing. I'm never going to take a side about whether you did or didn't. You're your own team, you've got your own circumstances.

JOHN MORRIS (Two-time Olympic gold medallist): Now, if the boycott was happening at this stage of my career, I definitely would see it differently. But when you're young and you're brash, and you haven't had as much experience playing on tour... Things were different for me and our team back then. What they were just trying to do, Kevin Martin and the newly formed Players' Association... They obviously weren't being treated fairly. And I agreed with that.

CCA was making making a lot of money on Briers, and we were the stars of the show. But curlers weren't making anything from it. We'd have to take a week off work and not make a cent. I think I found it really hard to see that angle back then and just because I hadn't really been through it all.

CHAD McMULLAN: There were a couple of teams who broke rank. They were in when we were on the phone. But as things shook out, the Canadian Curling Association started calling them, offering them things, offering them jobs, sponsorships - in the sense that they could be used to promote events. So a few teams did break rank over the process.

KEVIN MARTIN: Guy Hemmings was a big name back in those times. He was actually ranked 21st at the time. So we didn't need Guy, for the 18 out of the top 20. But he's a big name and he said he would sign on.

Later, he phoned me at home and said, "Hey, Kevin. You know I will sign on with you. I will. But here's what I just got offered from the CCA if I don't sign with you. I get a guaranteed amount of money to do a curling teaching tour across Canada." The Guy Hemmings tour - and they paid him a lot of money to do that tour. And what a successful tour it was!

It was a three-year deal, and you know, they did that tour. But he said, "I won't do the tour if you need me." And I said, "Actually, the whole thing is about getting the players to be financially stable, for teams to be stable. So, no. Thank you very much for calling, but no, we don't need your signature."

Then he did the Guy Hemmings [Rockin' The House] Curling Tour and got paid very, very well for it. And he didn't sign with us. But what a great guy. I've got nothing but respect for Guy Hemmings.

CHAD McMULLAN: The unsung heroes in all that were Team [Greg] McAuley, from B.C. They won the 2000 Brier and were now carded athletes, and were getting paid monthly from the CCA or Sport Canada, and it was pretty considerable. If they had come back to the group and said that they were going to lose their funding, and they had to stay with the CCA, the group would have said, "You know what? We'd do it too. You've gotta do it." But they didn't. They worked out a deal with IMG because they believed in it.

GEORGE KARRYS: It was tough because there were active lobbying campaigns to change minds.

CHAD McMULLAN: In that initial period, I was probably on the phone 18 hours a day, from sunup on the east coast, until sundown in B.C. because it was one thing after another. Everyone was calling, "I heard so-and-so is bailing. If they're bailing, then I'm bailing too." You'd have to calm him down, then call the other person and ask, "Are you bailing?" They'd say, "What are you talking about?" It was like herding cats for weeks.

GEORGE KARRYS: Russ was making noise about being on the fence and not necessarily wanting to join. IMG told the players, and me, that we're nothing without Russ Howard. He was running the sport at that time. He was the name, not Martin. Guys were sending emails to Russ, asking him to reconsider.

WAYNE MIDDAUGH: If Russ had still been in Ontario, I'm pretty sure he would have been on the side of the guys doing the boycott. But the fact that he'd moved to New Brunswick, and it wasn't that hard to get to the Brier every year, he wanted to go to the Brier!

GLENN HOWARD: To be honest with you, I was kind of a little disappointed. I wanted him to. I wanted him to stay onboard. I think just to him... I don't want to put words in his mouth... I think the fact that he was down in New Brunswick and it just wasn't as much in the forefront as it was in Ontario or in Manitoba or in Alberta. I think he loves the Brier. He didn't want to miss the Brier.

And I get that and he was getting older, and this sort of thing. But, I truly believe if he was at home if he was playing with me, I think he would have boycotted.

CHAD McMULLAN: He'd just moved to Atlantic Canada and it's very different from what he was used to. Those guys didn't play on tour, they didn't see value in the tour. They played every year to go to the Brier, and that's it. So now he's there, and he wants to do this, but he's getting pressure from his teammates, from people on the street, saying "What are you doing? How can you do this?"

I also think he thought that he could just do both. He kinda did, and it didn't sit well with the rest of the group, that's for sure.

KEVIN MARTIN: You bet. When I write *my* book, then you're going to hear all about that.

DON BARTLETT: Russ was horrible. Like, he just didn't seem to get it. Like, Russ, you either can play in the Brier, or you can't play in the Brier. Those are your two choices you can't have both. You can't be on our side and still play in the Brier. And he didn't get that. He was thinking, "Why can't we do both?" You can't. That's our bargaining chip, not playing in the Brier.

News articles from the time state that Russ Howard had originally signed the Grand Slam contract, and was suspended by the World Curling Tour for two years when he decided to enter the New Brunswick playdowns. He told CBC Sports, "It just doesn't make any sense at all. All we've been doing as a small town team from New Brunswick is trying to do the right thing for curling. Nobody can convince me that boycotting the Brier is the right thing to do." [5]

GEORGE KARRYS: I found myself advising IMG internally, about what to do and what not to do. Unfortunately, they didn't listen to me. They jumped right into a media war with Warren Hansen, fingers pointing, spit flying. They did it wrong, I think. It may have blown up anyway, but IMG didn't need to be complicit in things blowing up.

WARREN HANSEN: Quite frankly, what I was actually trying to do, at that point, was trying to bridge the gap between the athletes and some very stubborn people on the the CCA board... in particular a CEO who didn't want to give an inch.

KEVIN ALBRECHT: We offered them 25 percent ownership of the WCT Tour for no equity, That's right...for free. They didn't even want to discuss it. It was at that point I knew they did not want the good-faith negotiations that they lead us to believe they wanted, and the meeting ended.

I recall their childish and petty nature and the [Canadian Curling Association CEO] Dave Parkes ending the dialogue by saying, "You'll be out of business in a year, I guarantee it."

---

[5] Howard suspended by WCT -
https://www.cbc.ca/sports/howard-suspended-by-wct-1.353729

CHAD McMULLAN: It was mostly he-said, she-said. I just remember reading things that would make me cringe. A lot of the things that were said were not professional. You might have expected that from the athletes, to sling some mud back and forth... and some of them did... but not from upper management of the groups. I remember tempers going through the roof, on both sides. Things were said that shouldn't have been.

The press would call these guys, and we'd tell them to go through us. But the press had private numbers for all the players, so they'd call them directly and talk to anyone. So the next day, you'd hear that this had happened, and this guy said whatever.

RICHARD HART: But then suddenly, it turned into a boycott. I don't know who did that, but I suspect I know who was responsible. It left me with a bad feeling. We were trying to create something, and we were proud of that.

CHAD McMULLAN: Kevin Martin and the players' board were in right from the beginning. They were part of the decision-making with IMG. Kevin Martin had an extra close connection to Kevin Albrecht, the head of IMG. We knew that that handful of teams, represented by these five guys, were all in.

Then it was a matter of reaching out to the rest, and doing it fast.

CRAIG SAVILL (Two-time Brier and World champion:) That was a tough one. We [Team Morris] made a decision pretty early on. I didn't get as much pressure as John did. He got a lot of phone calls from a lot of people. Certainly when we were on tour, a lot of people would talk about it. To us, the Brier seemed like everything. To get to the Brier was the goal we grew up chasing.

JOHN MORRIS: I got a call from Kevin Martin. He said, "Okay, here's what we're doing. We want to do a boycott, and in order for things to change we have to have all these teams on board."

So we had just won the World Junior Championships, so we weren't even really into it. We were just, sort of, breaking through into men's. So the fact that he wanted to boycott a Brier was huge. We hadn't even been to a Brier yet. That was always the big carrot for us as well... so that was sort of tough to grasp.

KEVIN MARTIN: I called Johnny, but no different than when I phoned Al Hackner, and Rick Folk. Many people that weren't in the top 20 anymore, but were people that mattered in the game. And Johnny didn't even know what was going on. He was just out of juniors. So I talked to him and he was nice about it, saying, "I don't even know what you're doing. I don't know, I just want to curl."

I suppose that's like when they asked me my opinion back around the Olympics and the Free Guard Zone rule, when I was a kid. The same thing... John, in that case, was like a kid. "I don't really have an opinion and if I did, nobody would listen to it anyway."

JOHN MORRIS: We had one sponsor, and it was Bruce Saville. And Bruce Saville was such a fantastic sponsor. We weren't getting a lot compared to what teams get now, but we were just up from juniors, and it was like nwe could actually almost play a year for free, or at least get some of our expenses covered, which was fantastic. Bruce was a big supporter of curling across the board. He sponsored a few teams... us, Kevin Martin and Eddie Werenich.

I am friends with Kevin, but I'll tell you what he said to me at the time and it really rubbed me the wrong way. Kevin Martin said to me, because he and Bruce were tight.... but he said to me, "John, if you don't join this boycott now, Bruce Saville's going to pull the sponsorship."

And I immediately called Bruce. I said, "All these big dogs want us to boycott our dream. We're just out of juniors, like, we don't care." We don't care about this, we're the just World Junior champs.

I'm like, "Did you you tell Kevin that if we don't boycott, you're pulling your sponsorship?" He goes, "No, no, no." Bruce is always a straight shooter. He said, "Never did I say that." Completely set the record straight. So that upset me.

I asked Kevin Martin if he had any memories of such a call, or potentially tampering with John's sponsorship arrangement.

KEVIN MARTIN: I actually don't. I really like John! We're really close friends. I don't know... I don't remember any of this, but knowing my personality, I would have probably tried to have him understand the importance of players sticking up for players. I think that's really important as your life goes along.

You know what I mean? If you're going to become a big name in a sport, the last thing you need is to be the guy who helps yourself in a positive way, or go against your comrade. You know, I would have put it that way. I guess it could be viewed as a bit of bullying, I suppose, but I just wanted to make sure you understood the consequences of not going with the players.

JOHN MORRIS: If that phone call from Kevin hadn't happened, or if maybe a different person than him calls our team, and they explain the situation better... if that had happened, instead of Kevin trying to pull this off on us, you know, maybe we would have boycotted.

But that was enough to upset us, and to be like, "Screw that!" So I think it actually had a reverse effect.

I think he was trying to put the heavy on us. Instead, we were a young team with a lot to prove and we didn't like being told by someone, "You're going to do this," and especially the way it was done. So that's what happened.

KEVIN MARTIN: It was tough to start with. Then Glenn Howard, Jeff Stoughton, Kerry Burtnyk, Wayne Middaugh, Pete Steski, the Lyburns [Willam and Allan]. They were really focused on it. They said, "You know, this makes a lot of sense." And once it got started, we had a group of really strong, well known, smart individuals that bought in, and away we went.

GLENN HOWARD: Kevin Martin obviously was instrumental in the whole thing. He gave us a call. He says, "Glenn this is what we're doing." And we said, "Done. Yeah we're in, Kevin. I'm in for sure." And I know there are only a couple of the big teams who didn't. Obviously Randy didn't do it.

DON BARTLETT: The year before, at the Players Championship [2000], was the first time all the teams got together and we discussed it. Like, "Okay, next year we're going to boycott." Dave Nedohin [of Team Randy Ferbey] was there and he got up and gave just an excellent speech. He was fairly new at the time to the great teams, and everything. He got up and said, "You know, guys. I support you guys, our team supports you guys, we're behind you a hundred percent." And I thought, "Man, a young guy giving this speech? Good for you, right? He gets it."

And then the next year they win the Brier. Of course, now they're in the uncomfortable position of having to give up a lot of funding... So it was very uncomfortable for them, to be in that position. I get that now, but at the time, I'm thinking, "Wait, why aren't you on our side?"

JEFF STOUGHTON: A lot of people ragged on Ferbey, but are you telling me that if you were getting Curling Canada funding, and Sport Canada funding, that you'd give all that up? I don't think so. I totally understand where they were coming from, not choosing to stay with the Slams. I don't have any ill will towards any of the teams who chose either way.

SCOTT PFEIFER (Four-time Brier champion): Well, we [Team Ferbey] won the Brier in 2001, and with that, the Canadian Curling Association, at that time... we became part of their national team program. We had signed an agreement as national team athletes.

RANDY FERBEY: We had the most to give up, The Slams were, at that time, an idea. We didn't know where they were going to go. They wanted us to boycott the Brier, which is totally ridiculous. The biggest event in Canadian curling and we're going to boycott it? I still think it was done very very poorly, quite frankly.

They think that if they didn't boycott the Brier, then the Slams wouldn't be where they are today and I say that's a bunch of bull, because they would be there.

CHAD McMULLAN: They were on the list. At least for the first round of calls. That was a tricky one, because he'd just won. Ferbey was the poster boy. It was around that time where they were just starting to promote the players more. That's another thing we were pushing for. IMG recognized its athletes who drive the game. Tiger Woods was driving the PGA. CCA needed to do a better job of promoting them, and they were just starting to do that.

So they were the poster boys. They already had that in the bag. It also didn't help that Ferbey and Kevin Martin were public enemies No. 1. That really didn't help. It probably got way uglier in the press than it ever should have. The tiniest thing gets out, and the press makes it bigger. Then the retaliation gets even bigger. So it just got really out of hand.

KEVIN MARTIN: I don't think he [Ferbey] was an opponent of the Grand Slams. It's just that they were sponsored by the Brier, and it was a lot of money to not sign. So they're guaranteed a really nice income for not signing. So it's not anybody's fault. You know what I mean? They padded their pocket.

During the boycott years, Russ had already moved to New Brunswick, so he didn't have a very good curling team. And then, Randy was the only team in the top 20 actually in the playdowns. Yeah really. You know, they won for fun.

JEFF STOUGHTON: I don't think you can look back on it and say, Martin would have beaten him one year in the provincials. You don't know. Us, or Burtnyk, could have gone to a Brier one year, and maybe beaten him, but again, you don't know. But to achieve what they did... it shouldn't be blemished because some of the so-called better teams weren't there. There's never a guarantee that any of us would have beaten them. It's not an open entry!

KEVIN MARTIN: There's no question that going against the players certainly hurts, you know, the way players think of that team. No question. Because you know, winning championships when there's nobody to play against, is not that good of a championship.

WAYNE MIDDAUGH: I was at the Brier in 2001, I was one of the teams they beat along the way. It is what it is! That's the way they decided to go, and they continued playing in Briers. And for a couple years, for lack of a better word, they had some pretty easy Brier wins.

RANDY FERBEY: Those are the kinds of statements is still kind of get to me quite a bit, you know.

Just because they boycotted, it doesn't mean they were automatically entered to win the Brier. I mean there were always different teams going back then. They say things like, "Oh, well we weren't in the Brier." There was no guarantee you were going to get there anyway!

GEORGE KARRYS: But what a good team, and they could have won them anyway. The first Brier they won was full strength...

I'd like to think the guys who joked about asterisks back in the day would probably agree that there's no need for an asterisk now. It was unnecessary and uncalled for. That was all political posturing.

JEFF STOUGHTON: I don't think anyone can argue that they weren't a great team. If they do... they're not that smart.

SCOTT PFEIFER: I just honestly think we might not have been the four most talented people but we knew how to get the best out of each other. And I think Kerry Burtnyk, before us, was the greatest example of how to get four guys who might not, on paper, be the best guys, or the best throwers on the ice, but they made each other better and I would say modelled ourselves after them.

RANDY FERBEY: I mean, the best team in the Slams was Kevin Martin, but Kevin Martin was not guaranteed to get to the Brier, or win the Brier playdown. We beat him in the Alberta playdowns many times. So there's no guarantee that he is going to get there anyway.

REID CARRUTHERS (2011 Brier and World champion): A title is still a title no matter what the competition is. If I have to beat the top team on tour in the final, there isn't going to be an asterisk because of who we played in the final. Showing up and winning a Brier is a lot different than showing up and participating. They still had to win the title.

GLENN HOWARD: It's not any fault of Randy or the team. They made a conscious team decision that they didn't want to do the boycott. They loved the Brier, they loved the national championship, and there's nothing wrong with that. I do believe, though, that the field was watered down, there's no question about it. But then, I would go to the grave saying this: They could easily have won the four Briers had we all played in them.

KEVIN MARTIN: So you really need an asterisk. And I can't imagine anybody arguing that with me. I mean, how is there not?

RANDY FERBEY: So they've all said that we *might* have not won. Okay, that's a fair statement. But how many of the Slam events do these people win, that we weren't there for, that they might not win? Has anybody ever said that?

You know, that's still a boiling point to this day! Kevin Martin does not win "X" number of Slams... yes, they're absolutely a great team. But do they win all those Slams if we, and Russ Howard, and whoever else didn't boycott the Brier would have been there for all them?

SCOTT PFEIFER: I would say it was definitely a rivalry. I don't think that there is a lot of bitterness, I mean. There's always that admiration for each other's abilities on the ice, but as far as getting along off the ice, you know, some of the guys you got along with. But I know Randy and Kevin had a long history dating back to when they played together for about half a year.

REID CARRUTHERS: And without them... if they didn't go and play in the Brier during that period, would the Brier have continued growing? It still brought a spotlight to the Brier, and they were the marquee team.

I've been fortunate enough to go to four Briers, and to win one of them. Even if I'm lucky enough to go to six more, there's no guarantee that I ever win another one. For Ferbey to say that he's won as many as he has... how can you take anything away from him?

CHAD McMULLAN: Long story short... the route would have been a lot harder, but I don't want to take away from those guys because they're one of the best teams in curling history.

I had seen Chad around the Toronto Cricket Club during the Chisholm Bonspiels over the course of a few years. But one day (I'm guessing in summer of 2008) he emailed me and asked to meet up for coffee.

He wanted to start a school program called "Rocks & Rings." He had the equipment lined up, but needed some ideas for the actual program, and an instructor to run the first bunch of schools.

We met a couple more times, at least once with some teacher friends, and planned out the activities and lessons in a standard Rocks & Rings session. We launched in the fall, and I did 25 Toronto schools the first year. We were off and running, and I couldn't believe how fast he expanded after that.

Within a few years, Rocks & Rings was in cities across the country, and into the U.S. I stopped doing the schools and was now working with him more for his on-ice business, Rock Solid Productions, which actually included a trip to Brazil in 2010.

Since then, he's been all over the world promoting the sport, and we're still working together on various projects. Rocks & Rings, meanwhile, visits more than 1,400 schools every year, and has introduced curling to more than 1.5 million students.

I asked Chad when he knew they were actually going to get off the ground, and that the Grand Slam series was going to survive.

CHAD McMULLAN: Probably during the first Grand Slam, in Wainwright, Alberta... everybody was there playing. Sportsnet was there for the TV stuff. And the event was happening. Before that, almost daily it was another thing that made us think, "We're done. This thing is over." It was almost a daily thing, where we thought we were sunk... and then we'd pull it back out of the fire.

They were a ton of work for everyone involved. Whether it was the event staff, IMG, the players' board... it was a ton of work by everyone. It was like a union trying to keep everybody on the same page, trying to keep everybody informed. That's the thing that's most amazing... we actually *did* stay on the same page for that whole period.

I don't think we'd have the Grand Slam of Curling, or the TV coverage, any of the sponsorship stuff at the Brier, a uniform playdown situation... I don't think you get any of that if those guys at the time didn't stand up and do that. None of it would exist.

After all was said and done the Grand Slam of Curling series had commitments from 18 top skips, while the Brier playdowns went on without them. Ferbey would win two Canadian championships during the "boycott years" which lasted from the start of the 2001-2002 season through the 2003 Brier.

WARREN HANSEN: We had a meeting at the Brier in Calgary in 2002, with all the players that were there to discuss this whole thing. I can remember in that meeting, Russ Howard making some very strong statements about Kevin Martin. I remember we held another meeting at that Brier, we brought in Kevin Martin and Kevin Albrecht and a couple of other guys from their group. That was the beginning of discussions with them, and those discussions were pretty heated.

KEVIN ALBRECHT: I distinctly remember our first meeting with the CCA in a hotel in Toronto. It was Warren Hansen, Dave Parkes, and the CCA president. They came in angry and belligerent from the start. I was taken aback with the disrespect they accorded to Kevin Martin. I had never seen a sport's governing federation treat one of their athletes with such contempt.

WARREN HANSEN: Albrecht was pretty much an agitator as well. Albrecht never wanted those players to go back and play in a Brier ever again. Probably the thing that began to swing it back in the other direction was the players' group appointing a guy named Paul Boutilier from Halifax.

McMullan and Boutilier were probably the two guys that finally began to bridge the gap, and eventually brought the whole thing back into reality.

KEVIN ALBRECHT: IMG was sold in 2004 and I took a global position with the company in New York City. The new owners, a Wall Street leverage buyout firm, were significantly slashing the company's expenses and they had no interest in curling. I arranged for the President of the WCPA, Paul Boutilier, to meet with IMG Canada and work out an agreement for the WCPA to take ownership of the WCT and GSOC at no cost to the WCPA.

The WCPA, through Paul, ran the GSOC events for two seasons and considering the tremendously small resources he had at his disposal, Paul did the best he could to keep the events afloat.

Boutilier was able to bring a fresh perspective to the dealings largely because he wasn't as ingrained in the world of competitive curling. Although his parents were Nova Scotia mixed champions, he only played recreationally growing up, and eventually spent more time focused on hockey. He played seven years as a defenceman in the NHL, winning a Stanley Cup with the New York Islanders before moving on to the Boston Bruins, Minnesota North Stars, and Winnipeg Jets (before they moved to Phoenix, or back from Atlanta).

After he retired from hockey, he went back to curling, played in a few Atlantic Curling Tour events, and eventually was recruited to negotiate on behalf of the Players' Association.

PAUL BOUTILIER (Executive Director - World Curling Players Association): You know, it seemed to be maybe it was the right time. I thought, "Maybe maybe there is a way to find a solution, without that attached emotion that I didn't have."

CHAD McMULLAN: Paul Boutilier got involved as head of the Players Association. He was way more open. We could actually get a meeting with the CCA. They'd talk to him. I remember we met and played golf, and tried to sort things out. All that happened because he was president. Kevin [Martin] was too controversial. He was too far gone with them, they wouldn't even meet with him. I don't even think we tried too hard with Kevin, because we knew it wasn't going to happen. But with Paul in there, that's when things started to thaw.

PAUL BOUTILIER: Change is always hard. So it was that type of situation, and it comes down to getting to know the people and respecting the viewpoints on both sides. And certainly working towards the betterment of the game. I think that's the one thing that everybody had around the table... the idea of what's right for the sport in the longer term... and to see everything evolve to where it is today.

WARREN HANSEN: One of the things which I was probably a key driving force behind was... maybe we can't do it with those events right now the way you'd like it. Why don't we create some new events, where we can do things differently, because there isn't the same historic context? So those two events were the Canada Cup and the Continental Cup.

RICHARD HART: We weren't asking for anything from the other side, but things happened as a reaction: The Canada Cup was formed, the Continental Cup was formed, there was sponsorship revenue sharing at the Brier, athlete assistance funds were created. But we never went to them with those demands.

Eventually, things were sorted. The Slams would continue, and the CCA was forced to make a series of concessions, for both men's and women's curlers. Another Olympic cycle was underway, and all parties were anxious to settle the dispute and look ahead to 2006. If they hadn't worked it out, one could wonder

95

how - or if - Grand Slam teams would have been included in the CCA's Olympic Trials process for Torino.

KEVIN MARTIN: Everybody on our side was pretty happy. I think I can tell you for sure that a really good friend of mine, Warren Hansen, wasn't overly excited about how it all went. But we're still super close friends. You know we sit and chat quite often about this.

In the 2003-2004 season, all the "boycott" teams were back in the Brier playdowns. Surprisingly, most of them didn't reach the Brier. Randy Ferbey won Alberta, and Kevin Martin didn't reach the final. Mike Harris beat Glenn Howard in the Ontario final. Brent Scales took down Jeff Stoughton to win Manitoba.

At the 2004 Brier in Saskatoon, Nova Scotia's Mark Dacey took down Ferbey in one of the most dramatic comebacks ever. Dacey was down 8-3 playing the eighth end, but took three, forced Ferbey to one in the ninth, and took three more in the tenth. He had to draw the button to win. ▶ *⁶*

The Ferbey Four would win another Brier in 2005; their fourth in five years.

Looking back, it was a tumultuous time, but by most accounts, necessary. The CCA introduced two new events, changed its restrictions on sponsorship cresting, and agreed that Brier and Scotties profits would be shared with the players, and later evolved into performance-based payouts.

Meanwhile, the Grand Slam of Curling and the CCA figured out how to schedule their events so they didn't conflict. Provincial playdowns were limited to specific weekends, and slowly but surely, the two sides learned to co-exist, if not cooperate.

BRAD GUSHUE (2006 Olympic gold-medallist, two-time Brier champion): We were never actually asked to boycott, but I was certainly part of that generation. And we benefited from it, probably more than any

---

⁶ 2004 Brier Final - Dacey vs. Ferbey - http://www.youtube.com/watch?v=YNSNX2zH7-g

team. When the boycott went on, we were never asked, which was nice. So we had the freedom to go and play in playdowns, and then we were young enough, and still good enough, that we got some invitations to some Slams. You know, when one of the original Slam teams couldn't make it for whatever reason. We actually we got to fill in.

So I played a number of boycott era Slams and I also got to play in the playdowns. So, you know, I fully understood what those guys were doing. And like I said, we've benefited from it once some of the changes were made with the Brier, and the whole game really.

REID CARRUTHERS : I was still pretty young when that was going, and probably didn't really understand it all. But thinking about what they did at that time, it certainly did make a lot of sense. You had to take a step backward to move forward. We had those couple of years where you didn't have every single marquee name in the Brier. There were still some memorable Briers, but at the same time, you look at the list of the players who did boycott, and did stand up. It's pretty remarkable when you look at some of the names who were willing to do that, and commit to what I think is the greater good... having a successful tour as well as having a successful provincial and national championship.

MIKE McEWEN (Three-time Manitoba champion, seven-time Grand Slam champion): I'll be honest; I didn't really know what was going on and why, but I got to understand later on, as we got into Slams much later, and understanding how the association events like the Brier playdowns and all that worked, and then having the separate tour and the Grand Slam series. I now very much understand why they did what they did. And I'm really glad and fortunate.

I think that they created the Grand Slam series, it moved the yardstick, so to speak, for the players' ability to negotiate. So, I really understand why they did it and I think it worked out long term for where the sport would go.

COLLEEN JONES: The Brier was already a ratings winner. The women were still trying to build our product. We couldn't boycott, we had barely built our product.

Even though they had Canadian Women's Curling Championships since prior to 1982 [when Scott Paper joined as a sponsor], it was not the event it is now. So my hunch is, the women were going to go and say, "Let us try to build our product."

JOAN McCUSKER: The women weren't organized, we had no leader, and we weren't invited. Those things go hand-in-hand. Had we been organized as a players' group, maybe we could have knocked on the door of the Players' Association, which was all men's teams... they might have invited us in. If we had representation, or a voice, they might have invited us. But we weren't organized, we didn't have that, and that's our bad.

COLLEEN JONES: But I thought, "Good for the men!" They had a product, and we were still building the product. So how can you boycott something that hasn't quite started?

The women wound up winning in all that, because everything the men got, the women got too. The men took all the risk, and the women benefited... because curling has done a terrific job of being pretty much equal when it comes to so much of it. They just took a big risk and it paved the way for a lot of change in curling. So good for them.

PAUL BOUTILIER: Without that emotion, you just sit down and get to understand the points of view. You certainly work with everybody... you create a path, and with regards to men and women, I think it was really important at that time that, as we walked through those days, we had to do it with both genders together, and walk our way through the path towards where they're at today.

Even though the Grand Slam folks and the CCA settled the bulk of their differences in 2003, some bitterness still lingers in the old guard of each camp.

Boutilier stepped down from the Players' Association after the 2007-2008 season. Hansen worked for Curling Canada until 2015.

Even when I started writing for Curling Canada in 2014, the words "Grand Slam" were still a bit taboo. You'll rarely, if ever, hear them uttered on a TSN broadcast during the Brier or Scotties. They might refer to a particular "tour stop," but that's as far as they'll go.

MIKE HARRIS: I have a bet with Cheryl [Bernard]. I text her all the time. I tell her I'll buy her a bottle of her favourite champagne if she can get Vic Rauter to say "Grand Slam" on TV. Just once. We [Sportsnet and CBC hosts] don't care, we mention Brier, Scotties, Canada Cup, and all that on Slam broadcasts all the time. More curling is good for everyone.

HOW I MET COLLEEN JONES

I worked at CBC News in Toronto from 2004 to 2010, and she would occasionally visit for work as she was, and still is, with CBC in Halifax. I remember bumping into her, introducing myself, and having a *very* brief conversation about curling, which I'm sure happens to her every day of her Hall of Fame career.

We crossed paths several times in the decade that followed at CBC, Curling Canada events, the Oslo Cup in Norway, but we never shared much more than a "hello," and I'm pretty sure that it was a long time before she put my face to my name.

The thing I remember most about "getting to know" Colleen was a time she wasn't even there. I went to the Mayflower Club in Halifax to coach at the Whitecap Curling Camp and I tried to count her banners hanging from the rafters. You couldn't see them all, let alone count them. Row upon row of provincial, national, and world championships. To this day, the most banners I've ever seen in one place... and on 95 percent of them was the name "Colleen Jones".

We chatted over the phone as she was driving home from work, from CBC in Halifax to Lunenburg, N.S..

CHAPTER 4:
THE 2000s - THE JONESES

While the men were locked up in a bitter dispute over payouts, sponsorship, and calendars, no such "boycott" existed in the women's game. Their bonspiel schedule went on as usual, the Scott/Scotties playdowns went on as usual, and eventually national champions would be crowned... again, as usual.

What was unusual about this time was that from 1999 to 2004, the same team kept winning... except once. Colleen Jones and her Halifax foursome of Kim Kelly, Mary Anne Arsenault, and Nancy Delahunt won five out of six Scotties titles, and added two World championships along the way.

COLLEEN JONES: We practised a lot... I guess we were a workhorse team. We enjoyed each other. The chemistry was so good, and I think that's true of all the great teams. They have this incredible chemistry and trust and belief in each other. And when you get that, it's magical. And I think you literally see it in every top team. We were always excited to be on the ice. When you're watching, you can tell that a team just loves it out there. We definitely had that.

CATHY OVERTON-CLAPHAM (Five-time Scotties champion, 2008 World champion): They didn't travel a lot. They stuck to home and practised, and really focused on the Scotts.

COLLEEN JONES: Yeah we were all business. We signed a contract with each other. You know, this was not a job to us, but it was a job! We had rules that we had to follow, and we knew we needed to sleep and all that. We loved that process.

We brought in a sports psychologist, Ken Bagnell, who was not associated with curling at all. He may have been the first. But he approached the sport like other sports, and made us do the same.

If you look at what was going on in our lives outside of curling, it was who we were. We had our careers, we were all moms. And we loved being on the ice and going to play. But it was all work when we were there. Because we weren't going to *not* be with our family if we weren't taking what we're doing the right way, seriously and professionally.

JOAN McCUSKER: They didn't try to win anything else. Their entire year was focused on re-creating the conditions at the Scotties, which was usually really straight ice. They'd try to recreate that at the Mayflower, and they'd practise the out-turn hit that Colleen was going to throw to win the Scotties.

MIKE HARRIS: She caught flack for not playing cashspiels, they didn't play on tour, they didn't win any money. But they didn't care about that stuff. They were clearly built for winning Scotties.

COLLEEN JONES: But we actually had unbelievable bonspiels back here in the east. At the time we had way more sponsorship for big bonspiels, at our home at the Mayflower... Dartmouth, N.S. had a big one, Moncton had a huge one... There were just more events to play here, back then, and they were pretty hardcore.

JOAN McCUSKER: I think they were really smart for bringing Ken Bagnell in to coach. He got the team to buy into what the role of a skip is, and what the chances of winning are if you can make her comfortable, and just never question what she calls. It was so effective!

COLLEEN JONES: It was recognizing what your strengths are, and managing the end to get to the shot you want to play. And it was no secret that I always wanted to play the out-turn hit. And I do marvel at the number of times I had an out-turn hit for the win... but yeah, I definitely would try to orchestrate that. You'd still have to be flexible and open, because it didn't always work out like that, but I was always thinking, "What's my shot going to be?"

So for me, I was just making sure I had a shot. And I think that's what I got from watching that much of Sandra's game. Yes, she had an incredible shot in the Olympic Trials, but most of her shots were pretty routine!

SHERRY MIDDAUGH: Having played so much against Sandra, I didn't see very much difference in their styles. Maybe I'm totally wrong. Maybe it was more obvious because Colleen was blatant about how she was going to do it. But seriously, why change your style when you're winning? Unless you're forced to. But why would you change?

In the ladies game, you see a lot more misses. Games can be lost on a miss. Colleen never really put herself in that position. I remember she made some key draws against us. You're thinking you might get lucky if she doesn't make this, but she usually did.

COLLEEN JONES: We got progressively better, from when we went to the Scott in 1999, we got a little bit better in 2001. We still weren't as good as the team we grew into in 2003, and 2004. By then, we were just a solid, solid team.

Nobody can doubt the record of Colleen Jones as a curler, but still, she faced more than her share of criticism, most of which was just silly. People poked fun at the way she chewed her gum, drank from her water bottle, and used her East Coast slang... "Just a titch less ice!" or "That's a pistol! Pistol!"

But it seemed that what bugged people the most was the open style of game she played. As she said previously, the only thing she wanted was an out-turn hit to win. And because of that, there weren't usually a lot of other rocks in play.

RICK LANG: You have to give her credit. Look at the outcomes she got, and how she got it done. I'd be envious of a record like that, and I think we all should be. It's unbelievable what she pulled off. Did I enjoy watching her style of game? Absolutely not.

MIKE HARRIS: For someone who's won six Canadian championships, she's somehow still underrated. She takes a lot of flack for the stupid stuff, like the way she chews gum. Who cares? She's an unbelievably nice person. So what if she threw a lot of out-turn hits? She makes them! It's clearly working for her.

JILL OFFICER: Every team has their own strategy, and that was their way to approach the game. It worked for them. You can't deny that it worked for them. She played to her team's strengths. At the same time, it's not like they couldn't play aggressive. They just didn't do it all the time. You gotta do whatever works to win the game.

SHERRY MIDDAUGH: It didn't seem like it affected her too much. She just went about her business. But it's not like she couldn't draw. She could draw you to death. At the Scotties one year... '03 or '04, suddenly she starts drawing, with full guns. And you're just like, "Whoa, what's this?" And they still won!

PAUL SAVAGE: She dominated the Scotties for years, but it was sure difficult to watch her play. I mean, the entertainment value was limited. They were rock-solid takeout artists, and they'd hit, hit, hit until the other team made a mistake, then draw for two. That was their style.

RICHARD HART: Kelly Scott tried to steal that playbook through the mid-2000s and it worked pretty well for her.

B.C.'s Kelly Scott was very successful by playing a similar style. She won the Scotties in 2006 and 2007, won the Worlds in 2007, and nearly won the 2005 Olympic Trials.

JOAN McCUSKER: After Sandra died, we made it back to the Scotties in 2003. We decided we were going to mix it up with Colleen. But the team in front of her was so good, she still had open hits. If you're going to mix it up with them, you'd better be on... or they were going to make you pay.

RICK LANG: I'd sit in my living room and scream sometimes because of the conservative nature of the game she called. But you gotta give people credit for playing their own game, playing to their strengths. It's smart! But was it boring? Absolutely. I don't know if I've ever disagreed with a skip more times . from my couch than with Colleen Jones.

IAN TETLEY: If you'd won once, then maybe you don't deserve much credit. But when you win six, you've gotta give credit where credit is due.

I can't think of a time when Colleen Jones had to make a stupendous shot to win something. They were just far more patient, and she knew her opponent would miss, then eventually they did, and she took the opportunity and would capitalize.

JEFF STOUGHTON: Colleen was at so many Scotties, and represented Canada so many times. And though she finally won a Worlds, Sandra was continually winning. You don't look at somebody's faults when they're World champion and Olympic champion. Whereas Colleen suffered some losses in finals, and struggled once in a while... maybe that's why people looked at it and critiqued her.

JOHN EPPING (Three-time Grand Slam winner, Canadian Mixed champion): They were for sure underrated. I think people were harder on Colleen, for every aspect, because they didn't like the style of game, they made it about her as a player. I think people were so hard on her, they wanted to forget her. She's one of the most decorated female curlers to ever play the game.

RANDY FERBEY: Is she one the best players, one of the top five players, or top five team ever to play the game? Absolutely. She did what she had to do. She won by hitting, whether was boring or not. She did what she had to do. End of story.

Six Scotties wins, two World championships, 21 Scotties appearances. That's just in women's. There's also a Canadian Senior Championship, and a World Senior Championship. Oh, and also two Canadian Mixed titles. Boring or not, Colleen Jones is hands down, one of the most (if not the most) successful curlers of all time, and frankly I think more credit is owed.

HOW I MET JILL OFFICER

My first personal memories of Jill are vague. I recall meeting her at one event or another in passing, but we didn't have much interaction.

When Team Jones went to the 2014 Olympics in Sochi, I was there working for Olympic Broadcast Services (OBS). I'd see them around the venue, and wish them good luck... but still no great personal connection.

It was only a few years later, when Reid Carruthers started his summer camp in Winnipeg, that I really got to know Jill. I had dozens of camps under my belt, so Reid asked me to be part of the staff to help things run smoothly. He paired me up with Jill, a curling camp rookie, as my coaching partner.

We hit it off right away, and worked well together. It was a pleasure to finally get to know her a little, to learn more about the team's methods and training process, and it was oddly gratifying hearing - from an Olympic gold medallist - that she really enjoyed my presentations and coaching style.

We sat down for a chat in Winnipeg, during the second edition of Camp Carruthers.

Following five Scotties titles in six years, Colleen Jones' Nova Scotia foursome made two more appearances at the Scotties before disbanding. In 2005, Jones's Team Canada lost a tiebreaker to New Brunswick's Sandy Comeau... which ended the team's streak of four consecutive Canadian titles, and earned them an arena-wide standing ovation. In 2006, they lost in a semifinal before pulling the plug on the Hall-of-Fame squad.

As fate would have it, 2005 wasn't the end of the Jones era. It was more like the passing of a torch... so a different Jones era could begin. While Colleen Jones was putting a bow on her sixth Canadian title, Winnipeg's Jennifer Jones was about to start her own run of championships, and 2005 was her coming-out party.

In only her second Scott Tournament of Hearts, Jennifer Jones faced Ontario's Jenn Hanna in the final.

JENN HANNA: Going in as a rookie team, you know the schedule before you show up there. So we were nervous and excited, and just this young team... just hoping we could split the week and be quite happy with that. Maybe make a run, hopefully for a tiebreaker, into playoffs. But then we saw that first game. Not only did we have Colleen. We were going to be on television. Yes, the nerves set in pretty early.

It was a relatively close game. I remember halfway through, thinking we might actually win this game, and being... I don't know if I'd say excited about that, but just sort of unbelieving of it, I guess. But probably the thing I remember most, is after the game was over... I'd won the Hot Shots that morning, and then we'd gone out and played Colleen, and beaten Colleen. And all of a sudden I was thrown in the middle of a media scrum, the first ever media scrum I'd ever been in.

Everybody was asking questions like, "Who are you guys?" and, "Where did you come from?" and "Did you think you could beat Colleen?" And, "You won the Hot Shots, what are your expectations for the week?" And all of a sudden our whole plan about showing up and flying under the radar... that was a big deal for us. One of the things that we were counting on doing was pitched out the window quite early.

While Manitoba sat at the top of the standings with a 9-2 record, Ontario snuck into a four-way tiebreaker. After beating Alberta's Cathy King, they beat New Brunswick's Sandy Comeau (who had already knocked off Nova Scotia in the tiebreaker) to qualify for the playoffs.

LORI OLSON-JOHNS (Three-time Alberta champion, two-time Grand Slam winner): We [Team Cathy King] were actually in a tiebreaker against Jenn Hanna and on the other sheet, Sandy Comeau was playing Colleen Jones in the other tiebreaker. And in the ninth end, Sandy had come through a port and made some incredible shot to take four points on Colleen's team, and that was essentially the end of the game. So they took their little in-between-end time out and then decided to shake hands. So as they're leaving the arena the crowd is giving them a standing ovation. And this team, the champions that we've known for however many years, are kind of at the end of their career. I think they'd made an announcement, so we thought maybe that was the end of that team as we knew it.

And so as they're leaving the ice Jenn Hanna's sister Steph was in the hack. I think it was either her or maybe Dawn [Askin, later McEwen], and they called a time out because of the distraction of everything going on. We're in our final end, and I think it was their last time out. But they knew enough to wait, and nobody got frazzled. I look back at that game like "Wow. What composure for that team to have to just do that, and nobody be upset about it."

And it was basically just to let this amazing moment happen and give credit to it. And then Cathy King, who was my skip at the time, starts bowing to Colleen Jones, and Colleen bows back to her. It was just legends of the game just showing their respect, it was really an incredible moment.

JENN HANNA: Every game we played for the last half of the week was do or die. We couldn't afford to lose any more games and we had to hope for a little bit of help, and things just sort of worked out that way. But you know, I think when you're in those games and you play those back-up-against-the-wall games, you start feeling momentum.... The more games we got under our belt the more times we were able to play on television, the more comfortable we were getting... and the more comfortable we were getting with the ice and all of the fans.

That game against Cathy King... she and I have talked about it since. The shots made in that game were something else. I think she said to me at one point, "I don't think I have *ever* played that well in a game in my life, and lost." We were going back and forth, making doubles and runbacks, and it was it was pretty spectacular... and fun. It was a lot of fun.

GERRY GEURTS (Owner of CurlingZone.com, Grand Slam of Curling statistician): Jenn Hanna is a big-game player, it seems. She wins the tiebreakers, wins the playoffs, and comes up big when it matters.

Jennifer Jones told TSN, "That week was such an amazing week, and everybody was playing well. That final was actually one of our worst games, and probably my worst big game. I remember saying after the ninth end, 'All we need is a shot. I promise, if there's a shot, we'll make it.'"

Manitoba trailed by two coming home, with hammer. Ontario sat one on the button, with a few guards in front of the house... and one Ontario rock hanging way out on the wings, just off the circles.

CATHY OVERTON-CLAPHAM: I remember I had missed my shot earlier in that end, to sit three. Obviously, Jen [Jones]wouldn't have had to make the in-off if I had made mine. We did see it [the potential in-off] after I had missed my shot. And we both had talked about it, but we didn't want to look over on that side of the sheet and give it away.

CHELSEA CAREY (2016 Scotties champion): Being from Manitoba, we were watching that for sure. I was like 19 or 20... we were obviously cheering for Jones. I remember thinking that I couldn't believe that Jenn Hanna didn't go into the house, instead of throwing a guard. If she just draws the eight-foot, Jones has no shot. The game's over. And all week, she had been drawing the pin for fun. They were just this unbelievably good draw team for that whole week. So when she was not throwing the draw I remember being shocked. So even before she threw it, when she called the guard, I knew that Jennifer was playing the in-off, and even back then, we knew that was her kind of bread and butter.

MIKE HARRIS: I remember Jenn Hanna throwing the wrong shot. If she puts another one in the house, Jones has nothing. It was an incredible shot, but it shouldn't have been there.

GEORGE KARRYS: I had a feeling she was going to make that shot. I was there with CBC, with Mike [Harris] and Joan [McCusker] and Don Wittman. I just had a feeling she was going to make it. I put my head in my hands a bit, because she beat a good Ontario girl. I saw what Jenn planned to throw... the guard on that last one. Just thinking, *"Go in! Go In!"* What are the odds? But you're giving her a chance!

While it's certainly true that a well-placed draw would have made it impossible for Manitoba to score two to tie, throwing the guard forced Jones into the wide in-off, which if made, would be for as many as four... and the Scotties championship.

JENN HANNA: I've had a lot... well maybe a couple of people, okay... more than a couple... but I've had a few people say to me, "Why didn't you put another rock in?" The truth is we tried to on my first one, and I was light. And then it was at a point where, flat-out, I threw the shot I knew would give her the hardest shot to make, and I was playing the percentages.

GERRY GEURTS: To force your opponent into the only shot they have to win is never good. If it's the only shot they have, there's no debate. They didn't have any other options so now they're 100 percent committed to the shot, they're 100 percent focused, and they know it's the only thing they can do.

KAITLYN LAWES (Two-time Olympic gold-medallist, two-time World champion): They were playing in Newfoundland, so the game was on early in Winnipeg. I played in a Sunday morning junior league, and we were all there watching that last end before we went on the ice. I said to everyone in the curling club, "She's going to make this shot." And they all looked at me like I was crazy.

CATHY OVERTON-CLAPHAM: And the funny thing is before she went to throw, I knew that we were making that shot. You just have that feeling. But during that whole game, I felt that we were still going to win that game. It was never a doubt that we're going to win that game, and I think that's probably maybe why she was going to make the shot.

JENN HANNA: I've watched the video, and I can see me... I was standing on the ice, and then I got back up on the back boards, and then I stepped back on the ice again. And that was really the first time I felt super, super, nervous in the second half of that week. Because all of a sudden, I had no rocks to throw - it was out of my hands. I finally felt the "Oh my God, what happens if we win?" And that was really the first time that hit me. And that's when the nerves set in."

MIKE HARRIS: I talked to Cathy O after... she said she knew Jennifer was going to make it. What are you talking about? It just goes to show you how great athletes find a way to get it done. What a shot!

JILL OFFICER: I remember sweeping that rock, and being worried about tripping over the boards, because I was on the side that was running out of room.

LORI OLSON-JOHNS: At the time, all the teams marched out after the last shot of the final, when the game is over. Everybody got to march out. And so all of us players were peeking through the bleachers on the sidelines, watching that last end play out. It was pretty incredible to see that play out in front of you.

KAITLYN LAWES: Then she makes it... I remember that moment. They [2017 Team Jones] don't like that I say I was a young junior when I was watching that, but it was a powerful moment for women's curling.

BRAD JACOBS (2014 Olympic gold-medallist, 2013 Brier champion): What a shot... that shot, when I see it on TV, still gives me goosebumps. To see the reaction they had, and how happy they were. It was just an incredible moment. That's my favourite shot!

We could NEVER throw that shot inside out. We'd never leave the rock on a shot like that. I have no idea how other teams do that. In my opinion, it's a lot harder, but I guess you get a little more spring on the roll. I like the outside-in and hit the low side all day long.

JILL OFFICER: When it hit, I was watching for the rock to have enough momentum to move the other one far enough for us to get the four points. Then I remember going crazy, uncontrollably screaming, and flailing around. I started bolting down the sheet towards Jen, still going crazy, my microphone fell off. Then after that, it was kind of a blur. ▶[7]

Jennifer Jones, Cathy Overton-Clapham, Jill Officer, and Cathy Gauthier were Scotties champions. It was Gauthier's third title, and the first of many for the rest of the team.

JENN HANNA: She made the shot she needed to make to win it. But looking back on it, at the percentages... She was out-curled that game and the odds were that she wasn't going to make it. Did she make the shot she called? She made a great shot. 100 percent. So it's hard for me to look back and say, "Should I have done something different?" Would I have done something different had I been able to rewind, and not knowing the outcome? I probably would have thrown my guard again.

RICHARD HART: Like so many of the big shots, she was forced into it. She had no other shot. And it was like, "Okay, no choice to make here. No pressure!" She goes and makes this incredible shot, wins the Scotties. And really, that was the birth of Jennifer Jones. Once you've made a shot like that, no one can ever take it away.

BRAD JACOBS: Until then, she hadn't won the Scotties, and since then, it seems like she's won everything. She's had so much success.

---

[7] Scott Tournament of Hearts 2005 - http://www.youtube.com/watch?v=J5hUqUH1XoE

LORI OLSON-JOHNS: Many people don't realize what else factors into winning a championship like that, in terms of funding, in terms of support and resources, wearing the Maple Leaf, and being able to return the next year. Half the battle is getting through your province and earning that right. And so by winning that game, it just created that momentum for her.

After that, Jennifer Jones became the face of women's curling for the next decade and more. She'd appear in 11 more Scotties (as of 2018) and win six of them, tacking on two World championships and 15 Grand Slam titles. In 2014, Team Jones also captured Olympic gold for Canada... but we'll get to that later.

Jenn Hanna continued to play competitively, off-and-on, with a variety of teammates over the next decade. She had three children during that time, and although she appeared at the Ontario provincials nearly every year, she wouldn't return to the national Scotties until 2016, after defeating world No. 1 Rachel Homan (also playing out of the Ottawa Curling Club) in the provincial final.

HOW I MET JENN HANNA

Although I know our paths had crossed multiple times prior, the first time I actually remember talking to Jenn was at the Ottawa Curling Club in 2012. I was in town shooting a video for the CCA, and went to meet my friend James Grant and maybe catch a bit of his game (James was an enthusiastic new curler, even though I'd curled with his brother Steve since juniors).

Anyway, following the game, we end up sitting at a table with Jenn. I think we played that game of trying to figure out if we'd actually met before. She knew who I was, and I knew who she was, but we weren't sure if there was ever an official introduction.

The only other thing I remember from that conversation is that I told her that she threw my favourite shot ever at the 2005 Scotties. With the last rock of the 10th in the round-robin versus Saskatchewan, Jenn went through a barely-there port and tapped her own rock to the button for the win. It kept her playoff chances alive, and eventually Ontario fought through two rounds of tiebreakers, a 3 versus 4 game, and a semi, to reach the Scotties final.

It's one of those shots with no room for error, on weight or line. Perfect team shot. I show it a lot to the groups I coach at various camps, especially when I'm talking about communication and managing a shot.

The rest of the night was a bit of a blur thanks to James.

CHAPTER 5:
THE 2000s - SALT LAKE & TORINO

In the first decade of the 2000s, there were also two Olympic Winter Games. In 2002, Salt Lake City, Utah, hosted. In 2006, it was Torino, Italy.

In each of the preceding four-year periods Canadian curlers were still working on developing a formula to qualify for the Olympic Trials, peak at the right time in December, then represent Canada at the Olympics in February. The 2002 Games were just the second attempt at an "Olympic cycle." The Trials were held in December 2001 in Regina.

KELLEY LAW: When I got my Olympic team together for 2002, we got together in '99, that was already the goal... to go to the Olympics. And win the Worlds, win the nationals, and all that kind of stuff.

Julie [Skinner] had already been to an Olympic Games. The other two hadn't. But Georgina [Wheatcroft] had won a World championship. And me, I'd won some provincials, but hadn't won a national at that point. So I just kind of went, "Okay, whatever! Let's do it! Let's make it our goal!" Even though I was also thinking, "Do we really want to make that our first year goal? Yes, of course we do. We want to go all the way." I think you have to have that type of mentality in every position in order to be an Olympian.

SHANNON KLEIBRINK: I was playing with the three girls from Sandra's team that year. The qualifying process still involved winning a single spiel. I remember we had a shot to win the Autumn Gold and it picked. After that we didn't really have another chance at it. We didn't get real close.

KELLEY LAW: When we won [the 2000 Scott] in Prince George, our first national, we'd only played a handful of games together, so we were kind of working out the kinks in front of everybody on TV... I think we played 15 games - with tiebreakers and all that - to win the national, so it wasn't easy. And there were points where it came down to one shot here, one shot there, or we're out. And we just kept rolling... Again we were still fairly new as a team. So 2001 in Sudbury, we lost that final to Colleen Jones, which was really bad, but good in a way. Because we changed our strategy for Regina, and that became our focus.

We didn't take anything for granted. We got a sports psychologist, we trained even harder. You know, in terms of physical strength, the diet was huge... because I used to almost fall asleep halfway through the game. My coach would bring me out of coffee and a chocolate bar. My energy level was just really, really low. So we changed a bunch of stuff. And so we were the strongest that we've ever been in in Regina and felt really good.

WAYNE MIDDAUGH: I think we won three of the four events we played in just before the 2001 Trials. But then we get to the Trials, it was weird... we couldn't get a feel for the ice, one guy would have a bad end. It seemed like every end, one guy would miss a hit or one guy would miss a draw. We just didn't seem to be at our level.

We tried different things in prepping every time we went. One time we played a ton going into the Olympic Trials, the next time we only played a little bit going into the Olympic Trials. The next time, we played different events. We did it a little bit differently every time, but for me, it's one of those disappointments I look back on... and I can't figure out why we didn't play better.

DON BARTLETT: I remember that one, or the next one... Middaugh won five of the 10 qualifiers. Like five of the 10 spots he won, so second place kept getting all the entries into the Trials.

JOHN EPPING: Look at Wayne Middaugh. Probably the worst record in Olympic Trials history, and he was a favourite at three of them. He's gone, 2-7, 3-6, 2-5, and 2-5.

SHERRY MIDDAUGH: With all his successes, that was something that bothered him. It was success, success, then it would come to the Olympic Trials and they wouldn't do well. It was a different mentality so they might have pressed a bit more, played a little bit tighter. It is a totally different mentality, a totally different pressure.

KERRY BURTNYK: I'm not sure I would say that I was more prepared [than 1997]. But I think that having the experience of going through it once before was a big benefit going into the second one. So I'm not sure there was something different in terms of preparation. But I think from a mental standpoint, I knew I had a better idea of exactly what to expect going in as compared to the first time. If everybody was being honest, I think they would say that it ended up being a much stronger mental task the first go-around than any of us expected going in. Because, of course, none of us had gone through it before so we really couldn't expect it to be that hard mentally.

RANDY FERBEY: You know, there's so many great teams that have gone to the Brier, or not gone to the Brier. Think about how many great teams have not gone to the Olympics. That comes along once every four years. Now if you're not at the top of your game for that one week, well then you ain't going to win because there are still going to be eight to 10 great teams playing in the Trials. Unfortunately for whatever reason, we didn't play that well. Maybe we rested on our laurels a little bit more than we should have. But now I look back at it. I blame myself for a lot of the stuff that we did or could have done or didn't do. But still today, it's a very very tough thing to win.

SCOTT PFEIFER: I actually remember when we were sitting down watching the 3-4 game at the 2001 Brier, and because Kerry Burtnyk beat Guy Hemmings, that got us our spot in the 2002 Olympic Trials. But I remember our team sitting there and cheers-ing with a glass of champagne. But at that point, that was our first Brier we had been at, so our focus was on winning that Brier. And quite honestly, the Trials at that point were almost an afterthought.

CRAIG SAVILL: I've always loved the Olympics, even well before curling was an Olympic sport. When curling was introduced, I never really thought the Olympics was a possibility, because at that point, as a junior, I didn't even think the Brier was a possibility.

I thought those teams were so good, and you have to be in the sport for so long to reach that level. It was always the Brier. Then Mike Harris goes in 1998 and wins a silver. Then in 2001, and we actually get to the Trials, I started thinking that it was really a possibility... actually getting to the Olympics and actually playing in it. Not just watching it every four years.

John Morris, Joe Frans, Craig Savill, and Brent Laing were fresh out of juniors, but were making a splash at the Regina Trials.

CRAIG SAVILL: We were pretty feisty. We had a chance to make the playoffs that year. We were playing Howard. We were three up, and gave up four in the last end against Russ and Glenn.

That was a game where we played really well, and then had four missed shots in a row. I hate pointing fingers, but it was completely the back end's fault. It was three whiffs and a freeze that bounced off... and that was it.

WAYNE MIDDAUGH: The weird thing that week was that Kerry Burtnyk started 0-3 and we end up seeing him in the final. And the other one was Johnny Mo being up three coming home on Russ and Glenn and they took four.

CRAIG SAVILL: It was one of the numerous times John got off the ice and said he's never playing again. If we win that game, we're in the playoffs at the Trials. We came in with very low expectations of how we were going to do.

JEFF STOUGHTON: We didn't have the best week. It was sort of a blur... it is what it is.

At the end of the round robin, Kevin Martin's team sat in first place, securing them a spot in the final. Manitoba's Kerry Burtnyk and B.C.'s Bert Gretzinger were tied for second, and played the semi to see who would face Martin's squad in the final. Jeff Stoughton, Russ Howard, John Morris, and Randy Ferbey were all tied for fourth with a 5-4 record.

DON BARTLETT: They [Burtnyk] were playing really well. I mean, the whole team did. And we didn't want to play them in the final, that's for sure. I don't remember who they played in the semi but we were hoping that team won.

Burtnyk won 8-6, which earned him a spot in the final against Martin.

DON BARTLETT: I think it was the fourth, and we were drawing against five, against Burtnyk in the final. And we had to go away from centre. It was one of those where you had to start down the middle and draw to the edges of the eight-foot because they have five all around the 12-foot, maybe one half in the eight.

And I remember we're starting down the middle, or just outside the middle and there was a spot where it stayed straight. It would run, and a little bit off the line it would curl, and it was a spot where if you started it, it would go nuts to the outside. So it was one of the few times where I said, "Kevin, take just take a little less ice because this might hang, this might run here."

So we get down to the end, and it's coming over the hogline and I'm looking up at where we are, going, "Oh no, did I just cost us five or six points? This is really curling!" And we just stopped in time. We had, like, three quarters of the eight-foot to get our one. But man, was it was panic mode from hogline in.

The thing that stands out most about that game was how well Don Walchuk played. He was a one-man wrecking crew. Holy crap, we were in trouble early a lot and he would fix it, pretty well the whole game, and anytime he didn't, Kevin did. It was a really good performance from our back end.

Tied coming home, Martin had the hammer. With a draw to the four-foot, he won the game and the right to represent Canada in Salt Lake City. Unlike Albertville, this time Martin, Walchuk, Bartlett, and Carter Rycroft would be playing for a full-fledged Olympic medal.

KERRY BURTNYK: Well, my best description later that evening, or the next morning probably, was that I felt like I was standing in the middle of a road and got run over by a semi. It was a real devastating blow. Easily the biggest disappointment that I had in all the curling that I did. And not disappointing from a standpoint that I felt the result should have been different or anything like that, just to be close to something that was that important and then to literally have it taken away on the last shot, which I have no control over. It was a very bitter pill to swallow.

KELLEY LAW: We were always going one game at a time. Keep knocking them off. You can't look at the week and say, "We're going to win this!" because it's all a good teams. And obviously, they're all there because they won something as well. So yeah, it was just one game at a time, and as we got closer and closer, then the dreams became reality. At the end, we didn't let down, we just kept ourselves moving forward, and we weren't ever nervous or scared. We were excited. ▶[8]

On the women's side, B.C.'s Kelley Law beat Saskatchewan's Sherry Anderson in a fairly one-sided final. The 2000 Scotties and World champions (not to

---

[8] Law vs. Anderson - 2001 Canadian Curling Trials Final - http://www.youtube.com/watch?v=Mm-r8cMjZes

mention the 2001 Scotties runner-ups) would be wearing the Maple Leaf in Salt Lake City. Law, Julie Skinner (formerly Sutton), Georgina Wheatcroft, and Diane Dezura (née Nelson) would try to repeat what the Schmirler team had done in 1998.

GERRY GEURTS: Leading up to the Olympics, they were playing in a Slam in Gander and Kelley hurt herself. She sprained her ankle on the dance floor. I think Carter Rycroft was involved? They were out on the dance floor having a good time, and I guess she stepped weird, and sprained something.

KELLEY LAW: Well, we had a decision to make on whether we were going to go to Switzerland. We could play a spiel in January there, or we could go to Gander, Newfoundland and play with the guys. My choice was to go to Switzerland, but some team members said, "We don't want to show our hand. So let's go play the men, and maybe we can pick up some stuff. We don't have to win the thing, but it will be good experience."

So we did that, and I was exhausted and we were just at the club after after a game, and it was my birthday. My girls are like, "You can't come all the way to Gander and not go for dinner and a drink with the guys!" because Kevin Martin's team was there. So anyway, I got up on the dance floor, and I think I was this caught my heel wrong and it just bent. You could actually hear the crunch over the music.

Sure enough, Law had sprained her ankle on a Newfoundland dance floor. There is no doubt she wasn't the first to do so, and would certainly not be the last. She was, however, likely the first (and only) to do so less than a month before she was due to compete at the Olympics. She was able to resume practising 19 days before the Games began.

KELLEY LAW: Now if that was my right ankle, I wouldn't have tried. I wouldn't have been able to kick out of the hack, and sort of bend it in that vulnerable position behind me. But because it was my my left ankle, the physio guy that I worked with - just about every day... He said, "You're most protected in that position like that." It took me about 45 minutes to get back in the hack that first day back. It was kind of like I was cliff diving. I was standing at the top going, "No, I can't do it." It was just awful. He says, "Yes, you can." So he had to talk me through it, and obviously it wasn't as bad as jumping off the cliff.

But oh, it was bad. It hurt.

GEORGE KARRYS: Kelley Law's team was all hot. They've got Bruce Allen who manages Bryan Adams for his whole career, super agent... and he's got a deal with a couple of hotel companies, and a casino. If they win Olympic gold, they're getting bazillions. It would have been the first million-dollar endorsement for a curler.

KELLEY LAW: Obviously, when you're injured, you're not in your best state of mind, and you're not feeling like everything is great. But yeah, I did the best I could. We still won the round robin, then came up against Great Britain. They were pretty fired up. And normally, if we play them, we'd beat them eight times out of then. But yeah, you never know when you go into an Olympics what you're going to be faced with.

Law's team wouldn't have a chance to play for the gold medal, after losing a tight game to Great Britain's Rhona Martin in the semifinal.

KELLEY LAW: We all had to talk to our coaches and our psychologist who was there. They said you know you got to go out and win. And I remember Kevin Martin coming up to me and saying how important that game is, and how important that bronze is. Imagine going home with no medal. "Reset your mind, and then go out and do it." He goes, "You want to be on the podium no matter what color it is."

The Canadian women beat Erika Brown of the U.S.A. in the bronze medal game, while Great Britain took home the gold by defeating Switzerland.

KELLEY LAW: It's not fun losing. I know we did feel a huge sense of accomplishment by getting the bronze. And like I said, we had to reset because we sang about winning gold for two years. That's what we had our sights set on, and that just didn't happen.

KERRY BURTNYK: By the time the Olympics was on, I certainly was well recovered from how I felt in the first day or two after the Trials. But actually I had a couple of young girls at that time, and we sat and watched the opening ceremonies. One of them, without realizing what she was saying, said, "Gee daddy, just think, you could have been there!" And for a moment, it reminded me a little bit of how I felt immediately after.

DON BARTLETT: At that time we were probably 0-7 against [Sweden's] Peja Lindholm. They were the only team in the world we couldn't beat. Every other team, you know we win half the games, or sometimes three quarters or whatever. You can beat any team, but that was our Achilles heel.

Midweek, we played Lindholm and, of course, he beat us again. But we were 8-1 after the round robin. Pål Trulsen [Norway] is playing his last game. If he loses we play them in the semi. If he wins, we play Sweden in the semi.

Trulsen is down two playing the ninth. He gets two in nine and steals 10. Now we're going to pay Lindholm in the semi. The only people you really don't want to play because they've got our number.

Leading by two, playing the 10th end with hammer, Martin and the Canadian team were in good shape. Only a steal of two by Sweden stood between them and an Olympic medal.

DON BARTLETT: Kevin's can see probably a good third of a rock, maybe a little more than that, and we're just going to pick it out. And if he picks it out, we win the game and we're playing for gold. He makes the shot. I don't know if I've ever been that excited. Carter was right beside me. I just grabbed him and I said, "We're Olympic medallists!" I felt really good about it.

Canada was guaranteed silver, and would face Norway's Trulsen for gold.

DON BARTLETT: And then two days later I got the worst feeling of your life. You go from the highest high to the lowest low, two days later.

KERRY BURTNYK: Basically Kevin Martin had the same shot to win the gold medal as he had to beat me. And in my mind, unfortunately he made the wrong one. Made it against us, but missed it for the gold medal. I'm sure he had a bit of a feeling that the next day similar what I felt like after the Trials.

DON BARTLETT: All I kept hearing was, "Why didn't they throw the in-turn and use the backing? He just threw it, follow him down! Play the same shot he did, and if you're a little heavy, you run into it."

If you're curious, you can look this shot up on YouTube. It's simply called Canada - Norway, 2002. If you're searching, include "Olympic curling." It's a Norwegian version of the broadcast, and it's in glorious 2002 Standard Definition. If you can tolerate the blurriness, fast forward to the 3:00 mark. Trulsen's in-turn comes to rest biting the back four-foot, and Kevin wastes no time putting down the broom for the out-turn draw.

DON BARTLETT: Well first of all Kevin's in-turn is straighter than anybody else's. So now we've got to take less ice and we're playing a different line. Now, you're bringing the centre rock in the play. Number two, we played the whole end to play the out-turn. It was the exact same shot we had to win the Trials. So you know he's ready to make it.

And there's two or three other reasons why we didn't play the in-turn. People don't really know about them. That was one thing that really bothered me. All of a sudden, everyone's an expert. ▶[9]

GERRY GEURTS: Why did he draw to the open side instead of using the backing? Well, if you need the backing, you're probably not going to curl up to it anyway. So it was a big debate at the time. I think he got cut up for that, even from people who knew curling. He got a little wired, and threw it a bit

---

[9] Norway - Canada, Salt Lake 2002 - http://www.youtube.com/watch?v=Hdajkgijpo4

too hard and Trulsen wins. You see Kevin, and you think he's one of the great clutch curlers, but I think that's learned. You have to learn how to win those games.

Martin was a bit heavy, and the sweepers backed off. As the rock approached the house, it curled toward the Norway stone in the top eight. The sweepers reluctantly got on it for line. It grazed the yellow Norway rstone, and spun two inches too deep, just hanging off the back of the four-foot, just outside the Norway counter. Norway took home the gold, Canada would settle for silver.

KAITLYN LAWES: I remember watching Kevin Martin miss his draw to win. I was thinking how heartbroken he must have been, for missing on something that he'd worked on for so long.

Kevin Martin is arguably the best in the game, when you consider his longevity, and what he accomplished in his career. It's amazing how much that motivated him to get back and really be the best.

DON BARTLETT: I don't know how I know this, but it took eight months to get over it. Eight months. I did a lot of drinking. I went to a doctor later that year and he said, "You were just self-medicating. That's your way of getting over it." I did a lot of drinking and after a while I got together with one of my friends. He said, "You're becoming a bit of an alcoholic here!" And I said, "I kinda like it!"

After eight months, I was just like, "Okay, that's enough. Get on with your life, shit happens." So I got on with my life. To this day it still hurts. I'll wake up dreaming of it once or twice a week. You know, how close you got. You could have had the gold.

Oddly, out of all the interview subjects, very few had specific memories of the 2002 Olympics. Perhaps it was because it was four Olympic cycles ago, but perhaps it was because curling wasn't really the big story of the Salt Lake City Games.

Figure skating dominated the headlines for most of the event, as Jamie Salé and David Pelletier were screwed out of a gold medal by a corrupt French judge. The allegations, ensuing investigation, and controversial confession from the judge led the Olympic news every day. The Canadian pair had their silver medals upgraded to gold later in the week.

The other big story was Canada's first gold medal in hockey in 50 years. No matter how popular curling is in this country, everybody gets swept up when a hockey gold is on the line... especially when Canada its their first in a dozen Olympics.

Regardless, the Canadian curling men brought home their second silver in as many tries, and the women brought home the bronze. Canada's medal count at the Olympics was a perfect 4-for-4.

HOW I MET WAYNE MIDDAUGH

Wayne Middaugh was my favourite curler growing up. He was on TV winning Briers and Skins Games, and making highlight-reel shots seemingly all the time. He won the Brier in 1993 and 1998. I was 17 years old in 1998.

So it was a little surreal when we signed up for the 2000 Ontario Zone playdowns, and I had to play him for the first time, at the ripe old age of 19. I think we were playing at St. George's Golf & Country Club (Wayne's home club for competitive purposes).

The reason I remember that is because I was so nervous and the ice was so fast, I couldn't throw a guard. Every rock slipped into the top of the house, and there was no offence to be seen for the whole game. My skip, Tom Butters, was hardly thrilled.

I've played against him several times since, and only once came even close to beating him. At the 2007 Provincials, we were hanging in late in the game and had a very unfortunate pick derail was was shaping up to be a good end.

We finally caught up on the phone, and he was awesome. He talked for an hour and a half, and I felt bad for taking so much time. It seemed like he would have been happy to tell stories all night.

After the completion of another Olympic quadrennial, the strangest thing started to happen... people started to treat curling like a sport. A sport played by athletes. Athletes who spent time in the gym. Athletes who worked with performance consultants, nutritionists, and sports psychologists. This was no longer your grandpa's game where the national championship was sponsored by a cigarette company... times were changing.

DON BARTLETT: You get to meet other athletes at the Olympics. I remember was looking at all these athletes, and they are just ripped, absolutely ripped. We were curlers and weren't really athletes. And I think that might have been the start of Kevin's thinking. "Well, maybe it's time to change our sport."

After that, he made us go to the gym. Walchuk and I didn't want to go because we're older, but we went three times a week. One thing I remember, it really made you feel good. You know you feel good after you work out. And then you started eating healthy. You didn't want go do all this work, then go have a cheeseburger. You really felt good about yourself, and that's something I never really expected to happen out of it.

WAYNE MIDDAUGH: It didn't change then. It didn't change until the Olympic Trials became more of a big deal. It wasn't '98, or '02. It maybe started in the Gushue year, 2005 to 2006. I went to those Trials as Glenn's fifth player. I was probably in the best shape of my life because I had skipped for a long time, I had just gone through the whole thing where Joe Frans tested positive for cocaine... I knew before the summer, I wasn't going to those Trials.

Indeed, Middaugh's second Joe Frans was banned from competitive curling for two years following a positive drug test at the 2005 Brier in Edmonton. In an e-mail to the Canadian Centre for Ethics in Sport, Frans wrote, "This is a complete shock. I don't believe it. I drink a lot, I'm a curler, but I don't do drugs. I partied hard at the Tim Hortons Brier, going to the Patch (a licensed area) every night. I did go to the smoke hole often because I like to smoke when drinking... I also went to many after-parties all week long. I don't remember seeing cocaine or anyone smoking it. I am at a loss."[10]

WAYNE MIDDAUGH: So when Glenn asked me, I made sure I was physically in really good shape that year. I didn't know if I'd be sweeping or skipping or whatever... Between games at those Trials, I'd go and ride the

---

[10] Ontario curler banned two years -
https://www.cbc.ca/sports/ontario-curler-banned-two-years-1.569315

bike. Every day, I'd go to the gym. Every day at the Olympic Trials... until they lost their fourth game, and it stopped right there.

Since then, teams really started to change. They started to focus on fitness and health, and the whole experience of how they go to the Olympic Trials, how they approach each event, how they work with coaching, and everything. To me, it's too much... but that's just my opinion.

REID CARRUTHERS: Not to discredit anyone who took fitness seriously before that, because there were lots of good sweepers before then who put a lot of effort in and got themselves in shape. It seems to have been a slow progression from something that was kind of important, to something that's now essential.

Can you beat the top four or five teams in Canada at the Olympic Trials if you're not in shape to do so? I don't think so. The fitness level has been raised, and it gets higher every year.

SCOTT PFEIFER: Once we played in the 2001 Trials, and then you go and watch Kevin Martin in his big game in 2002, the Olympics obviously then became a major focus for us. We knew we'd be sticking together from between 2003 to 2006 so we kind of put a four-year plan together and really wanted to beat him in 2006.

JILL OFFICER: We had kind of started the fitness stuff, because we now had the resources. But that was only one summer of training. We couldn't possibly have been fully ready to experience that. So after that, we had a little more time to put into that kind of stuff. We had more resources for fitness, sports psych, nutrition... all that stuff became more available then.

JOHN MORRIS: With the inclusion of the Olympics, I started feeling like I wanted an edge over my competition. When I went to my first Brier in 2002, we lost to Ferbey in the final. And we'd had a good Brier, but at the end of it, we were a little bit burnt out. And I said I never wanted to feel like that again in a final. You know it's a long week, like the Trials or a Brier. I want to be as fresh at the end of the week as I felt the first weekend. So I started really changing my preparation.

And so not only did that physical edge occur, but also I find that there's a really great effect you can have mentally, from not only proper, nutrition, but also proper consistent training. So I felt that I was really mentally sharp. That mental toughness, that I may have had sometimes in the past, now it was like I could pretty much turn it on, on demand.

BEN HEBERT (2010 Olympic gold-medallist, three-time Brier champion): Although there were Olympics in '98 and '02, I felt like '06 is when things started to change. Now I say that because that's when it changed for me. For Kevin Martin who won in 2001-02, it may have changed for him then. But I feel like the curling world, at that point, saw what was going on with the Olympics, and for '06-'07 things really started to change.

COLLEEN JONES: We were close when Kelley Law won for Salt Lake City and that was probably our best option because... or maybe not, no. The one after that, Torino, I guess we went in pretty favoured because we were Canadian champions four times in a row, and we'd just won a World championship.

Those Trials were in Halifax. It didn't work out! You know that sometimes that's the way it goes. I think we over-prepared for it, but that's curling sometimes.

SHANNON KLEIBRINK: 2005 was a year that we actually thought we had a team going in where our expectation was we could make the playoffs, and possibly win it. We had put a lot into it. That was sort of when everybody was in the gym, starting with the sports psychology, adding all the extra elements of the game that we hadn't maybe had in the previous four years. So we all felt like we had put everything out there, done everything we possibly could to win that trial.

AMY NIXON (2006 Olympic bronze-medallist, two-time Scotties champion): I didn't think we were going to win. I just fully expected we could win, just to be clear. I didn't think we should have been ranked No. 1. I really was just thinking, "Let's make playoffs and see happens." But I absolutely prepared myself to be in Torino.

Kleibrink's team (with Amy Nixon, Glenys Bakker, and Christine Keshen) started the week with a win, but then lost three straight. In a 10-team round robin, four losses usually leaves you out of the playoff picture.

AMY NIXON: I remember the moment that were 1-and-3, and I knew that was all the losses we could afford. And I remember we really had to come together as a team. "You've got to believe." It was a lot of that all week.

It was probably the best thing for us, being 1-and-3 because we weren't the most cohesive team, and we needed something to make us cohesive. And that was exactly what we needed to pull together and claw back almost from the brink.

Kleibrink strung together four wins, knocking off Colleen Jones, Sherry Anderson, Sherry Middaugh, and Jo-Ann Rizzo. Her final round-robin game was against Stefanie Lawton, and carried playoff implications. Lawton was 6-2, while Kleibrink was 5-3.

If Kleibrink won, she'd have the head-to-head over both Lawton and Middaugh, who would be forced to break a tie for third place. A loss, and Kleibrink would face Middaugh in the tiebreaker.

Kleibrink beat Lawton, who went on to beat Middaugh in the tiebreaker. Kleibrink would beat Lawton again in the semifinal, which meant she'd be facing off against No. 1 ranked Kelly Scott, who would go on to win the next two Scotties Tournament of Hearts.

Up two in the 10th end, two early mistakes got Scott's B.C. foursome in trouble. Kleibrink kept the pressure on and Scott was forced to abandon her defensive strategy and start drawing and freezing.

SHANNON KLEIBRINK: The whole game we were just thinking, "What do we have to do to win now?... now we're down two... now what do we have to do?"

Somehow we made a comeback in the final and my team made some incredible shots.

CHERYL BERNARD: Shannon is a true competitor and a great athlete. She never really gets concerned, she never gets ruffled, never seems fazeded. She plays a pretty defensive style of game. She was able to do that, and continue doing that, even with the four-rock rule. She'll make most of her shots, but she'll also get some misses from the opposition... and they'd always capitalize on them. She's a real matter-of-fact player on the ice. Great thrower, could make the big shot if she had do.

Amy Nixon, who was with her for three of those Olympic runs, is a super competitor too. Their back end was really strong and competitive.

SHERRY MIDDAUGH: Shannon's not shiny. She's not in your face. She goes about her business. She's not flashy. Just always gets the job done.

While it wasn't flashy, it was textbook. Needing two to tie, and three to win, Kleibrink kept her guards in play, and a few miscues by Scott's team (including a near-but-not perfect game-saver with her last shot) allowed Kleibrink a hit for the win. It wasn't a gimme, however, as there were a few ways it could have gone wrong.

Needing to move Scott's last draw (which had just rubbed a stone on the way by, to remain visible), Kleibrink had a choice to either pick it out through the crowded four-foot, or nose it and risk a jam on a rock in the back four.

If the pick runs wide, you jam. If the nose hit runs wide, you jam... but there were also guards in play on the narrow side. Tick a guard, you lose. To make matters more complicated, they were playing a particularly straight piece of ice. They opted for the nose hit.

AMY NIXON: I remember the moment that we were standing in the house for the last shot. Shannon is looking at it and says, "... but if I miss it that way, we lose!" And I said, "I know."

SHANNON KLEIBRINK: Well, our team has just had this motto that we would believe until the end that we would win. So I don't even remember that game, thinking that we were out of it. We were only down two coming home and we all know that anything can happen in big finals like that.

And so we were lucky enough to score four in that last end and we didn't even have to play an extra.

After a bit of panicked sweeping, her stone snuck by the guard, and hit as close to the nose as possible. Scott's rock ticked the backing on the way by, but the shooter had already stopped dead. ▶ [11]

People who talk about it like to mention what an exciting finish it was when Kleibrink took three to win the Olympic Trials. It was actually a shot for four. The backing that was ticked stayed in for fourth shot. Oddly, Shannon Kleibrink is the only person I talked to who said it was four. I checked the tape, and she's right!

Even the Curling Canada media guide has it wrong, likely because that's what the officials posted on the scoreboard. Regardless, it was enough points to win.

JOHN EPPING: It seemed like destiny. Giving up three in the 10th to lose... that was a collapse.

---

[11] 2005 Tim Hortons Roar of the Rings - http://www.youtube.com/watch?v=n3B_Cpm1pQc

AMY NIXON: The other thing that is an incredible memory for me, is that my dad was coaching us. Before we went, we'd been looking at all these provincial jackets in the closet... he came out when we won, and he grabbed me and hugged me. I said, "Dad, we got a Maple Leaf!" He started crying and said, "Thanks, Wee."

According to Amy, "Wee" has been her nickname since she was a child. Anybody who follows her on Twitter may already be familiar with her handle: @Wee_Nixon.

JOHN EPPING: Imagine that team [Kelly Scott] wins the Olympic Trials. Suddenly, they've won two Scotties, a World championship, and the Olympic Trials, probably a medal, then you've got to put her in the mix for everything. That team was solid. They were really good. They should have won the Olympic Trials. They were the best team.

I agree with John that Kelly Scott's team in the mid-2000s doesn't get the credit it deserves. Perhaps because they were sandwiched between the two Jones dynasties, or maybe because they ONLY won two Scotties and a World championship, Team Kelly Scott gets looked over too easily.

HOW I MET SHERRY MIDDAUGH

I'm judging when I first met Sherry on a pair of shoes. They were BalancePlus Deluxes, with the lace flap, with quarter-inch teflon. Whenever those shoes arrived (I'm guessing in 2005-2006 or so) was my first real interaction with Sherry.

At the time, my friend Kate Hamer was curling with Sherry and they needed their team website overhauled. Kate, knowing that I handled a few other web projects, asked if I could do it, and how much it would cost.

Considering it was a pretty small job and wouldn't take too long, I said the cost would be a new pair of curling shoes... which they'd acquire from their equipment sponsor, BalancePlus, on my behalf.

Anyway, I managed Team Middaugh's website for a few seasons, which gave me a few occasions to chat with them here and there, either at tour stops or the now annual Players' Championship Grand Slam stop in Toronto... which happens to take place about 400 metres from my house. We'd occasionally play a game of pool at Mick E. Fynns, the pub across from the arena which acted as the unofficial "Patch."

I was up in her neighbourhood for a golf outing, so I asked if I could meet up and interview her and Wayne. Wayne was at work, but Sherry poured me a Caesar and took me out to the boathouse deck where we talked curling overlooking the beautiful Georgian Bay.

At the 2005 Trials, there was also a men's representative to be crowned Team Canada. But first, you had to qualify... and some young lads from Newfoundland decided to do it the hard way.

MARK NICHOLS (2006 Olympic gold-medallist, Two-time Brier champion): We're in a tough spot, flying in and out of

Newfoundland, compared to some of the other teams that are more centrally located, that's for sure. But we knew if we wanted to get to the level of Kevin, and Randy, and Jeff Stoughton, and Wayne, and all those guys... the only way was to travel and play in the events that they were at.

BRAD GUSHUE: Obviously the cost for us getting off the island is a big hindrance for us, and a lot of teams. But really, the other big thing that a lot of people forget about is the time. For us, when we go west, anywhere really west of Toronto, you have to add an extra day on each end.

GERRY GEURTS: He essentially has to fly two and a half hours and *then* start travelling like everybody else does.

MARK NICHOLS: We didn't have a lot of cash in those days. In 2005, we had lost the Brier 3 versus 4 game to Jay Peachey, and if we had won that game we would have had a Trials spot.

And then going in that fall, there was one spot left at the Canada Cup East in Ottawa. But we didn't have a lot of money and you know, we played as much as we could. We ended up getting a loan from some family members so we could get there.

BRAD GUSHUE: We had a bad fall. So all the money that we had from from sponsors and winnings was pretty well gone. So I booked one-way tickets because that's all I had money for, to go to Ottawa. We got a friend of our team, who worked at a hotel up there, to give us free rooms, but it was about 40 minutes from the rink. So we had to commute a long way once we got up there. I didn't tell the guys that we we only had one-way tickets.

MARK NICHOLS: And you know, the rest of us went into that not knowing we had no money to get home. Brad ended up booking the flight after we won the final and booked that spot to the Trials.

BRAD GUSHUE: We celebrated pretty good after we won, and I told the guys the story because I got right on the phone with Air Canada to book four tickets home.

And also, from that event, we made enough money to go to the actual Canada Cup, and we did well there, which then qualified us for the the Players' Championship, where we ended up losing the final to Kevin Martin. But we still won $30,000.

And really, that three or four event circuit that we went on really got us into the top level, where we were getting into all the Slams and able to play just about any event we wanted. So I'm really glad that we took that risk and yeah it definitely worked out!

MIKE HARRIS: Brad had never won a bonspiel. Except for the one in Ottawa that got him into the Trials.

I can't take full credit, but I know I mentioned to Brad that he needed to bring someone on to help teach him a bit. I don't want to say it was my idea, but I'm pretty sure I suggested that he talk to Russ.

MARK NICHOLS: We asked for Russ to come aboard to kind of help us leading into the Trials. And he went to a few events with us. We kind of played a five-man team with him, we rotated through, tried a few different positions and lineup orders. It seemed like when we had Russ in the lineup we were obviously playing a little bit better.

EARLE MORRIS: There was a big event a few weeks before the Trials, in Port Hawkesbury, Nova Scotia. And here's this new lineup with Russ Howard. But sometimes he played and sometimes he didn't. They hadn't figured it out yet. They were still trying to figure out how it would work the best.

I was, as much as anybody, thinking, "There's no goddamn way you bring in a guy who's 50 years old to play second! That's never been done in the history of curling. It's not going to work."

MARK NICHOLS: And shortly before the Trials, we had a team meeting. We brought up all our options and Mike [Adam] accepted to go down to fifth man to let Russ play, and give us what would have been our strongest lineup going into the Trials.

GLENN HOWARD: I was stunned when that all came about, I didn't know. But I'll tell you, and I don't know whether Brad would admit it, but I don't think they win without Russ there. I think Brad was still wet behind the ears, he was still learning the game. I think he learned a ton. Russ was the voice of reason, he skipped. He knew Brad's strengths and weaknesses, he knew the game, he was he was the calming sort of influence.

Brad and Mark had all the talent in the world, and they still had that youthful exuberance... it was the best move Brad ever made. I don't know, but I'd like to think that he would admit that. Because I just really believe that Russ brought them over the hump. Brad still had to make the shots and he did... but he could just kind of focus on making shots.

CRAIG SAVILL: Let's be honest, I don't think that team wins the Olympic Trials without Russ. At that point, Brad was a young skip, and I think his strategy has much improved since then. Back then, maybe it wasn't as good. Russ coming in and taking off the pressure, let Brad just concentrate on shooting.

Russ handled the line calls, and watching the ice, and calling the game. That's huge for a young skip.

JOHN EPPING: Brad did the right thing to win when he brought in Russ. The pressure it takes off Brad to deal with the strategic part was huge. The Trials are probably more stressful than the Olympics. What he did there... that was a great move.

BRAD GUSHUE: When we decided Russ was going to be part of it, which is about a month before the Trials, I knew that he made our team a little bit better. And calling the game, I just felt like we were brought up another notch. Certainly at the Trials, his calmness and his experience really came out, and kind of fed through the team. We all just felt super confident, and that we had a real chance. We went into every game feeling like we were going to win and knowing we're going to win. And that's such a great feeling to have.

GLENN HOWARD: Russ called the game, and did everything he needed to do. He deflected stuff. Russ was the wily veteran when it came to the media. He dealt with all that, and they left Brad alone, which is exactly what he needed at that age. And it was the perfect recipe, and I don't think they knew it at the time, but when it happened, and it was over, it kind of hit me... that was the best recipe going!

RICHARD HART: Nobody knew how to evaluate that team, and what Russ Howard brought to it. Brad made all the shots, and Mark and Jamie [Korab] were fantastic. But Russ Howard was a game changer.

JEFF STOUGHTON: They picked up Russ to play second, and call the game. We played them in a Slam, and something else. I think there were two or three events where we'd seen them and played them, and they weren't "there." They may not admit it, but most of the other players felt the same way. They may not have said it... I said it.

When asked about the field at the upcoming event, Stoughton told reporter Paul Wiecek of the Winnipeg Free Press that he believed Gushue had "no chance" of winning the Trials.

RICHARD HART: When Jeff Stoughton said "no chance" to win, he didn't properly evaluate the impact that Russ was going to have on that team. That being said, I think he made a perfectly fair statement, because nobody correctly factored in the Russ Howard component.

MARK NICHOLS: Jeff just kind of got caught in the spot where he said what a lot of people were actually thinking. It kind of got blown up out of proportion, but I guess we used it as a bit of that bulletin board material that could get us motivated and fired up.

JEFF STOUGHTON: I'll never look back and say I shouldn't have said anything. Obviously, our team, Brad's team we know each other really well now. I know it took a couple years to get over things from his side. Because... it's an insult. Let's not cover it, for what it's worth. It was a bit of a surprise that they did so well... I don't think I'd ever want to take anything back.

BRAD GUSHUE: I don't want to make it any bigger than it was, because in all honesty, what he said was no different than what anybody was thinking. I hold no ill will or animosity towards Jeff for that comment. But certainly at that time, that was kind of the last thing we needed to get us fired up and get us going. And when I read that article, I actually cut it out of the paper and put in the bottom of my bag, so when I got dressed in the locker room, it was looking right at me, and it was just a little bit of motivation because we felt like we had a chance.

It probably wasn't as good a chance as teams like Kevin, or Randy, or Glenn had. But we certainly felt like we could win. And when I saw that, it was kind of the last little kick we needed to go out there and do it. And then just pure fate, I guess, we played him in the final. And yeah, it was a big part of it.

But I don't want to make much of it because, like I said, when I saw it, I was smart enough and had enough perspective to know that this is what everybody is thinking. And it's probably a fair thought for him to have. Just maybe don't say it to a newspaper reporter.

MARK NICHOLS: We had shown glimmers of, I guess, high quality curling through the fall, but the results didn't really show it... I didn't disagree with people putting us towards the bottom of the pack in terms of the quality of the field. But you know, we've seen lots of events where guys go out, they just catch on to the ice, they start playing well, and the next thing you know, they're rolling and that kind of happened to us.

JOHN EPPING: The big guns didn't show up that week. Ferbey, Martin, didn't show up. They didn't make the playoffs. Johnny Mo kinda walks through and has a great week, then loses to Stoughton in the semifinal.

MIKE HARRIS: In the final against. Stoughton, Brad wants to play a shot, and Russ wants to play the *right* shot. I was doing the commentary and I said, "This is exactly why you brought Russ Howard to be on your team. If he doesn't listen to Russ, he gives up three." Back then, the coaches bench could listen in on the commentary, and they end up calling a timeout.

Toby McDonald goes out and says to Brad, "This is exactly why we brought Russ Howard to be on your team. Listen to him!" The coaches can't listen to the commentary anymore.

JEFF STOUGHTON: People talk about the final. I know people have written about how it's a motivational thing. It can help you, sure. Or not. I look at it like... I missed a shot in the fourth end, and it cost us the game. And that's how the game goes.

When you look back at your career... that was the year. The team was playing so well, we were so confident. And it was probably one half-shot over the whole game that did us in. That was it.

MARK NICHOLS: The funny part about all that he goes and makes those comments, and next thing you know you're going toe-to-toe with him. I know we had a great game against him in the round robin. They were going through that whole event really good. And we got into a lead in the final and then just barely hung on at the end. ▶ [12]

---

[12] 2005 Tim Hortons Roar of the Rings -http://www.youtube.com/watch?v=JBNdxxYrxXM

HOW I MET BRAD GUSHUE

Following two Canadian Junior championships, a World Junior championship, and his first trip to the Brier, Brad was invited to coach at the Trillium Curling Camp in 2003. Summer camps are fun, and the staff usually stayed up too late and goofed around.

Not Brad.

Even in 2003, as a 23-year-old fresh out of juniors, he had his sights set on the Olympics. Most nights, he'd sit around with the coaches, play a game of cards, maybe have a drink, and then disappear quietly. We'd look around and he was gone.

At breakfast the next morning, we'd find out that he'd been up early, gone to the gym or out for a run before we headed to the curling club at 8 a.m.

After a few nights of his "ghosting" act, we got used to it. So imagine my surprise that on the last night of camp, the only one when I went to bed before *anyone*, there's a knock on my door at 2:30 a.m. It's Brad and Paul Webster (who went on to become a National Development Coach for Curling Canada) - they needed to express how disappointed they were that I'd quit the party on them.

That's right. Brad Gushue called *me* out for not partying enough.

About six weeks later Gushue and Kleibrink made their way to Italy for the 2006 Torino Olympics.

SHANNON KLEIBRINK: It was incredible. I think what I remember most is actually the opening ceremonies and walking in as a part of that bigger Team Canada, wearing the Maple Leaf on your back. That to me was the pinnacle of the Olympics, before it even started. So yeah just really a great honour to be a part of that event.

BRAD GUSHUE: It was obviously super exciting. Just amazing to be part of that event. You know for anybody that hasn't been there, that's probably the best way I can describe it. It's just one cool moment after another cool moment, day after day. You meet certain athletes, you get to go to certain places. Even just the food court, within the Olympic Village, is amazing because you know you see stars every second. Then outside of that, you get to meet famous people, and world leaders. Really, it's an incredible experience.

MARK NICHOLS: Obviously, we knew that we had to kind of continue doing what we were doing leading up to the Trials. But the pressure was completely different. Because you go into a Canadian curling Trials as an underdog, or as a lower ranked team. Then you go into the Olympics, where Canada is now a favourite every time they step on the ice. So the pressure you feel is just completely different and nothing you can even describe until you're actually faced with it.

BRAD GUSHUE: As for the curling part, we didn't feel comfortable, really, the whole week. The ice wasn't great. I know Russ had a really hard time because it was straight at the beginning of the week, and he got so frustrated that it wasn't the same kind of speed and curl that we had at the Trials. Because you go to the biggest event in the world, you expect the best conditions. And that certainly wasn't the case.

We realized that he was dealing with the pressure the same way we were. And that's why our team was different at the Olympics, than it was at the Olympic Trials... we really had to get the most out of each other, like we had to fight for it. At the Olympic Trials, everything was just smooth and easy and everything was clicking. At the Olympics, we all had to help each other get through some struggles and some down moments.

PAUL WEBSTER (National Coach, Olympic Team Leader - Curling Canada): Kleibrink's team had some sickness to deal with that week. It seems like illness is also part of the Olympics. It's like an international petri dish you put together, and hope you don't get sick. If you do, you just hope you recover faster than the other guys.

SHANNON KLEIBRINK: We had a couple of players go down with illness and we had to use our fifth player [Sandra Jenkins] quite a bit, and that was a little nerve racking. But we were able to get our third, Amy, back for the semifinal. And we were lucky enough to stand on the podium at the end of it. So we remember some of those challenges. There were days when we thought Amy wouldn't even be able to play at all, which after four years of training, and finally getting there... That was kind of disappointing.

MIKE HARRIS: Shannon is an awesome player, but her team wasn't that great. In fact, the team was sometimes a disaster. They had the only player I've ever heard of to sleep through a game at the Olympics. Christine Keshen wouldn't answer the door, they couldn't get her up. So they just went to the rink without her.

PAUL WEBSTER: Because we're a sport that deals with established teams, and routines, and more mature athletes, there's the assumption that people will look after their own things. Kleibrink's team had that assumption, even individually. So people get to the rink on their own schedule, and so they get out there and... they're missing a player.

AMY NIXON: I know Christine went to sleep, and I was responsible for getting her back to the arena. She didn't answer the door, or pick up her phone and we couldn't get in to her apartment because nobody had a key.

So we went to play our game, and she didn't show up. Well, Christine is Christine. You just have to know her... she's a delightful human, but you know, just a bit random sometimes, which I know is difficult to explain.

SHANNON KLEIBRINK: You know, that didn't bother me at all. It maybe bothered some more than others, but I was just happy she got there in the second end, and I was just happy to see that she wasn't hurt. She tended to go out for runs, and my fear was that she's gone for a run somewhere and gotten lost or kidnapped. It all worked out fine. She made it to the rink for the second end, there was no damage.

AMY NIXON: I was certainly not impressed at the time. We're in the locker room right before a game. Christine is nowhere to be found. Now, I'm in a position of running on out the ice, and yelling at Paul Webster in the stands to go find her, which is bullshit, right?

PAUL WEBSTER: So into my little blue minivan I go. I think I honked a few times when I got there for good measure, and then I go knock on her door. I remember a sense of frustration... I guess that's why we have a fifth player. Well, not *why* we have a fifth player. But it is one of those things. Life happens at the Olympics, and mistakes happen. Part of our job as a support team is to make sure we can recover, and if we can, how to best facilitate the team moving forward.

SHANNON KLEIBRINK: In her defence though, she was sick. She just had laid down for a nap with her earplugs in, and didn't hear the alarm.

AMY NIXON: So Paul went on his mission, banging down the door, and eventually and showed up with her. I mean, frankly I was livid... like livid. And I knew, all the way around, she'd done something to not show up on time, that she was likely okay. But Shannon is Shannon, and was absolutely convinced that Christine was dead in a gutter somewhere. That's not what you want your skip to be thinking before a game at the Olympics.

What can you say? I would say it was an example of probably a team that wasn't super cohesive and somebody went off on her own and then wasn't accountable for it. And it was obviously highly stressful and embarrassing for all of us, and absolutely less than ideal. It shines a light on a team that's probably struggling to have some level of cohesiveness. At a time when the stresses are higher than ever, it's not ideal, that's for sure.

PAUL WEBSTER: As a coach, you don't think you are going to have to deal with something like that, but at the end of the day, you figure out how best to deal with it to make sure the team doesn't feel the pain as much. Everything goes off Shannon's back, like water off a duck. She's probably one of the athletes that you just never see stressed. And I just think that with the rest of them, there was a lot of head shaking.

BRAD GUSHUE: We got off to a good start and then we lost to to Italy and Finland, which are two teams that we were obviously expecting to to beat. And then we're 4-3, and of our backs are against the wall, and we have to play New Zealand and the U.S.A. The U.S. had a good team with Pete Fenson, and we beat New Zealand and then we go to face the U.S. and we get a call in the morning that Jamie [Korab] is too sick to play.

Mike Adam, our fifth man, has to jump in and play in a do-or-die game. If we lose that, I think we might have been in a tiebreaker, worst case, but I think we also could have been out. Anyway, he played a great game, and we played a great game and ended up squeaking it out.

PAUL WEBSTER: Brad got ill with whatever flu was going around, and he came to me asking for assistance, but he didn't want his teammates to find out. He was young, but he's always been a mature athlete. He didn't want to build in an excuse about why he wasn't going to perform well, or he didn't want his teammates to think that they had to pick him up. He wanted them to focus on their game. He's one of those athletes who wasn't looking for an excuse, he was simply looking for a way to perform, and he wasn't going to let anything get in his way.

So Dr. Bob McCormack, our lead doctor at the Olympics to this day, and I had to perform some covert operations to get Brad the medication he needed.

AMY NIXON: Dan Petryk went to the 1992 Olympics with Kevin Martin, when it was a demonstration sport. For some reason Dan was in my house, after the Trials, but before we went to the Olympics. He said to me, "No matter what happens at the Olympics, just remember a bronze medal sure would look nice in my trophy case now." Because they were fourth in Albertville.

We lost the semi, I did the media thing, and I'm in the locker room. I'm thinking, "You know, I'm not going to forget the bronze medal is still a medal, and it's important." It's something I can say with pride now, 12 years later and for the rest of my life, like it's something to be known for.

SHANNON KLEIBRINK: I think going into it the expectation was that of course, you want to win the gold. That's the goal. When you get there, considering the week that we had, there are so many challenges with people going down with Norwalk [virus], and then Amy having four or five days out sick, in the middle of the week, and using our sub in a couple of different positions. At the end of it, we were just really happy to have a medal at all. So I think our expectations changed as the week went on.

AMY NIXON: I certainly was not interested in being on the first Canadian curling team to not bring a medal home with them. That's also one of my biggest memories of the Olympics... the real palpable sense of relief.

Walking into the closing ceremonies, arm in arm with my dad, with a bronze medal in my pocket, that's another great memory.

MARK NICHOLS: We're the first Newfoundland-based team to have that sort of success, to win an Olympic gold medal. Honestly, when we were over at the Olympics we had no clue of the impact that we had on the province. As the Olympics were going on, we were so in our bubble, so disconnected from anything. I don't even know if I was on Facebook at the time, or I don't even think we had any means of communication or social media. You don't read the papers. You don't really know anything.

BEN HEBERT: We were watching Brad's gold-medal game, because we were curling in Newfoundland at a Grand Slam when Brad was in Torino. During the game, and I was playing with Pat Simmons, on the ice, and they showed the game on the jumbotron at Mile One Arena. So I totally remember that.

BRAD GUSHUE: We actually found out the day before. This is dating us but this is how it went down. We had a day off between the semifinals and the finals, and we were staying outside at the village. We were about about an hour outside of town so when we had the day off, we decided we were going to go into the athletes village for a couple of hours just kind of hang out. We hadn't really had that experience.

And they had an internet cafe, because at that point, we didn't have phones with internet. They weren't as accessible back then. But we went to the internet cafe in the athletes village, and we're just surfing around, and I remember Jamie went on the *Telegram* website which is a big newspaper in St. John's and across the province. And one of the headlines was that the premier was closing schools for the Olympic final game. And Jamie called us over to the computer to have a look, and I read it and immediately I got really, really, nervous because I knew that if we went out and shit the bed the next day, the whole province is going to be watching.

MARK NICHOLS: Next thing you know we get a call from the premier of Newfoundland and Labrador the morning of the final, and he's talking to Brad, and tells them that they're shutting down the schools in the whole province, so all the kids in the province can watch our gold-medal final. And you kind of sit there and go, "Holy smokes!" That's pretty amazing for them to shut down school for everyone to be able to watch.

BRAD GUSHUE: Mark really struggled throughout the round robin, and they had our practise facility right next to the actual arena. We went over there for one practise and Mark was kind of trying to soften his peels and kind of, you know, steer them. We went over there, and I just said to him, "Just start firing!" and all of a sudden, he kicked out and was throwing probably five and a half second peels. In the end, he went and nutted, I'm going to say... five or six in a row. You know, you could see just the glow came back in his eyes and he started feeling confident. And I left that practise feeling pretty good about our chances. He threw like 94 and 96 percent in the playoffs and made some big shots for us, and we ended up winning.

In the final, Canada faced Finland's Markku Uusipaavalniemi, who had defeated Great Britain's David Murdoch in the semifinal. In the sixth end, a few Finnish errors and an absolute gem from Nichols left Gushue with the easiest shot ever to put a gold-medal game away... and he missed.

MARK NICHOLS: They had lots of chances to get out of it. They could have gotten a rock in, or made a freeze, or anything like that... and they just didn't. My double-runback pick was was more fortunate than anything. We were playing a double peel and to try to open up their rock on the button. For me to end up picking it off the button was a bit lucky, but it still left the guard up there. They still had a chance to get out of that, and they never did. ▶ 13

When he wrecked on his last, and pushed us into the rings... and then rolled out. As soon as it was coming down the sheet, me and Jamie were looking at him like, "He might hit this guard!" And then he taps it, and Russ gets up there to sweep. Oh my God, I can't believe it. And then it goes through and honestly, my reaction was more shock than anything.

It's like, "Holy crap, we're going to win the Olympics!" Because you know, the game was pretty tight at that point. Next thing you know it goes from a close game to a big lead, and we just kind of had to finish off the game.

BRAD GUSHUE: We did a lot of work with the sports psychologist leading up to the Olympics. And I was so prepared in that game, in any game leading up to that, to draw the four-foot to win. I would have been able to draw the four-foot or draw the button to win that game, I believe, nine times out of 10.

So I'm prepared to be able to handle those emotions, handle the adrenalin and the thoughts that were going through my head. But not at one point over the four or six years prior, did I prepare to draw for seven to win the Olympics.

---

13 Brad Gushue leads Canada - http://www.youtube.com/watch?v=VqEFlwRaRZA

So when Markku's shot was coming down and he ended up ticking the guard. And I think he bumped us in and rolled out over the top of one of ours, and Russ was running around trying to sweep. When the dust settled, I looked around and I started counting on my hand, and I got to five, and then I had to go to the other hand. Because I really never ever though what happened could happen. So I didn't look ahead to say, "Well, if he misses the shot, we could score six or seven." That never entered my mind.

Brad and the Canadian men had to hit the house to score seven. That rock is, as we say in the biz, "still going." It really didn't matter, however, as the game was well out of hand, and the Newfoundland and Labrador foursome (with a little help from the Ontario/New Brunswick guy) had soon secured Canada's first gold medal in men's curling.

What made it all the more impressive was that Brad was only 25 years old. Russ Howard had turned 50 during the competition.

BRAD GUSHUE: When they turned around and shook our hands in the eighth end, then it was kind of like relief. That was probably the first emotion that I felt when we won, which is really so different from the Olympic Trials, which is pure jubilation. But at the Olympics, with all the pressure and the expectations on us at home, and we were struggling so much and it was such a grind to try and find your A-game, which we never really did... when we actually won it was like, "Thank God, we did it."

And then as the night progressed, and the excitement and the realization of what we actually achieved started to set in, and it fully set in when we came home and saw what was going on in our province that we knew we had done something real big.

Following his Olympic gold medal in 2006, Mark was invited to coach at the Trillium Curling Camp in Guelph, Ont., in the summer of 2007. We instantly hit it off as two of the younger coaches on staff, and a friendship developed.

In the following years he'd fly in to Toronto a day early so we could catch a Blue Jays game, or stay a day late so we could go golfing. One year we went to a Toronto FC game prior to the camp, and he bought a traditional team scarf. Normally that wouldn't be a big deal but this was a sunny afternoon in the middle of August, and it was about 30° Celcius.

Not ideal scarf weather, but he wore it anyway.

RICHARD HART: This was the first generation of curlers whose dream it was to win an Olympic gold medal. When we were young, our dream was to go to a Brier. Those kids didn't know any different.

The weird thing is, other than Brad's big win in 2006, he didn't do too much for a while. He had some good Brier runs, and probably won a few events here and there. But now, it's 12 years later and *now* he's in his prime. That's crazy.

GEORGE KARRYS: I asked Brad at a news conference, "What was your first curling dream? The Brier or the Olympics?" He said, "Olympics. I wonder if I'm the first."

That was on my mind. When was this generation going to start? People my age would be out the door, and the Olympic generation was going to take over.

CHAPTER 6:
THE 2000s - GOING PRO

Following the 2006 Games, teams quickly reshuffled to gear up for the next four-year cycle. Kevin Martin set a new standard by bringing in John Morris, Marc Kennedy, and Ben Hebert. The foursome took a different, pure business, approach to training, season planning, and competition.

Across the country in Ontario, Glenn Howard was working out the kinks with his two-year old team of Rich Hart, Craig Savill, and Brent Laing. In the mid-to-late 2000s, Savill and Laing set the bar for what a front end should be. And only a season or two later, many would argue that Kennedy and Hebert raised it.

All the while, curling fans were in for a treat at every event. With Martin and Howard leading the way, the bitterness of the boycott years fading, and the Olympic cycle in its fourth edition, curlers set their sights on the next golden carrot... being the home team at the 2010 Olympics in Vancouver.

JOHN EPPING: I think curling changed in 2006, when Kevin Martin got a new team. That was a Tiger Woods moment for this sport. With Johnny Mo, Hebert, and Kennedy... that team changed curling. The fitness, they treated it like a job, they worked hard at it constantly. They worked harder than anybody else in the sport. They set the bar.

JOHN MORRIS: I was sick of being top five. We were always like, "Okay, we're fifth in the world" or, "We're fifth in Canada now." I didn't want to to be fifth anymore. I wanted to be number one in the world... to dominate. That's how we made that lineup with Kevin.

It was probably the first time I didn't necessarily put a team together based on friendships. It was more, "It's time to win." And I didn't want to be a curler who, over the course of my career, had been close but never had been a champion.

KEVIN MARTIN: We had a four-year plan absolutely from the start. What worked? Well chemistry, definitely... and shooting. And you know, I think you're missing one really, really important part if you don't mention Jules Owchar. When you look at championship teams over the last 30 years, somehow he's coaching them all the time.

GERRY GEURTS: When that team got together - year one - the question was, "When is this team going to blow up?" I think there was a lot of volatility. Knowing John and how intense and competitive he is... knowing Kevin, and how he likes to call the game his way, you could see there was potential conflict there.

You could see it come and go, but that team had so much success, that they could make it work. It was four players who were professionals, and who respected each other enough and had the same goal in mind. They weren't all friends. They didn't really hang out, but they ended up making it work because they wanted it.

IAN TETLEY: I think they recognized that dysfunction could help function. The rumour on the street was always that Johnny Mo wasn't a good fit for that team, but they seemed to win despite him. I think there was a real maturity about how Kevin called the game with that team. As he aged, he became a better player and a better leader.

MIKE HARRIS: They became a professional team. They hired all the right people, and basically changed the game.

CRAIG SAVILL: Kevin is arguably one of the best curlers to ever play the game. He's had the most success. He's been an arch rival for the teams that I've played on forever. In the mid 2000s when I was playing with Glenn, our two teams were far ahead of any other teams at the time. We'd joke that we weren't going to start trying until the quarters or the semis. You'd look to see where Martin's team was, and if they were on the other side of the draw, we figured we'd see them in the final.

RICHARD HART: And from that point on, Martin started thinking about the sport differently, and built his team that went on to win in 2010. He was such an amazing hitter, but he had missed a draw to win [in 2002]. And he knew the only way he was going to win it, or any big event, was if he became the best drawer in the world, then he went out and did it.

He got two sweepers who were incredible - in Kennedy and Hebert. And trained himself to never overthrow a draw. Then he goes on to beat us by drawing the side of the button in a Brier final, and went on to win Olympic gold by coming up big on some big draws.

REID CARRUTHERS: It always seems like those guys are sweeping it. If they're not sweeping it, and they have to back off a shot... they look shocked. Because they're not doing what they're used to doing, and they know that if they're not sweeping, it might be that once in a blue moon time that he's heavy.

IAN TETLEY: Johnny Mo, wherever he goes, seems to breed success regardless of what he does. He may seem like a misfit, but at the same time, he brings the best out in everybody else.

EARLE MORRIS: They were all great, and Kevin was really in the groove as far as being strategic. The other beauty was, he was bringing another great skip on board so collectively they made some better decisions. Kevin's got a strong personality, so a lot of others would stand back and let him do his thing, and there would be an "oops" every once in a while strategically... but John wouldn't be afraid to say, "What about this? What about that?" So I think during that era, that was a strength for that team.

RICHARD HART: Glenn and Wayne probably throw the rock better than Kevin. They probably hit the broom and throw it better. In 2002, Kevin changed. He stopped trying to be a machine and throw everything perfectly.

Sometimes, it didn't even look like he was trying to hit the broom. Don't be wide, hook the crap out of it, and let Benny and Marc hold it, every time. Everytime he threw it light, they'd get it there, every time. I don't know how many times, you'd be sure he was light, and they'd get it there every time. That was a great adjustment that Kevin made. He never missed heavy, and made himself a better thrower.

EARLE MORRIS: One of the things that made a difference was you had two amazing brushers, one left-handed and one right-handed, so their power stroke was the first stroke from either side. And those two guys were really fit, so you had great sweeping. They worked really hard at the game, and they were confident in their abilities.

Kevin has always been good at putting together teams who could do something special. And bringing Ben on... I think he originally offered the position to Carter, but he didn't want to play lead. So they got Ben, and he's been dynamite.

BEN HEBERT: I got a call from Kevin Martin and John Morris in April asking if I wanted to play lead for them, and relocate from Saskatchewan to Alberta. I didn't have to think very long about it. And so I committed to them and then I moved up to Calgary just because of the job I had.

REID CARRUTHERS: You look at a guy like Ben, he's like a linebacker. We'd never really seen a guy like that in curling. And Marc is also in incredible shape. I always make jokes when I teach curling clinics and I talk about sweeping, and footwork, and body position, and how to get the most out of a shot. I say, "People think that Kevin Martin has gotten better with age. I actually just think he got smarter. He hired two guys that could manage the stone better than he's ever seen before." It's about putting it all together. I think he put together the greatest team in the history of curling.

WAYNE MIDDAUGH: Different. That's a good word for Kevin. He was one of those guys, fantastic strategist, and knew how to make shots on tough ice conditions. It didn't matter if the ice was great, or bad, he could find ways to make the rock go where he wanted it.

EARLE MORRIS: I think it was more of a case where you had the three young guys who would hang together, and then you had the Ol' Bear. They didn't always do everything together, which is fine, but they worked it out. It wasn't bad.

BEN HEBERT: That was an interesting dynamic. We were young kids. I was 22, Marc was 23. John was 27. But we were brash and cocky. We thought we were real good, but we weren't very good. Well John was, but Marc and I weren't very good yet. But Kevin was so good. I think just Kevin rejuvenated with the young guys... he saw something in us that I think that we probably didn't even see in ourselves.

JOHN MORRIS: So yeah, that's how we picked the new lineup and really took it up a notch. Essentially, we put together four of the most competitive guys I know, and that all had athletic backgrounds, so they know how to train properly. And guess what. You know, we clicked immediately, and still I feel like that team was probably the one of the best teams ever. I truly believe that.

BEN HEBERT: I can specifically speak for myself that I wasn't really a good curler when I started curling with Kevin. I thought I was a real good curler, but I really wasn't. Kevin taught us how to be good curlers and how to see the game. Mostly, though, how to practise.

I used to slide with my broom on the ice, when I started with Kevin. We had won everything our first half of the year... everything. We won our first 15 games in a row out of the gates, won two or three events. We won a Slam, maybe our first Slam ever as a team. We get into Northern [Alberta] playdowns, back when you still had Northerns before they added provincial spots for CTRS points.

And we're practising before Northerns and we've been killing it. There's no worries. Kevin asked me if I would mind sliding with the brush on my back. I said, "Why would I do that?"

He said, "Well if you want to be on this team, you're going to slide with the broom on your back."

And I was kind of like, looking around at Marc and John like, "Is this guy serious? We're cleaning up everything!" Now, I look back like he knew I could be better, my mechanics could be better. You know, whether or not I was having a good year or a bad year didn't matter. He knew I could be better if I did it that way, and he was right! He made me a better player with more consistency; just the mechanics are tighter that way. So he saw that. I made the change at that practise and I've never slid with my broom down since.

KEVIN MARTIN: Marc would be the first one to admit he was a really good hitter, but didn't have much of a draw game, when he first came on the team. And Benny was a really good sweeper, but didn't throw the rock very good. John's in-turn was super soft, but his out-turn was deadly when we first got together.

Well it didn't take long, and all of a sudden Benny's shooting averages 90 per cent, Marc seldom averaged as low as 90. And John Morris... like, he was just lethal. A lot of that has to do with chemistry but a lot of that has to do, I think, with the coaching as well.

If he didn't start great, Marc Kennedy got there in a hurry. He was a first-team All-Star at the Brier in 2007, 2008, 2009, and 2011. He was also the World Curling Tour Player of the Year in 2008.

Martin's "super-team" won the Brier and the Worlds in 2008, and followed it up with another Brier win in 2009... and while the foursome remained intact, they also tacked on a dozen Grand Slam victories. Martin has a total of 18. There was also the small matter of another trip to the Olympics.

BEN HEBERT: And a lot of the time, for better or worse, there are some things that obviously you don't agree with. But he's the boss, and that's how he runs his program. But, I look back at that now, and we were young and we were kids, we were naive and I'm glad we had that. Glad we had that leadership from Kevin to show us how to be professional.

While Martin's team was formed for the specific purpose of winning the 2010 Olympics, there was another team in that era who helped pushed the standards higher. Starting in 2006, Glenn Howard went to eight straight Briers, winning two. He also added two more World championship titles to his previous pair... not to mention 14 Grand Slam wins.

RICHARD HART: In our time, we had Kevin Martin and ourselves, from 2005 to say, 2010. There were two really dominant teams.

GLENN HOWARD: I'm proud, obviously, during that that time period, playing with three of my best buddies, nothing seemed to go wrong. We just played, we won a lot more games than we lost. We were ranked either first or second with Kevin for several years. It was almost like the Tiger and Phil Show, and it was just back and forth and super exciting times. And you know, I don't care what anybody says... winning is fun.

And when you're winning and you're on the top of the heap, or near the top of the world, it's just surreal and you just try to relish the moment. But also, we were experienced enough to know that it can end at any time.

JOHN EPPING: At the time Glenn's team with Rich, Lainger and Savill... they were right there, too. Their consistency was phenomenal. They were so good game in, game out. Glenn Howard's consistency was better than anybody's. But Kevin's work ethic, their explosiveness, the weight they could throw, the power of their sweeping, the way they managed the game - I think that changed our sport.

CRAIG SAVILL: It was great to be a part of that team and to have a front row seat to how good Glenn is. I still remember the first 'spiel we played together, the Shorty in Brockville [Ontario]. We didn't qualify.

But then we go out to Regina, and about three games in, I think to myself, "I'm getting kind of sick of saying 'Great shot.'" Every time, it was, "Great shot, Glenn" or, "Nice shot, Glenn" because he kept making everything. After the game, Rich said to us, "Boys, you're about to watch a show. When Glenn gets like this, just hold on tight. It's fun to watch."

GEORGE KARRYS: He's always been a technician. He was rock solid in his technique. It was really interesting to watch him graduate to that level at skip. He always made a semi and occasionally a final, lost a couple of provincial finals. It took him a while to not only find the horses, but also to feel comfortable at skip. He had a hall of fame resume as a third... before he even started skipping.

CRAIG SAVILL: When Glenn starts playing, he makes absolutely everything. He's a skip now, but he plays more like a third. Sometimes he's just like, "Tell me what to do and I'll do it." Not saying that he didn't make the decisions, but it's part of the reason he and Rich worked so well. Because at the end of the day, he didn't seem to care what shot it was, he just needed to know the ice and weight, and he'd throw it. That's worked well because Rich liked to be in charge, and would voice his opinions very strongly, and Glenn would just kinda say "Alright." And he'd make it.

PAUL SAVAGE: I often tease Glenn when I see him at golf tournaments and whatnot. I tell him, "It's really too bad you didn't start skipping about 10 years sooner!"

REID CARRUTHERS: Rich is an incredible player, and there may not have been anybody better in the world at the soft-weight, bumper-weight hits. It's one of the hardest shots in curling, and that team seemed to make all of them.

GLENN HOWARD: I feel like it was yesterday, and just some of the greatest moments in my life. You just cherish it, so you never forget it. Yet you realize what you've accomplished. The four of us quite often get together and we'll reminisce about old times like that. We had so much fun with those guys. Brent and Craig and Richie are just three characters, and to traipse all over the country, and all over the world with those three guys... we would rent an RV, or play golf together, we partied together, we did everything together and that was magical.

WAYNE MIDDAUGH: They were a great team, they had a great front end. It was like two teams. If you've ever seen Brent and Craig work together, they're fantastic. And then you had Richie and Glenn who were a team on the back end. It was like two teams that liked to beat up on everybody else. The front end was a bit better, and then the back end was a bit better. It was actually really entertaining to see.

CRAIG SAVILL: Brent and I had played together so long, and knew each other so well, it almost got to the point where we didn't have to talk. Knowing what the other guys needed from us, which we figured out pretty quick. I think Glenn made it easy on us, because he'd throw it so close and we'd just manage the rock all the way down.

REID CARRUTHERS: Glenn with Savill and Laing deserve credit. Glenn seems to make those guys sweep every one of his rocks. Even playing against them, I've always marvelled at how every shot is, "On, off, clean... on, off, clean." There are brooms going down, but it's always awfully close, and the weight is usually perfect.

JOHN EPPING: That's just a team that got along really well, you could see they really liked each other. And their consistency was just outstanding. Game in, game out. You had to curl really well to beat them.

And then later you add Wayne... and I'll argue with anybody to this day that he's the most talented player to ever play the game. Wayne's talent level is unbelievable.

BEN HEBERT: I certainly always had a lot of respect for those guys. They're such a good team. You'd look at that team, position by position up the lineup. I always knew whenever I ran into Craig, I was going to have to play really really good. I think the same thing with the back end too... John and Kevin against Rich and Glenn. You'd have to play your best against them.

It was funny... that was when there were only four Slams, and then the Brier. For the actual tour events, we didn't play them a ton because they'd stay in eastern Canada, and we stayed in western Canada for the most part. You know we didn't bang heads a lot.

PAUL SAVAGE: I look for it every year, the look in the eye hasn't changed. Every time Glenn gets in the hack, you can see it's still there.

CRAIG SAVILL: With that, Glenn is one of the nicest guys you'll ever meet. He's not a finger pointer. He's the kind of guy who could play 95 percent, and we lost, and that 5 percent was not his fault because we all shot 30 percent, he's going to say "I should have made that one shot a bit better and maybe we would have won."

BEN HEBERT: I remember a few funny texts with Lainger back in the day. I mean, we were always social buds with those guys, right? On the ice, I hated them, I hated them more than anything. And honestly, just because they were so good. And you know, Richie was a dick sometimes... but so was I. And so was Kevin, and so was Cliffy [Glenn]. So was Brent. Really, the only guys who weren't really dicks were Craig... no, even Craig could be a dick. But whatever, on the ice we got into some words sometimes, had a couple of fights, but for the most part, the actual mutual respect for each other's players was really high because we knew if we were playing them, we had to bring our very very best. I think they thought that about us as well.

GLENN HOWARD: I relished every time we had a chance to play Kevin. We'd giggle because we were fiercely competitive, but I firmly believe over those years the mutual respect was there. We probably all hated each other for a brief moment, but the respect was there because we knew that we were one and two, and you were banging heads all over. It was cool.

BRAD GUSHUE: I knew that Kevin's team was going to come together, and I knew Glenn had a really solid team and it was going to be real competitive. Our team kind of struggled from a commitment standpoint. The thing is, after you win the Olympics, it's a challenge to get motivated again, because you've already reached the top. And we had some players that just didn't put in as much work as what they did in the past, and then all of a sudden you do see Kevin and Glenn getting better and better, and we were were taking a step or two back. It was really, really frustrating from from my standpoint to see that, because I felt that we should have been a team that could have competed with them.

While Glenn Howard had a perfect three-for-three record at the World championships (later four-for-four, after 2012), Kevin Martin hadn't won a gold at an international major (Olympics or Worlds) in his first four attempts. That changed in 2008 when he won his first World championship. They returned to the Worlds in 2009.

CRAIG SAVILL: There was something in his head where he'd play international teams, wherever it was, and he couldn't win. You could tell it was in his head. He would just get lost, overthink things. For a guy who was amazing at angles, and seeing shots ahead of time, he just saw things differently when he was at the Worlds, or playing international teams.

IAN TETLEY: My memories of Kevin were always him making some stupid calls. Like in 2009 when he threw the rock away against Murdoch. There are these things that seem to happen to Kevin...

BEN HEBERT: Obviously hindsight's 20/20... I think Kevin saw something in his mind and Kevin's got an interesting mind. He thought that if he threw it away he was going to have an easy shot.

In the 10th end of the World Championship final, Canada is tied with Scotland, with hammer. After much discussion on almost every shot, Kevin Martin decides to throw his first shot of the end into the wall, instead of changing up the situation in the house. Scotland's David Murdoch played a tap freeze perfectly, which left Kevin with a tougher shot to win than he had anticipated. ▶ [14]

GEORGE KARRYS: I don't know how I knew it, but I knew he wasn't going to throw it. I'd seen it before from him. Usually out of the spotlight, like some cashspiel in Wainwright or something, but I'd seen him do that before. I was on the media bench, saying, "He's going to take a pass."

IAN TETLEY: He would always call some stupid shot, and you could always figure that if you waited long enough, he was going to call something stupid. But then you never knew when he was going to make a great one.

BEN HEBERT: And I think when the dust settled from Dave Murdoch making his little tap, Kevin was probably like, "Well, I didn't see that happening!" Kevin's last shot wasn't easy, no. But he missed it by a lot, he threw a brick.

CRAIG SAVILL: I still think he had a shot that he makes most of the time, and then nobody ever talks about it. We think he's brilliant for creating this "X" and throwing it away.

---

[14] Martin (CAN) vs. Murdoch (SCO) - 10th End -
http://www.youtube.com/watch?v=p0CshmRVE9o

BEN HEBERT: I didn't want to throw the rock away in the first place. John didn't, I don't think Marc did either. But you know, we were with Kevin, for better or worse, and he won us so much with his wizardry and his experience, and how amazing he was as player... he won so much. So the one blemish on us is that he made a stupid call in the World final.

Months later, Kevin was still convinced he'd play the end the same way again. He appeared on CBC during the Players' Championship and talked through the end with the telestrator. He kept referring to the "X," the arrangement of the rocks, which he believed left his stones in ideal positions.

In my opinion, throwing away the rock wasn't the problem. Only needing to score one to win, there were way too many rocks in play... both in front of the house (for most of the end) and in the four-foot. I know a lot of other coaches who agree... but shouting at your TV doesn't win you Briers and Olympics, so who am I to say?

BEN HEBERT: You know what? I'll tell you this. Obviously, that's one you'd love to have your resume. But, we wouldn't have been as good in the 2009 Trials and won those Olympics if we didn't lose that '09 final.

It made us a way better team because we were untouchable. We were by far superior. We had back-to-back Brier wins *undefeated.* That's mental! Undefeated in two Briers and that was against good teams like Howard, Stoughton, Gushue.... and not really any super challenge. We had some really good games against Glenn in those Briers and we rolled through playing great, and we were just flying.

GLENN HOWARD: We played them a couple of times that week, and we lost both of them. And I can remember coming off the ice, and I was smiling in the media scrum. They say, "Why are you smiling? Glenn, you just lost!"

I said, "Did you watch that curling?" And they go, "Well, yeah." I said, "That was one of the most enjoyable games I've ever played in my life!" And they said, "But you lost!"

I said, "That doesn't matter. It was amazing. All eight guys were making everything!" It came down to the last shot, Kevin had a draw to the button. But there were runbacks, and angle raises, and in-offs. It was incredible. It seemed like that every time we played Kevin.

BEN HEBERT: And so when you're flying high and winning everything, why change anything? Why would you work harder? You don't need to change when you're rolling. But losing that '09 final made us all recommit.

I quit my job, John quit his, Marc quit his, and we became full-time athletes for one year. We trained full-time in the gym, we threw a million rocks. I moved to Edmonton with Kevin and Marc, rather than being in Calgary and it made us a really good team in 2010. So as much as that loss stings and I still hate it... it made us better.

JOHN MORRIS: The bigger the game, the better we got. Man, that was a special team. I'll never forget that. I also think the way we trained and the way we approached the game is what really inspired a lot of our younger teams... that team with Kevin, Ben and Marc really was a very motivating team. Other teams pretty much had to make that decision. "Okay, we have to go to the next level. We have focus on these next-level things like nutrition, and working out, or else we're going to be left in the dust." And that's when curling really started changing.

IAN TETLEY: Whatever they did for preparation that year, a book should be written about that. It seemed like mentally, they were all in a great spot. It was almost like Kevin took responsibility for that. He seemed to have an unbelievable maturity and confidence, and it exuded through him. And it helps when your team is making everything. It makes your life a heck of a lot easier.

BRAD GUSHUE: They were the best two teams for sure, but even within that, Kevin was still another level above Glenn. And looking back on it, it was fun to play in that era and play against a team that was that good. But from my standpoint, those four years were frustrating because we were nowhere near as good as we should have been.

MARK NICHOLS: They're probably two completely different teams in terms of their makeup and stuff. They both knew how to win together. You know Glenn, Richie, Craig and Brent were like four of the best friends in the world. They were always laughing and carrying on, and they seemed to really enjoy their time together. And Kevin, John, Ben, and Marc were were just machines, and were so good that you knew if you didn't play well against them, they were going beat you.

HOW I MET BEN HEBERT

In September of 2015, my friend and longtime teammate Josh Johnston asked me to spare for him at the Stu Sells Oakville Tankard. I was playing for another team that season, and we weren't in the event.

There were two catches. One, we were playing on Saturday night at 10 p.m. And two, we were playing against Kevin Koe.

It would have been bad enough if the draw was running on time, but of course slow play, extra ends, and necessary ice maintenance meant that we didn't get started until closer to 11:30 p.m. Nobody was really excited about heading out at that hour.

Shockingly, Team Koe (with Marc Kennedy, Brent Laing, and Ben Hebert) was better than us. After they popped four, and stole two, we quickly shook.

Ben looked at me and said, "Thanks for not dragging that out, boys. I'll buy the drinks."

For the 2009 Olympic Trials, Curling Canada changed the qualification process. Instead of winning a single event to qualify, teams now had to perform consistently over the previous three seasons to earn their spots.

This was influenced by, but not directly caused by, a major omission at the 2005 Trials in Halifax. Wayne Middaugh (ranked second in Canada in 2004) didn't qualify for the Trials, while B.C.'s Jay Peachey (ranked No. 14 in Canada) earned a berth as a result of a third-place finish at the 2004 Brier (because winner Mark Dacey and runner-up Randy Ferbey had already earned their spots). By the time the Trials rolled around in 2005, Middaugh was ranked seventh in the country, while Peachey had dropped to No. 37.

The qualification system was adjusted to reward sustained performance over several years, instead of giving a coveted Trials spot to a team that had one good weekend at the right time. It would be tweaked again for the 2014 Olympic cycle, and remained relatively the same for the 2018 quadrennial.

What mattered now was the Canadian Team Ranking System (CTRS). Based on performances at World Curling Tour events, Grand Slams, Briers and Scotties, and Canada Cups, points were awarded based on results and the strength of field. Chasing points became a big motivator starting in 2007, and remains so to this day.

If you wanted to get into the Trials, you needed lots of points. To get lots of points, you had to play in the Grand Slams. To get into the Slams, you needed a certain number of points from other World Curling Tour events. Of course, the Brier, Scotties, and Canada Cup also came with big point payouts as well. Teams were now playing much more, trying to make sure they stayed in the top tier, within reach of those Olympic Trials berths.

Even so, in the new format, only four teams were directly qualified for the Trials, which was officially rebranded "The Roar of the Rings" in 2001.

On the men's side, Martin, Howard, Kevin Koe, and Randy Ferbey qualified, while the next 12 teams played in a triple-knockout tournament for the final four spots. In the women's event, Jennifer Jones, Shannon Kleibrink, Cheryl Bernard, and Stefanie Lawton were in, while the next dozen would fight it out for the last four spots at the "pre-Trials" which took place in Prince George, B.C.

Of the 12 men's teams in the pre-Trials, Jeff Stoughton, Pat Simmons, Jason Gunnlaugson, and Wayne Middaugh fought their way into the Roar. Crystal Webster, Krista McCarville, Kelly Scott, and Amber Holland made it through the women's side.

Coming off two undefeated Brier wins, there was no doubt that Kevin Martin's team was the favourite at the 2009 Roar of the Rings in Edmonton. Glenn

Howard's team was right up there, but Martin definitely had the edge, and the home-ice advantage.

But surprisingly, it was a different Alberta team that made waves that week. Although Jennifer Jones was fresh off back-to-back Scotties wins and a heavy favourite to win, Calgary's Cheryl Bernard was a human highlight reel for most of the tournament, and her team of Susan O'Connor, Carolyn Darbyshire, and Cori Bartel found themselves at the top of the heap after the seven-game round robin.

CHERYL BERNARD: We were ranked fourth in that field. Did I think we were going to win? Well, it's a bit of a cliche answer, but I knew if we played well, at the top of our game, that we certainly could. Our issue was that we'd never won a Canadian championship. We'd won some bonspiels, we'd done well in mixed, we'd won a big event in Japan, but it was never anything like that kind of pressure.

GEORGE KARRYS: I'm still impressed with Cheryl Bernard. She stood on her head to win the Trials, and the first few games of the Olympics.

CHERYL BERNARD: You never really know how you're going to react. You don't know if you can bring your A-game under that pressure, in your home province, with all those people watching you, with those expectations. And sometimes, it's your own expectations that you put on. We'd had a couple of really good years, and we did have some expectations that we could go win this. But our key was how to go out there and *not* put pressure on ourselves. There's always going to be external pressure that you can't do anything about, but the worst thing you can do is add your own on top of it.

To say Bernard played well would be a massive understatement. It seemed that she was making a big runback, an in-off, or a double almost every game, and scoring multiple points each time. And if there was nothing to hit, she could toss it on the button at will.

CHERYL BERNARD: I don't remember what it felt like at the time, but I remember really trying to reach deep and feel it again shortly after the Trials. So many athletes talk about that state of being in "the zone" or whatever cliche you want to call it, but you're always looking for it. I ended up making a lot of notes about how I felt because it had been the best I had played over a long period, under pressure. You'd get it over a spiel or something, but it's a different kind of pressure. So I really wanted to figure out how to find it again.

SHANNON KLEIBRINK: She had a great week. We had a pretty close game in the final. I think we were tied up coming home, and she had the hammer, and had to draw the four-foot, and of course, she nailed it. She had been playing well all week.

CHERYL BERNARD: I don't play well under a lot of pressure. I have to have perspective. I remember a couple times during the event thinking, "If it doesn't work out this week, and we don't win, I'm going to San Diego for a couple of weeks. A nice little break." That was my trick. Everybody has their own thing. I had to make sure that it wasn't everything in the world, and it became so easy... the four-foot looked like it was twelve feet wide. It was so easy, because the pressure was off. That was the trick for me... take the pressure off.

BRAD GUSHUE: If you ask Kevin, we were probably the only team that he feared because we were the only team that could beat him. In 2009, we we had a great record against him, and by a great record, we probably won four out of 10. But compared to every other team that played them, that was a great record. Even against Glenn, Kevin probably wins eight out of 10.

We had a real good year. We won a Slam that year, and a bunch other spiels. I think we got up to third in the rankings that year, and we didn't get through the pretrial. So when we didn't make it through, I remember talking to Kevin after. He said he breathed a sigh of relief because he knew that we were kind of a thorn in his side. And now it was just a matter of him getting through Glenn.

JOHN EPPING: I played with Wayne at that Olympic Trials. And there were only a few teams that stayed out and still partied until two or three in the morning. That's how we did it. That's Wayne's rule on tour... you're going to eat well, drink well, and sleep well, and that's what we did. We had a blast, we enjoyed ourselves, and were usually crazy tired by the end of the week. But we could survive on how crazy good Wayne Middaugh was.... not to mention Jon Mead and Scott Bailey. I couldn't have asked for a better team. I was surrounded by the best at 25 years old. I was spoiled.

Ferbey, Koe, and Burtnyk... somehow we'd always end up with those guys at the end of the night. Sometimes you get those teams that you end up playing 30 times a year, and for that Middaugh team it was always Kerry Burtnyk. We had so much fun with those guys... even though we'd play them twice every 'spiel.

BEN HEBERT: Honestly, we were super prepared for those Trials. Honestly, I never thought for a second that we weren't going to win... which, it's crazy thinking that going into the Olympic Trials. It's the best field on the planet. I mean Ferbey's team was really good. Stoughton's team was amazing. Howard's team was great, and we got them in the final. Wayne was there.

We were super prepared and we had steely-eyed Kevin who'd been there, done that. We knew what his goal was with this team leading up to 2010. I just look back at it remembering it like, we were just like robots.

That was a pretty epic week. It was all four guys playing well. Not just one or two, but all four cylinders firing.

RICHARD HART: We were undefeated going into the last game against Kevin. No Page playoff, winner goes to the final. The big dumping fiasco was that game, in the ninth end. At the time, that rock stopped in the back eight-foot somehow.

With Martin's first rock of the end coming over the hogline (and looking a bit heavy), Ben Hebert finishes his brush stroke by lifting straight up, instead of off to one side, as the rule requires. The stone immediately seems to slow down and curl, coming to a stop, hanging off the back four-foot. Some words were exchanged, but nothing came of it. ▶ [15]

It did set the stage, however, for Martin's next shot.

BEN HEBERT: Kevin made an awesome runback against Glenn in the round robin, for three in the ninth end. Really, we should've probably been in a semifinal because Glenn should have beaten us in the round-robin game. But Kevin was *nasty*. Kevin made a couple great ones... like a hit and roll, to freeze, buried around the corner guard, or else they're getting two in eight. Then he makes a runback double for three in nine. ▶ [16]

And after that we kill them in the final. But that was a huge, huge win for us. I remember that like it was yesterday. And honestly, I just remember being in the zone that week.

RICHARD HART: The final was unmemorable. We were never really close in that game.

JOHN MORRIS: Those are actually the toughest games. When you know the win is in your grasp, you've really gotta focus for the last couple of ends. Because until they shake hands anything can happen.

In the end, it was relief... and elation. Not to disrespect the Olympics, but the Trials are harder to win. You have more good teams, and the level of play overall is better. So mentally and physically, it's tougher. We knew that if we played like we just did, that we could certainly win Olympic gold.

---

[15] Hebert dumps on heavy draw http://www.youtube.com/watch?v=fjT3F3Gs1Kw
[16] 2009 Roar of the Rings - Martin runback http://www.youtube.com/watch?v=d_aNJ-G5iZo

Martin winning the Trials wasn't a surprise. But Bernard was by no means a favourite. It seemed to reinforce a trend that had been developing at previous Olympic Trials.

RICK LANG: Looking back on it now, we all know the Trials history. And very often the top-notch teams' performance doesn't match the expectations. There's a real pattern to that. Everybody else was playing pretty tight, and of course they're loose because they feel like there's no pressure.

JEFF STOUGHTON: Kevin would have been the favourite in 2010 for sure. He and Glenn were in the final, so that was fine. But 2006 and 2002, your favourite would have been Ferbey. And you know when you're playing somebody, you can tell when they've got "it." You could tell they didn't have it.

GLENN HOWARD: I think it was the same with Gushue in 2006. Same sort of thing. They were on the lower half of the of the ranks for sure. So the deal is that if you're under the radar, there's no pressure and away you go! If you think back, there's only been maybe one or two favourites that have won the Trials since the beginning. It tends to be under-the-radar teams. Kevin Martin, obviously, was a favourite, but it's been more non-favourite than favourites who win the Trials.

KEVIN KOE (2018 Olympian, three-time Brier Champion, two-time World champion): Funny things happen at those events. Some of the favourites just don't do well. It happens every year. I mean, you can try and peak every four years and it's not always going to work out. There's a lot of pressure and you're playing good teams. I think that some people aren't made to handle it as well as others.

EARLE MORRIS: The weird thing about Olympic Trials is that often the teams that aren't expected to do much, end up winning. Looking back at Harris, he was probably ranked ninth or 10th out of 10. And in 2013, Jacobs and Johnny Mo were the last two to qualify, and they end up in the final. It makes you scratch your head as to what format is best.

JEFF STOUGHTON: It is interesting that sometimes your expectations are just so high... like in the 2013 Trials, Jen Jones comes and wins in her hometown. I come out and stink the place up! There's no explanation for it. I felt really bad for the team, because I wasn't at my best. I couldn't get a grasp on the ice as well as I should have. I never played even close to good enough to contend... it was disappointing.

CHERYL BERNARD: Before that [2010], you still had a lot of teams who weren't full-time players, and weren't really groomed for the Olympic cycle. There were still a lot of teams who weren't built for that. Now teams are built for every four-year cycle. And in between they win Briers and Scotties, and Slams. So when you have the ultimate focus for that, you're not going to have as many underdog stories as a result.

I don't think you're going to see that much anymore. These elite teams are groomed. Because they play full time, they've won Canadians, and Worlds, and they've played with pressure before.

I don't know that you'll see it again. You'll see favourites win. They play full time, they put themselves in situations which allow them to play at the top of their game in the pressure situations.

KAITLYN LAWES: I think because it's every four years, something changes about their thought process. They change their approach. It's how they handle that feeling. Not many people get that, not many people are Olympians. Going into it, if you let that consume you, it can change how you perform. That's happened to several people over the years. It's the teams that go in with a "nothing to lose" attitude that seem to come out on top.

RICK LANG: Our season used to be done in the fall. If you were in the playdowns and you lost out, that's it, you were done. You didn't play another competitive game after January 15. All the respect to the guys who can go play 10 or 12 'spiels, and commit to the schedule for the whole year.

We had to be committed for three months, and you could work your life around it. All of a sudden, it's six months, and our interests just didn't fit our lives anymore, with our jobs, and our kids, and our families. We just couldn't fit it all in there.

CHERYL BERNARD: It was much more of a transition for us. We needed to switch gears, play better, practise more. It became much more of a full-time commitment... with not a lot of money. Now you see the top handful of teams getting by on sponsorship, they're on TV with logos everywhere. That's what the tour did. A team, if you have success, can get your sponsors on TV and make some money. They're not making any more money in winnings, because the prize pots haven't gone up that much in all the years I've played. But they're making a lot more in sponsorship.

SHANNON KLEIBRINK: I guess I've always kept it in perspective. It's not the be-all and end-all for me. Curling was not the most important thing. Family's first, and then a lot of other things can come before it. So I think I've played with a lot less pressure than maybe some other teams put on themselves. Because at the end of the day, you know, the sun is going to come out whether you win or not. I just always kind of play for the love of the game, I guess you would say. Even though we had put so much work into it, of course... it meant a lot to us that we played for the love of the game, I guess.

CHERYL BERNARD: The danger is this. A lot of teams are only Olympic-focused. You've really got to make some short-term goals because there's only going to be one team that's happy every four years. You need to have some Scotties, Briers, provincial wins or you're going to lose yourself, and be pretty disappointed in your career if you don't. It's a balance, and these teams really need to watch it.

CRAIG SAVILL: When we first started, there was never this talk of extra funding... or the paperwork you have to go through. The money changes as you get closer to the Trials, depending on your points. The whole process has changed because of this four-year cycle.

It seems like we have to go to the Brier because it's worth really big points, and it's good money for the team that wins. But you have to go, because it's points towards the Trials. Before, our goal was just try to get to the Brier or the Scotties. There's been a shift, which is a little bit scary to me because I cherish the Brier so much.

JOHN EPPING: There was still a good amount of partying in 2008-2009... but when Martin won those Trials, every other team said, "Okay, they've set the bar. Now we have to catch him." We had to do things a lot differently. People say that it changed for the worse, but you gotta look and ask, "How good is the curling right now?"

With the Olympics now in their fourth official cycle, the recipe for success was becoming a bit clearer. With the changing qualification process, it was obvious that the Olympic drive was now going to be a four (or more) year process.

What didn't change, however, was the piece of cheese at the end of the maze... Once you battled it out, persevered, and found yourself at the end of the cycle, there was an Olympic medal to shoot for. And in 2010, Canada was hosting the big show in Vancouver.

CHERYL BERNARD: I remember thinking when we won, "We don't even get to go anywhere!" Kleibrink's team got to go to Italy, and I thought that was the coolest thing. I had no understanding of how incredible it was to play in your home country with a Maple Leaf on your back. I don't think it really sunk in for us until the opening ceremonies, and we went, "Okay. Wow. We're Olympians."

BEN HEBERT: I look back now, because you only know what you know at the time... but Kevin having the experience of being at the Olympics prior, to us going there was huge. At the time, we were thinking, "Why are we going to do it this way?" or, "Screw that, let's do this instead."

He never really talked too much to us about his past and his experiences, or the reasons why he is the way he is. Like he'd tell us that this is how we're going to do something, we'd ask, "Why?" He'd basically say, "Because."

He was just like, "Here's how we're doing it." It's interesting, but I think now that I'm older, I'm 35 now - He was 39 when we were playing together, I was 27. Now I get why he knew what he knew, he lived it. He realized he didn't have to tell us why; he knew how to get it done.

CHERYL BERNARD: The very first game was against [Swiss skip] Mirjam Ott. The fans were crazy, you couldn't hear a thing. I go down to throw my first rock in my first game, and I was trying to tell them I was going to throw board weight. They had to lean down within a few inches of me to hear what I said. It was unbelievable, I'd never played in anything like that in my life.

Mirjam asked me if it was going to be like that all week. I just said "I don't know!" It was crazy. It wasn't even curling, it was more like a soccer game. I'd never seen anything like it. And it was that way the entire time.

JOHN MORRIS: It was just what curling needed. I think that arena sat about 5,000 people, but it sounded like 25,000. It was the best atmosphere for any curling event I've ever played in.

I know it was either the German skip Andrea Schöpp or Mirjam Ott... one of them was complaining about it. You could barely hear each other on the ice.

GEORGE KARRYS: I was amused with all the stomping in the bleachers, and people who don't know curling, stomping and cheering for curling. The athletes who couldn't cut it just getting frustrated by the noise. The Danish girls were in tears because they felt they couldn't throw a rock. Sometimes you gotta grow a thick skin because you're going to get a weird crowd. It happens at the Olympics.

JOHN MORRIS: A couple times, the crowd just started singing the national anthem... just in the middle of the game. And I remember in the final, Marc was about to throw and they start singing. He looked up at me like, "What am I supposed to do?" I checked our clock, we had lots of time, so I told him to take it all in. So we took a quick break, and respected the anthem! ▶ [17]

CHERYL BERNARD: I remember thinking during that first game, "Don't miss this. You may never get back here." Halfway through the week, the fans would just start singing "O Canada" in the middle of the game, and I remember taking a moment just to enjoy them singing and taking it all in. These fans were cheering for Canada, and we were Canada, so we just tried to enjoy every second of it.

JOHN MORRIS: It didn't really faze us. We loved it. We always got up for big games, big crowds. I would always prefer the raucous environment, instead of a place where you can hear a pin drop. And Kevin was our fearless leader and just carried us through, and all four of us played well.

BEN HEBERT: He just knew what was right, he was a leader, through and through, and he played awesome. Actually, we all played awesome. I think I might have been the shittiest one on the team! At lead... that's a good thing, right? Marc and Johnny were in the zone. You know what? At those games though, we were we were the best team by a mile.

Nikki [Sweden's Niklas Edin] was there, but he wasn't Nikki yet. He was still young. [Norway's Thomas] Ulsrud had a really good team. Murdoch had just beaten us at the Worlds, but after being so good in 2008 and 2009, he didn't have a great 2010. He just wasn't firing at the right times, and they didn't make the playoffs.

JOHN MORRIS: We weren't too sad when David Murdoch and Great Britain lost the tie-breaker. David kind of had our number for the previous couple of seasons, they'd beaten us a few times. So, we played Niklas Edin

---

[17] O Canada at Olympics Curling http://www.youtube.com/watch?v=IlO8iUUpVIY

instead. That team was pretty young. If we had to play his current team, or his team from the last few years, it might have been a different story.

BEN HEBERT: Vancouver was an interesting one, especially having just come back from [the 2018 Olympics in] Korea, and now being able to compare. We really didn't feel like it was the Olympics. It was weird. I'll tell you why I feel like that. When I was in Korea, we were in the Olympic bubble, and you're in the village, and everyone is holding your hand to take you here and there.

In Vancouver, we rented a house where we could bring our wives or girlfriends to hang out. We stayed in the village for two or three nights, and then we rented this house, and then after we won, we went back to the village for the last two nights. So we weren't really in the bubble of the Games. We had an amazing place close to the arena. We were comfortable, we didn't have to sleep in tight little village beds. We weren't grinding at the Olympics, we were just playing another bonspiel. We went to some other events, and cheered on our athletes. We'd go for a meal at the village, just to check it out. But we were really in our own little place, and so I look back at it like I didn't feel the massive pressure.

The Canadian women ran through the round robin with an 8-1 record, losing only to China. They faced Switzerland's Mirjam Ott in the semifinal.

CHERYL BERNARD: I remember playing the semifinal thinking, I don't want to play the bronze-medal game. *That* would be stress. When we won silver, it wasn't such a great feeling, because we didn't really get to celebrate it. That's the disappointing part with silver, you don't get to realize that you won a silver medal, because you lost that gold game.

For a team that had been in control all week to end up with a silver medal seemed cruel. But she wasn't the first Canadian team to do it... Mike Harris had done it. Kevin Martin had done it. Unfortunately, the woman who made everything all week missed two game-winners in the gold-medal game, each by a terribly small margin.

In the 10th end, Bernard had a fairly open takeout to run Sweden's Anette Norberg out of rocks for the victory. Her light-weight hit needed to curl another inch or two for a nose hit, but instead she jammed her target on her own rock, and left Sweden an open hit for two to force an extra end. In the 11th end, Bernard had a fairly routine double take-out for the win, but this time it curled an inch or two too much, and just grazed the second Swedish counter. ▶ [18]

CHERYL BERNARD: For me, it was difficult. I won't kid anyone. I'm a competitor. We had a great run that week, and I missed a double in the extra end by millimetres. I rubbed the second stone, that's how close it was. It took me a while to get back to normal.

It was the day after our Olympic final. We had a driver there, and we asked him to take us to Starbucks. We were all pretty down, and dressed in baseball hats and jeans, thinking nobody is going to recognize who we were. So we go into this Starbucks in Richmond, we order and we're waiting for our drinks. And the barista who is making our drinks starts to sing "O Canada" as loud as you can imagine. We're looking around confused, and then the rest of the staff joined in, and then all the customers stood up, and people came in off the street... and they sang the whole national anthem to our team.

I actually think it was because of those complete strangers that it finally sunk in that we'd won a silver medal. If I could ever find that barista it would be amazing. I need to thank her.

A month or so later, once we got our lives back together in Calgary, we met up with the team for coffee and I broke down. I said I was so sorry, and that I'd let the team down. And they all looked at me stunned and said, "We won an Olympic silver medal. That's incredible!" It was only after that, when I finally realized, "Yeah, this is pretty amazing."

---

[18] Curling Women CAN vs SWE - http://www.youtube.com/watch?v=KNVdQQYRGaI

Over time, from the people that supported us, and the people who were around us... I've learned more from that loss than I ever would have if we'd won. I have a great perspective on that now, but it did take a while. You can't be a competitor and be okay with that finish. If I didn't have a shot to win, it might have been a different story. But I had it... and you always have the "What if?"

Martin's team went undefeated through the round robin and knocked off Sweden's Niklas Edin in the semifinal. Norway's Thomas Ulsrud beat Switzerland's Ralph Stöckli in the semi to set up the men's final.

JOHN MORRIS: Our team didn't get very nervous, and if they did, they hid it well. One thing I always did to get rid of my nerves was work out, get out and do something physical. The game that day was at 3 p.m., I think, so it was perfect. I had time in the morning to go do a little exercise before the game.

So I went to work out, wearing normal clothes... I think I went to the gym at the local YMCA near our house. A few people came up to me and said "Aren't you John Morris? Don't you have a gold-medal game in a few hours?"

When I got back from the gym, it was lunchtime. And no one was eating. I was like, "What the heck?" Benny wasn't eating; he told me after he'd puked in the shower before the game. And what hit me most was that Kevin wasn't eating. I'd never seen him nervous.... Kevin always had an appetite, so to see him not eating was worrisome for me.

I was feeling great after my workout, so just to ease the tension, I made the biggest egg sandwich ever and I said, "Guys, you aren't eating?" It was probably eight inches high. We got a good laugh out of that.

Then I took Benny and Marc aside and said, "Guys, I think Kevin is a bit nervous, I've never seen him not eat. He might be thinking about redeeming himself for that draw in Salt Lake City. So we're going to have to be the best teammates we've ever been. We're going to make everything for him and leave him easy shots until he's feeling it." We didn't want him to be in trouble in the first few ends. We came out firing.

During these Olympic Games, Ulsrud's Norway team was more famous for their fashion choices than for their curling. Each game, the reigning European champions wore a different pair of outrageously patterned, colourful, pants. Sometimes they were striped and crossed like the Norwegian flag, and sometimes they were a little more abstract. For the final, they wore a red, white, and grey argyle pattern. They've continued to wear the pants for every major competition since, and several other Norwegian teams - including women, juniors, and wheelchair teams - have followed suit.

A Facebook page devoted to the pants sprung up almost instantly. Today it has more than 481,000 followers. The manufacturer, a company called Loudmouth Golf, credits the Olympic exposure to boosting sales by 40 percent.

Dramatic fashion aside, there was still a game to play...

JOHN MORRIS: By the fourth or fifth end, Kevin looked like he was comfortable again. And I think it was in the sixth, he made a tough freeze to bail us out of some trouble. At that point I knew, he was back, feeling good. After that, we were all clicking again.

It's also worth noting that the crowd was still quite rowdy, as they had been for all of the 12-day event. While most of the cheering was good-natured and appropriately timed, at one point a fan blew a horn in the middle of Ulsrud's backswing on an important shot in the fourth end. The crowd, apparently having learned that this was inappropriate behaviour, booed the fan mercilessly. ▶ [19]

It was an unfortunate moment, but it's hard to say what effect it had on the game. Norway was down by one in the fourth end at the time, and Ulsrud just

---

[19] Men's Curling Full Gold Medal Match - CAN v NOR -
http://www.youtube.com/watch?v=2rQzRMSR1x0

missed his intended shot. The immediate result of the end was a steal for Canada.

They'd steal again in the fifth, and led 3-0 at the break. Norway took two in the sixth, and Canada took two right back in the seventh end. In the eighth, Norway was forced to score one. In the ninth, after less than stellar end, Martin was forced to make an in-turn tap for one to reclaim their three-point lead going into the tenth.

JOHN MORRIS: You never want to count your chickens before they're hatched. I didn't want to assume anything was over until Kevin makes an open hit to run them out of rocks, and then they shake hands. But that was a pretty good feeling. I don't think that feeling will ever be beat. To win on home soil with guys you'd battled with for four years, with one goal in mind, was pretty special. Not many athletes get to see that come to fruition. I was so proud of our team.

KEVIN MARTIN: The gold medal in Vancouver, the first Brier win in 1991, the 18th Grand Slam. Those are the three biggest wins of my career... in that order. And the gold medal is very, very important. We worked really hard to get that as a team, and we were really tough at that time. We didn't we didn't lose many curling games for those four years.

HOW I MET JOHN MORRIS

I met John Morris in October of 1997, when we played him in our first game at the Ottawa Junior Superspiel (I believe we were at the Navy club). He was coming off a silver medal at the Canadian juniors, and we were a bunch of 16-year-olds who were representing the northeast U.S. - aka the Grand National Curling Club.

This was literally the first time we'd been on the ice since March. They'd probably been curling for a month by then. They killed us - and went on to win the World Junior Championships that season.

In 1998, we played them again at the Superspiel. Again, our first game of the year, but this time at Ottawa Granite. This time, it was a close game, and we were trying to decide whether we throw a maybe/probably-there missile to sit a pile, or guard to steal one in the ninth end. We opted to guard, which still bugs me to this day. It might be the only specific shot I've ever really wanted back in nearly 30 years of curling.

Anyway, we scored one. We come home tied, without hammer. According to my dad - our coach - we played a perfect end at 100 percent. But so did they. John had an open hit for one and the win.

Oh - and they won the World Junior title that season too.

CHAPTER 7:
THE 2010s - NEW BLOOD

Since Olympic curling was granted full medal status in 1998, there had been four editions of the Games. With each cycle, the approach became more scientific, the amount of preparation by each team increased, and as Kevin Martin's team showed in 2010, team formation became more nuanced.

At the same time, there were whole teams of younger athletes emerging... athletes who were buying into the long-term approach to the Olympics. The Briers and the Scotties were nice, but the Olympic medal was the real drive now. Gushue had already won a gold medal, but he and his team were barely 30. Mike McEwen won two Grand Slams in 2010, and he wasn't 30 yet. Brad Jacobs was in his late 20s and starting to make waves. Chelsea Carey won her first Grand Slam and another World Curling Tour event that season, as a 26-year old. Twenty two-year-old Val Sweeting would head to the Scotties in 2010 as the youngest skip to ever win Alberta. This was no longer an old-man sport. Curling was getting younger and fitter.

Perhaps no team pushed that envelope more than the foursome skipped by Ottawa's Rachel Homan. After winning a Canadian junior title in 2010, Homan won the Ontario women's title the following year, and finished fourth at the national Scotties... when she was 21. Homan, Emma Miskew, Alison Kreviazuk (later replaced by Joanne Courtney), and Lisa Weagle emerged from juniors fully prepared to compete with the best in the world.

JOHN MORRIS: I used to play with her brother Mark in juniors, and Rachel would be hanging around the rink, just a little rink rat. She'd be running around, and she'd always put on this face like she hated curling. She was probably literally like five years old. So I'd bug her, I'd say, "Rachel, are you ever going to be a curler?" and she'd shout, "Never!"

RACHEL HOMAN (2018 Olympian, three-time Scotties Champion, 2017 World champion): I grew up watching my brother, and he's 10 years older than me. So I grew up watching him and when you're that age, just watching sports isn't very exciting. You don't really know what's going on. You know, it was just too much sitting around. So to me, I thought it was kind of boring just to watch.

Finally, they asked if I wanted to play, and I said, "Absolutely." I was always so competitive, all the time. I wanted to play. I didn't want to watch anymore. I wanted to participate and play against other people.

So I was probably four or five when they let me on the ice. Then my second time out, I asked if I could skip. Of course, I had no idea what I was doing. But it just looked exciting to call the game, and to throw last rocks. It was meant to be, I guess?

But yeah, if you had asked me before then about the highlight of watching my brother curl... it was probably putting stickers into books. Curling wasn't exciting to me then.

JOHN MORRIS: I know that my dad [Earle Morris] coached them for almost 10 years. When I moved west, he'd tell me about Rachel and the team. And he was like, "You know, John, she is the next big thing. She has so much talent. She's going to be the greatest women's curler in Canada." I'm thinking he might be a little biased, because he coached them, but he was quite convinced of it.

LISA WEAGLE (2018 Olympian, three-time Scotties champion, 2017 World champion): I remember when Rachel was in Little Rocks, and I remember my dad was watching, because she was around the same age as my sister, and they were playing against each other. My dad said, "Watch out for this Rachel Homan, she's going to be really amazing." And that was really the first time I ever heard her name.

GERRY GEURTS: In 2005, I was working with the World Curling Tour, and running the Ontario Curling Tour championships at the end of the year. We go down the list, and fill out the lineups. This young junior team from Ottawa, skipped by 15-year-old Rachel Homan wanted to play. I said fine... I'm always of the mindset that it's good to promote junior teams, and include them as much as we can... So Rachel, Emma, she's also 15, I think. Ali Kreviazuk might have been 16, and Nikki Johnston. They went through this women's field at the Cataraqui Club in Kingston, and won the event. Anne Merklinger was there. Sherry Middaugh was there. Every top women's team was there, and Rachel went through like a buzzsaw and won the event... at 15.

The next year it was played in Cambridge and she won it again.

RACHEL HOMAN: When I decided just to curl competitively, I just wanted to be the best at that age group, or in that year. It wasn't really on the Olympic stage yet. It was exciting to watch people at the Scotties and the Brier, but you just think it's so far away from where you're at, when you're young. I was just trying to go as far as you could, for a 15-year-old or a 16-year-old.

SHERRY MIDDAUGH: I think they had a totally different style than you'd see in ladies play. They had a different skill set. They'd play much more like a men's team, and they had the skill set to back it up. I'm not saying she can't draw or anything, but she's got a hit game that no ladies team has. And she's got a different attitude... you didn't see a lot of young players walk on the ice with that confidence.

JENN HANNA: What sort of set Rachel's junior team apart from a lot of junior teams, at least at that time, and probably a lot since then, was their "We Belong Here" attitude. They never put out an air of, "Well, we're younger, so we're not supposed to win," or anything like that. It was always a "We Belong Here" attitude. And along with the attitude, there was a fearlessness like, "Not only do we belong here, but we're going to show you why we belong here."

JILL OFFICER: They were still in juniors, and we played them in the London [Ontario] bonspiel. I think they beat us in the semi or the final that year. We played them, and they were fearless. I don't think they were taught otherwise. It didn't occur to them that they could lose, or miss shots.

JENN HANNA: And I think that got to be a little bit of a scary thing to play against sometimes, if you want my honest opinion. Because when you're playing against somebody that thinks that they can make anything, it's hard to put them in an uncomfortable position because they're so sure of themselves.

GERRY GEURTS: You knew she was destined for greatness. It took them a while, longer than they expected, for her to win the Canadian juniors. Some of that was how they were coached maybe? You saw that team's destiny was to go to the Olympics, to be one of the best teams ever... not just to win a junior title. So there were some bumps along the way. Kudos to the coaching staff for taking the long-term approach instead of looking for short-term gains.

I think it was 2007 or 2008 when they beat Jennifer twice in the London spiel. They might have been 16 or 17 then.

GEORGE KARRYS: They were just going from bantam to junior, they were that young... and they beat Jennifer Jones *twice* in that spiel. I put them on the cover of *The Curling News*.

RACHEL HOMAN: During that London 'spiel, our parents kind of looked at the draw and said we had to play the U.S. champions the first game. If we won, we had to play the World champion at the time, Bingyu Wang. And then, if we won, now we have to play Jennifer Jones. So our parents didn't really have high expectations for us that weekend. You're in a tough bracket.

I mean, I'm really glad that we could compete and just see how it went. And we played really well and qualified, and won the whole tournament. We had to beat Jones twice that same tournament. It's kind of crazy to think we were so young and able to perform really well and consistently at a young age.

CATHY OVERTON-CLAPHAM: We played them a couple of times in London. Great team, even then. They were great. I remember going, "Holy shit! These girls are going to be good." And they weren't scared at all, very similar to how they are now. Obviously they got better. It was hard to imagine them being better than they were at that time, but they were an amazing team even at that time.

CHELSEA CAREY: I remember playing in Ottawa, at the Canada Cup qualifier, when I was playing with Barb Spencer. I didn't know who it was at the time, but we were playing Rachel, and she was like maybe and 14 or 15. We outplayed the front three, but she was so good, she was staying with Barb, so she kept making shots and keeping them in it.

We were tied, coming home, without. And we had just a wall of guards, and one rock on the top of the pin, and and another one, not quite in the four-foot. And on her last shot she made a 15- or 20-foot, angle runback… and *stuffs* it for the win.

And I came off the ice and my dad called me, and he said, "How did it go?" I'm like, "I don't know who the fuck this kid is, but she is going to be so good!"

LISA WEAGLE: They had just finished up in juniors, they'd just won a World silver and I knew that Lynn [Kreviazuk] was too young to move up to ladies, and would probably continue playing junior. So I approached Rachel and said, "If you're looking for someone to play front end, I'm interested." And that's kind of how that all came about.

RACHEL HOMAN: We were a little bit lucky to be that successful in that time frame. We were putting in the work, and we believed in ourselves, and wanted to see how far we could go at the provincials. We didn't expect to win [Ontario in 2011] that's for sure, and when it all came together it was just really exciting and a really cool moment for our team.

LISA WEAGLE: So we played Krista McCarville in the Ontario final, who had won the year before. We won that, and got to go to the Scotties. So that definitely surpassed what I thought would happen for me *ever* in my curling career. I'd always wanted to go to the Scotties, that was the goal. But being able to go in my first year with the team was pretty incredible.

SHERRY MIDDAUGH: For most people, they get their confidence by having success, but with Rachel, it was always there from the get-go. It's a great attitude to have. I went to the 2011 Scotties as their fifth player. Their coach, Andrea Ronnebeck, thought I'd be helpful because I'd been there before. I'd never seen such confidence... and they backed it up.

LISA WEAGLE: I think we won our first five games in a row or something like that. And I think people started to take a bit more notice of us, and we started to believe in ourselves a little bit more. And we made it all the way to the semifinal. But we lost to Amber Holland from Saskatchewan; she went on to win it. But we were in the last group, and I started to change how I was thinking about being there and wanting to compete. After that, I really wanted to win.

JILL OFFICER: They were totally built that way. There was obviously potential seen in them by somebody... either Earle or somebody else, but they put that crew together, and built them from the ground up, and spent that time with them.

CHELSEA CAREY: You know, they entered a lot of womens' spiels as juniors. You've gotta pay your dues that way, and just she's always been somebody who doesn't have a whole lot of fear. I think that works really well for you when you're playing against teams you shouldn't beat... to just be fearless like that.

EARLE MORRIS: I think it starts with Rachel. She is an absolute phenom. She's always had no fear. It was a coach's dream from that perspective, she was fearless. And you'd just have to pull her back a bit so she didn't go high octane all the time. If it was up to her, she's go full offence 24-7. It's in her DNA and she was so good at it.

There were a lot of times where you'd want to call a timeout, but then she'd make some double-raise, triple-takeout or something, and you'd think, "There goes another teachable moment down the drain." You had to learn to let her go.

LISA WEAGLE: The next year, we made it to the provincial final and we lost it to Tracy Horgan [now Fleury], and I think that experience also pushed us even harder. We hired Earle, he had coached Rachel and Emma in juniors. In 2013, he came on as our coach and he was one of the greatest coaches ever in curling, and probably in sport. He was able to just demand that next level from us, and change how we train, and change how we curled, and that was kind of the year that the "tick" started happening as well. We just started to believe in ourselves that much more.

While most curling fans are familiar with Homan's heroics - which led to two Sandra Schmirler Awards as the Scotties MVP - lead Weagle quietly flew under the radar... until 2013. At the Scotties in Kingston, Ontario, Team Homan employed the "tick" shot so frequently (more than 70 times over the week, including nine times in the final), and Lisa made so many of them perfectly, that the curling world unofficially renamed the shot "The Weagle."
▶ [20]

---

[20] Lisa Weagle - 2013 Scotties - http://www.youtube.com/watch?v=IHkN3GQpkWM

LISA WEAGLE: It was really organic how it came about, and it really came out with the concept of tolerance, knowing the right way to miss the shot. For me, as a lead, if I'm trying to freeze on a rock at the top of the button, and there's a guard in play, the tolerance would be to hit the guard and open the front up. And so we were doing that in practise, and working on that, and we started to realize that making that tick shot sometimes would actually be a pretty good thing strategically, because then you have two corner guards, and you leave the centre open.

We started to realize that this was a strategy that we typically use in the last end of a game, but what if we started using it at other points in the game?

And it worked for us because Ali, Emma and Rachel had such an amazing big-weight ability, we'd be able to make the peels and the runbacks. So we had the tools at every position to be able to play with the strategy a little bit more.

Making a tick isn't really a high-percentage shot, maybe around 60 or 70 percent if you're really good at it... but there is some pretty big reward when you execute. And also, at that time people didn't really know how to defend against it, because it's not something you see a lot. You never played a tick in the second end of the game. So we were using it in some spiels. I remember we went to Saskatoon, and we were using it quite a bit there and experimenting with that. So when we got to the Scotties in 2013, we had been using it, but I don't think a lot of people had taken notice of it. So it came as a bit of a surprise.

GEORGE KARRYS: I've been saying that for years. We're going to get a team of Serena Williamses, and they're going to be tanks, and they're going to throw Howitzers, and win a shit-ton of games. The closest thing I've seen to that is Rachel Homan's team.

JENN HANNA: Moving from juniors into women's play, it struck people particularly... because there hadn't been really anybody like her, or her team, and they all kind of played like that. So I think that's probably the springboard that made Rachel so successful. It's this fearlessness... It was like, "Forget the draw for one. Let's play the 20-foot runback for four, because I know I'm going to make it."

CRAIG SAVILL: They stuck together for a long time. Rachel and Emma have been together forever. They've circulated a front end around. They work really hard. They practise a lot. They practise as a team a lot, which helps. They bought into a system as well.

SHERRY MIDDAUGH: She's pretty much had the same core for a while. She didn't do it alone, and she hasn't had to switch up too many pieces and dynamics along the way.

EARLE MORRIS: When you've got somebody as amazing as Rachel, the athletes who play for her really want to play for her. So they all work the same way she does. They prepare so thoroughly. You look at high performance... strategy, tactics, mental toughness, team dynamics, healthy lifestyles. They've got it all covered in spades. There's probably no team that's fitter. No team that works harder. They just get it.

RACHEL HOMAN: There's no guarantees in sport. We made playoffs at our first Scotties, and didn't even win the provincial the next year. There's a lot of great teams, and a lot of competition, and it's tough to get out of your province, especially for those bigger provinces that have a lot of depth. To have the opportunity to be able to go back a second time and win it in 2013 was a feeling I'll never forget. It was kind of shocking when we really felt like we were the underdog, as if we were going to win. I thought it would take everything in us to beat Jen [Jones] in the final. She played really well that game and the whole team did, and we kind of kept to our game and everyone played really well.

Team Homan would win the Scotties in 2013 representing Ontario, and again in 2014 as Team Canada. The World championship eluded them, however, as they finished with a bronze in 2013 and a silver in 2014. They'd win another

Scotties and finally a World championship in 2017 - just days before Rachel's 28th birthday.

While Rachel and Emma Miskew have been together since they were 12 years old, the front end has changed over the years. Since graduating from juniors to the women's ranks, there has been only one lineup change. After winning two Scotties in 2013 and 2014, Alison Kreviazuk left the team to move to Sweden to be with her boyfriend Fredrik Lindberg of Team Edin. They're now engaged. She was replaced by Joanne Courtney, who had been playing with Val Sweeting in Alberta.

GERRY GEURTS: You can't blame Rachel for wanting to scoop up the best sweeper in the game, and you can't blame Joanne for wanting to play with Rachel Homan. The problem, again, was timing. It left Val without a player too late in the game to go out and find somebody that she really wanted.

Sweeting ended up recruiting fellow Edmontonian Lori Olson-Johns out of a brief retirement to replace Courtney. Other than the one switch at the second position, Homan, Miskew, and lead Lisa Weagle have been teammates for eight years.

JOHN EPPING: The full unit is what's necessary to win at the top level these days. And they're treating it like it's everything to them. They're impressive. I played mixed doubles with Lisa. Every time we played, even if we won, she was always asking, "What can we do better?"

GEORGE KARRYS: Rachel threw a bazillion rocks... and they could throw the big weight. Before Weagle and the tick game came along, they were just outgunning everybody by throwing the heat. It was a huge differential for them.

JOHN EPPING: The big weight ability from both back enders is massive. And Rachel's touch game has gotten better from when she was younger. I think it's just a fact that your draw weight gets better, your touch gets better with age. Her consistency level has gone through the roof.

MIKE HARRIS: Rachel, Jennifer Jones, Colleen Jones, and Sandra Schmirler... all the best hitting teams of their era.

RACHEL HOMAN: You have to love the game and you have to be doing it right. I think we're so fortunate to play the game that we do and we're so fortunate that everyone loves to watch it on TV, and it's really growing and we're excited to see future generations get inspired. All the leagues are full and there's waiting lists to get into our clubs now. That didn't used to be the case before, so I think that the game is growing and it's just getting more popular, and it's exciting that more people are playing. We're going to take the game to the next level, and I'm kind of excited to see what happens next.

HOW I MET RACHEL HOMAN

Almost every good junior curler in Ontario attended the Trillium Curling Camp at least once or twice. Granted, there are a few exceptions, but Rachel Homan wasn't one of them.

She attended the camp as a teenager... probably around the same time she started winning women's World Curling Tour events. She was never in my groups though, so I didn't get to know her at all. Later, she worked at the camp and that's probably the first time we actually "met".

In the years that followed, our paths would cross again and again at OCT events, charity bonspiels, and eventually the 2013 World Women's Championships in Riga, Latvia, where she wore the Maple Leaf and I was coaching Switzerland's Silvana Tirinzoni.

That was her first World women's championship. She finished with a bronze at the age of 23.

It wasn't like young teams were taking over. Experienced teams were also re-jigging their lineups to include a bit of youthful energy. Just like Martin had picked up twenty-somethings Kennedy and Hebert leading up to 2010, other teams started to follow suit in the cycle that followed. While Jeff Stoughton picked up Reid Carruthers, and later Mark Nichols, Brad Gushue was reworking his lineup with some young bucks as well.

MIKE HARRIS: At the Players' Championships [the last big event of the year], there's always people sitting in the corner, whispering about next year.

At the end of the day, one of the parties is surprised. There's no easy way to break up.

REID CARRUTHERS: The spring of 2010, we [Team Stoughton] had our first talk about curling together. The goal was literally to win a World championship *that* season. We won the Brier and the Worlds that year, and played four full years together with Team Stoughton.

JEFF STOUGHTON: In 2011, we built that team to win that year. It was a big goal for a brand new team.

REID CARRUTHERS: This learning experience that I was given was something I wish for every young curler. It's unfortunate that there's only one Jeff Stoughton, one Kerry Burtnyk, or one Glenn Howard. The actual opportunity doesn't present itself very often, so I wanted to make very sure that I didn't waste it.

Getting to learn from Jeff, and not just him... Jon Mead, Steve Gould, and Mark Nichols... they're all the consummate professionals to learn from, on and off the ice. The preparation, event management... That's something I'd never seen before. They did everything like a professional team would do. It was easy to latch on and believe in him as a leader.

BRAD GUSHUE: That was interesting, in 2010-11 when we had tried the experiment with Randy Ferbey, myself, Ryan Fry, and Mark. It just went disastrously wrong. And after that season, I think we all kind of knew that we went down the wrong path, and we all thought we've gotta try something new. We all knew changes were coming.

MARK NICHOLS: We had some really good teams where we just couldn't find ways to consistently win... so my plan was to take a break from everything outside of work and family. Honestly, the year I took off, I didn't miss curling at all.

BRAD GUSHUE: Then Mark said he was stepping away. I think he was a little bit tired of me, and maybe my constant kind of pushing, and wanting to get to the top of the game. He wanted a break from that and maybe try something new. And I really think his stepping away from the game was always going to be temporary.

MARK NICHOLS: I threw rocks one weekend with Glen Goss. He asked me to spare in just a weekend 'spiel. So I played with them for a few games and those were the only rocks I threw until the Players' Championship that year with Jeff and Jon. Jon Mead was actually the one that called me and asked if I'd consider playing with them at the Players' Championship, because they were looking at making a change for the following season.

JEFF STOUGHTON: He did it on his own. He did move here. They moved to Winnipeg and bought a condo, and were here for two and a half years and soaked up the community.

MARK NICHOLS: I had no plans of going back, but when Jon Mead and Jeff Stoughton reach out, your ears perk up and then you start thinking, "If I do this, what could it lead to?" So I went to the Players' Championship. I enjoyed hanging out with those guys, Jeff, Jon, and Reid.

BRAD GUSHUE: And then when he got a chance to come back with Jeff, I think it was kind of a breath of fresh air, and an opportunity for him to go and learn from someone else and experience a different team, and a new dynamic.

MARK NICHOLS: Ultimately they gave me a bit of time to get some stuff in order, and see if I wanted to make the move to Winnipeg. And obviously, my wife Colette would have to be on board. And she was actually the one that convinced me that I should go back and play, and have an opportunity to play with some of the best players that ever played the game... It was one of those situations where I couldn't say no.

JEFF STOUGHTON: People asked him, "Why are you playing lead? You've been a third your whole life," and his answer was amazing. He said a gold medal is the same no matter what position you're playing. It was nice to hear that his expectations were that high.

MARK NICHOLS: Those few years in between were tough. I didn't enjoy playing against Brad and the guys on tour. I didn't enjoy our games when we played against them in the Brier. It wasn't fun for me to play against those guys, especially Brad. We had so much success together through the years and now basically we weren't talking, just curling against each other. I didn't enjoy that.

JEFF STOUGHTON: Mark said when we first played Brad in the Brier in 2013... I don't think we played him in anything before that, that year... it was hard. They basically grew up together. He said he really tried to externally pump himself up to be excited about the game, but it was hard to play against him. I think after the first one it was better. But he's got a Manitoba jacket on now, I'm sure it was strange for him.

BRAD GUSHUE: Really, for me, it was a blessing as well, because I made the decision after that, that I was just going to really take it down to the studs and rebuild. And then we brought in Adam Casey and Geoff Walker. At that point, Fry stayed on board, but nobody had heard much about those two. But I wanted two guys that were going to put in the effort and worked as hard as I did at the game. I felt that they had talent, just by what they did in juniors. I'd seen them play a little bit in men's and there were some technical issues that I felt I could help them work through. And the big thing was if they were going to come down to the rink every day and put in the work.

I realized that these were two guys that were willing to put in the effort. So we started with that team, and then Fry kind of went on a different route, then we brought in Brett Gallant, and all of a sudden we had four guys that were on the same page and put the same effort in working our asses off with the same goal... and it felt really, really good. The problem was that those guys weren't quite there yet. They had the talent, but it hadn't been kind of cultivated yet, to turn them into the players that they are now.

It was clear times were changing. The cycle from 2010 to 2014 certainly made a younger generation more visible, but the "old guard" wasn't quite ready to get out of the way yet.

JEFF STOUGHTON: Kevin Koe won in 2010, we won the Worlds in 2011, and Glenn won the Worlds in 2012... and then that's it. So maybe it's a bit later than that. We lost the Brier final in 2013, and got the bronze in 2014. But sure, the McEwens were getting tougher to beat, and the Eppings, and the rest of the crews. It seemed like it was the last big event for those guys.

JILL OFFICER: Into the early 2010s... you see a lot more young people showing up at the Scotties, and playing on tour. I certainly noticed that happening, and started to recognize that I was now one of the older ones on the tour!

BRAD GUSHUE: For me the big youth movement was more in the 2010 to 2014 cycle, with with the emergence of Rachel, and Jacobs would be another one. You know John Epping kind of came on the scene, and Val Sweeting. That was really when we started to see some new teams and new blood, and some younger teams that kind of came out of the gates ready to compete right away.

MARK NICHOLS: I approached Brad towards the end of that Olympic cycle and asked him if he was looking at taking on a new player. I told him that Colette and I were moving home for sure, because we were expecting our first child.

So I just threw it out there. And I said, "Listen, no hard feelings if you say 'no,' but I'm willing to come back to to your team if you want to take me." That was kind of the way it happened.

BRAD GUSHUE: Mark told me he was looking at moving back. He played the last couple of years with Jeff and he'd played really, really well. I felt that bringing in him might bring that extra bit of experience. With us back together, it was a guy that I knew was at the same level as I was from an experience standpoint. So we brought him back in and then I had to make the tough choice of who is out. And it was probably one of the toughest decisions in my curling career.

And obviously Adam [Casey] was the one that we chose and Adam had worked his ass off for me. He was a good friend and I really, really enjoyed playing with him. So that was a hard decision, and he took it like a pro, and he's a first-class guy. But of all the decisions that I've had to make in my career from a personnel standpoint, without a doubt that was the hardest one.

REID CARRUTHERS: Mark and Brad are professionals. Brad was a little bit shocked when Mark semi-retired and took a season off. To see him back curling, but with a different team, was probably another shock. Like most solid teams, you reach a point where you need to shake things up a bit. Now you see that team... they'd never won a Brier before, but they made it very clear that was on the bucket list. They spent some time apart, maybe recharged their batteries a bit, and renewed their desires. Now look at them... winning back-to-back Briers. They're the best team in men's curling.

In Ontario, there was another change brewing. In 2011, Rich Hart, the longtime third for Glenn Howard, decided to take a step back from the game. Glenn didn't have to look very far for a replacement. It turned out his Tuesday night teammate had "retired" and was available...

WAYNE MIDDAUGH: I never retired! Everybody thinks I retired early, but I never retired. I kept playing, I just didn't win!

Glenn and I, and his wife, and Sherry, we all play in a major league together in Penetanguishene. It used to be a men's major league, and we asked if we could play in it with our wives, and they said, "Yeah, I think you guys will be competitive enough!" We've been doing that for 17 or 18 years now. Since then, other people asked if we could make it open, and now it's an open major cash league.

So Glenn and I have been curling together through all of that. Even when we played against each other... in a provincial final or something, we'd go play with each other on Tuesday night! Normally whoever won the game had to play second that week as a punishment.

Glenn and I have always been friends, and never once has there been animosity or issues between us. He's the easiest guy in the world to get along with. If you can't get along with Glenn Howard, there's something wrong with you. It's not Glenn, it's you.

Glenn was playing like 10 events a year, and I was playing maybe six. I was actually playing with his son Scott at the time. Glenn said he needed a spare for the Canada Cup in 2010, so I said "Sure, I'll go play!" That was the first time I played with Brent and Craig, and all of a sudden we won. We beat Kevin Martin in the final, and we all played pretty well, and it was easy. Then Richie decides to take some time off to figure out his career and all that, so they said it was an easy decision to call me up and ask to play.

I said to Glenn, "That might have been one good week. I've never actually played third before." I wasn't sure if I was going to figure it out. Glenn and I sat down, and he convinced me that all I had to do was try to make shots, like I was throwing skip rocks. Just try to make each one perfect, try to play 100 percent every game. Once I took that attitude, that it wasn't anything different, and that I simply had to try to make shots, it seemed to work out okay.

Middaugh would join Glenn Howard for the 2011-2012 season, along with Craig Savill and Brent Laing. They won the Brier and the World championship that year. For Glenn, it was his fourth World championship... in a fourth separate decade. He'd won in the 1980s, 1990s, 2000s, and 2010s. How's that for longevity?

Aside from the shake-ups on the men's side, there was a major change on the women's side as well. In 2010, fresh off a Scotties championship, Jennifer Jones and team decided to part ways with longtime third Cathy Overton-Clapham.

In her place they picked up two-time Canadian junior champion Kaitlyn Lawes, who had been playing in Alberta with Cathy King for her first season of women's curling.

KAITLYN LAWES: How do you turn down an opportunity to play with the top women's team, arguably, in the world, at the time? And to have that experience, get to learn from the best, play with people who are motivated, people who inspired me? It was a no-brainer when the opportunity presented itself.

JILL OFFICER: The process of making that decision was incredibly difficult. A lot of people still think that it wasn't a team decision, but I'm telling you, it was. Obviously with the exception of the person who was let go, the rest of us were fully on board with each other to make that decision.

CATHY OVERTON-CLAPHAM: Obviously, they were trying to make their team stronger, and do what they had to do, looking ahead for the four years. It was big news, obviously, because it hadn't really happened before, and maybe just the timing of it, too. We'd just come off winning the Scotties, and losing the World semis. We won a bronze that year, so you know it was big curling news at the time.

CHELSEA CAREY: I remember the reaction being very supportive of Cathy and very anti-Jennifer. Certainly, it seemed that Cathy was the victim, from what we know. I guess my attitude on it was always that there's a lot of stuff that goes on within teams that that we don't know about… I guess I just have a hard time with that. I felt like Jennifer was too vilified for it, because we just don't know what went on there.

Jennifer Jones told Global News at the time, "These decisions are always extremely difficult, and Cathy is a great friend. She's been a huge part of our success in the past, but the focus is really now on 2014, four years from now. We felt like we needed to make a change." ▶ [21]

---

[21] Team Jones drops Cathy O - http://www.youtube.com/watch?v=IIaxlpXijI8

JEFF STOUGHTON: I want to win. And when you want to win, you try to put people around you that you feel you can win with. That's all Jennifer did. It seemed like Jennifer and Cathy's expiry date had passed as teammates, and it was time to move on to find someone else she could win with.

JILL OFFICER: We knew it was going to hurt, but we felt like we were leaving ourselves in a situation when we were hurting ourselves more. It's like ending a marriage or relationship... you know it's going to hurt the other person, but you're hurting yourself more by staying in that situation. That's truly how we felt. It was really difficult.

And it was difficult afterwards too. We had a lot of media attention and negative publicity about it, and we kept taking the high road, taking the high road. It was really hard for a good period of time, and we just kept supporting each other, and we worked with our sports psychologist, and eventually got through it. And in hindsight, taking the high road kind of paid off for us.

CHELSEA CAREY: I mean, while I understand why that would be people's reaction, I thought it was probably a bit unfair, just because no one actually knows what happened. Certainly it was a bit of a game-changer in the whole "curling as a business" kind of a situation. I think now we are more used to it just because teams change all the time now. That was kind of the first high-profile one though.

GERRY GEURTS: The problem was, from an outsider's perspective, that it wasn't done right. It was left too long. So she didn't really have a chance to find a team. Cathy was kind of stuck. She still wanted to play, still wanted to compete, so she had so find a way to create her own team.

CATHY OVERTON-CLAPHAM: I think maybe in that situation there wasn't any ... I don't know what the right word is. There wasn't any evidence that maybe there was something wrong, or that a change needed to be made. Also, the timing of it wasn't great. I didn't know anything about it. We were having a meeting, which I thought was to talk about next year. I was told then, so you know there was a lot that I had missed out on. We were going to be Team Canada at the Scotties, and teams were already formed at that time.

JEFF STOUGHTON: You see it all the time on men's teams. Even Jon Mead and me, we didn't play for a few years, then got back together. And at the end of our careers, same thing, we wondered if we were getting the best out of each other... and we thought, probably not, so let's move on.

Nothing wrong with that. Cathy could be at the top of her game, but if Jennifer and the team don't feel that it's putting them in a position to win, then why keep doing it? It's a professional decision, not a personal one. And I think it was tough, because it feels very personal.

GERRY GEURTS: The interesting part was that Jennifer and Cathy played in events all year long, and never had to play against each other... until the 2011 Scotties. It really got blown out of proportion, and it created a little more animosity in the story.

JILL OFFICER: I remember our sports psychologist asking us "Can you still win the Scotties if you lose that game?" And the answer was yes. That really gave me perspective on that. If we had to lose that game, we had to lose that game. We were still in the final, and we lost that game by a quarter of an inch.

I'm not going to say it was easy... but I was really relieved when it was over.

I remember watching that game from a hotel bar in Winnipeg. I was supposed to be in Florida, but bad weather changed my travel plans, so I was stranded at the airport Sheraton. Cathy O was the crowd favourite at the Sheraton bar. The Charlottetown crowd was obviously with her as well.

Cathy O's Manitoba team beat Jones' Team Canada 8-5. In the post-game interviews, the reporters tried to dig for more fuel to feed the media fire, but Jennifer wouldn't take the bait. She was pleasant, and professional, and said all the right things. "They outplayed us and they deserved to win... I've always said Cathy was a great player, and she played really well tonight." ▶[22]

CATHY OVERTON-CLAPHAM: Obviously, I was very close with Jennifer, and obviously, it's not the same relationship as it was back then. But you know, at the end of the day it's a curling game.

Cathy O continued to be a fixture on the women's tour with a variety of teams. She won Grand Slam events sparing for Scotland's Eve Muirhead, and Alberta's Val Sweeting, and reached another Slam semifinal with Switzerland's Silvana Tirinzoni. In 2017, she joined former provincial rival Chelsea Carey to make an impressive run at the Roar of the Rings, and also added one more Grand Slam championship to her resume.

Team Jennifer Jones lost the final of the 2011 Scotties to Saskatchewan's Amber Holland, but went on to win two more Scotties in 2015 and 2018, as well as the gold medal at the 2014 Sochi Olympics.

---

[22] 2011 Scotties Draw 14 Media - http://www.youtube.com/watch?v=tHITjT4dShc

HOW I MET CATHY OVERTON CLAPHAM

Like anyone familiar with curling, I knew who Cathy O was. I'd seen her on TV winning championships both with Team Jones, and as a super-spare for a number of other teams. What I didn't know before I met her was how much fun the five-time Scotties champion was off the ice.

I met her at the Whitecap Curling Camp in 2013. After several years in Halifax (and Saint John, N.B., before that), the Curl Atlantic camp was being staged in Charlottetown for the first time. Cathy was also invited to be on staff that year, and after the Sunday activities wrapped up, we were all anxious to have a beer in the coaches' lounge and unwind.

There was only one problem: no beer. It was about 8:30 p.m. on a Sunday in P.E.I. Beer and liquor stores closed at 6 p.m.

Robbie "Doc" Doherty, a Charlottetown local, chimes in and says, "No problem. Just go to Slick's." It's worth noting that at this point, Doc had not yet been to any of his three Briers, and supremely enjoyed the role of class clown in the Whitecap world.

So Cathy O and Adam Casey (fresh off a couple of Brier runs with Brad Gushue - prior to a few more for P.E.I. and Saskatchewan) decide, we're going to find a local bootlegger - Slick - who apparently has cases of beer stacked in his garage for just such an occasion. I get recruited as the driver, because I'm the only one who can drive a stick-shift, and that's the only option available to borrow. I swear this isn't a crummy Canadian "Smokey and the Bandit" knockoff, although perhaps it should be.

Doc gives us directions in the special P.E.I. language that involves no street names or landmarks, but Casey seems to think he knows where we're going. We get lost, again and again. Doc gives us more directions over the phone - again with no street names or landmarks - until we find a long dirt road lined with abandoned, rusting cars. At the end is an old farm house, which we say immediately looks like *every* house in a *Criminal Minds* episode, which meant there were probably lots of bodies buried in the garden.

I'm trying to approach the house slowly, except the dirt road has so many ups and downs and potholes, that I end up stalling a few times, or revving the engine loud enough to wake some of those bodies in the garden.

Eventually, we get to the house, convinced that this is the worst idea ever. We give Casey some cash and send him to the door, and immediately turn the car around for a faster getaway.

Cathy and I think this is somewhere between hilarious and terrifying, and she says, "There's no way this works. It doesn't even look like anybody is home."

He knocks. The light comes on, and immediately he's invited in. We're sure that's the last we'd ever see of Adam Casey. Two minutes later, he comes out with a case of Canadian, a 12-pack of Coors Light, and four extra bottles clanging around on top (because that's the exact number we could afford, apparently).

We drive away in disbelief, laughing hysterically as I stall the car a few more times, and finally make it back to our residence, and enjoy a well-earned beer.

That was the first day I met Cathy O.

One of the biggest team shuffle bombshells was yet to come. Following the 2012-2013 season, John Morris left Team Kevin Martin. Just eight months before the 2013 Olympic Trials, this was a move nobody saw coming. Most casual observers would have guessed that the team would stick it out for one more season and finish the four-year cycle, but apparently that was not to be.

The reason was simple. The team that had won everything wasn't winning anymore.

RICHARD HART: Everybody hits a point in their career when you want to do what you want to do. John's a free spirit, and he wants to do what he wants to do. I'm not surprised it lasted that long, but if they hadn't have won gold in 2010, they would have been done on the spot. When they won it, he stuck around for the payday. Who would walk away from that opportunity?

CRAIG SAVILL: John is a bit unpredictable. I kinda thought he'd stick it out, and maybe be miserable a bit longer, for a chance for some more money, and go to the next Olympics. I thought that's what would happen. Obviously John didn't care that much... he wanted to like curling again, and enjoy himself.

EARLE MORRIS: I remember when I knew it was going to happen. I was at the Players' Championship in Toronto watching. It was the end of the 2013 season. They hadn't been playing well, Kevin and John, in particular. They were struggling together. They had a really ordinary game, and I was waiting for them in the players area when they came off the ice. John whacked a garbage can and said, "I hate this game." He wasn't having any fun.

BEN HEBERT: We won in 2010, so we didn't really have a choice but to play together the next year. We still had a really good 2011. We won as much that year as any other, but didn't win the Brier. We did not have a good season in 2011-2012. Didn't make the Brier, because we lost to Koe in the Alberta final.

WAYNE MIDDAUGH: Winning. Winning is the driving force behind it all. When you're winning, you can deal with anything. Personalities, idiosyncrasies, how they eat, sleep, if they snore... if you're winning, not an issue. All of a sudden, if you start losing some of those games, every one of those little things starts to grind on you. You can only last so long.

EARLE MORRIS: When you got to the last year or two... they just weren't cooking the same way. And maybe the input wasn't appreciated as much as it was, once upon a time. Or maybe there was too much input, because John was saying too much, trying to make good things happen. It just wasn't good.

GERRY GEURTS: In 2013, Kevin missed some events after he had surgery. You could see some cracks forming. They weren't as good as they had been, and it was going to break down. The old adage is, "winning solves everything" and they'd been winning, which is why it lasted the seven years it did.

BEN HEBERT: Kevin and John, when we are winning, are sunshine and roses. And if we're losing, they are really different. No different than a lot of the top players when you're losing. Some aren't as fun to be around, myself included. But Kevin is difficult. And you know him and John didn't see eye to eye. John wasn't working as hard, no question. We won our big thing, our Olympic gold, and after that he wasn't putting the time in, and Kevin didn't like that. John wasn't playing as good, Kevin wasn't quite as good, and it was just kind of slippery slope, I guess. We played together for a long time. Tough personalities clashed, and so John decided to step away, and made way for a new guy.

JOHN MORRIS: I would just say we weren't playing as well as we were back when we were thriving. Kevin had an injury, a hernia. My passion, my soul, I would say was I wasn't there. I was just going through the motions. And for me to be a successful curler, I have to be fired up. I need some good energy out there. I really want to win for myself and my teammates, and I guess that fire and that passion wasn't there with that team... I guess what happened was I felt like if we played together the next year, we would have just gone through the motions again.

EARLE MORRIS: At that point, it was clear that John and Kevin had a disconnect, and they weren't able to resolve it together. They needed some sort of facilitator. A better option would have been to have someone say "Hey guys, we just have to pull together for another year. Why can't we figure out what's getting in the way and sort it out so you guys can be great again?" Because that was an incredible team... but it was not going good.

JOHN MORRIS: I didn't want to sewer those guys. That was the toughest part of it. That conference call with the guys was so hard, I was actually in tears for some of it, and it was really tough. But I told the guys that I think that if I'm not on the team anymore that they can get someone who would allow them to to thrive... and secondly I thought that if I took some time off, or joined a new team, I felt like I could get my passion back, and my soul back. So I felt like it was actually going to be, you know, for the betterment of both teams.. my future team which turned out to be with Jimmy Cotter, and for Kevin's team.

EARLE MORRIS: It was done in a professional manner. It gave the Martin team enough time to get someone, and John sat back and got somebody too. And it's interesting how that worked out, because at the Trials that year, John was second, and Martin was third.

REID CARRUTHERS: To me it looked like they got to the point where it's hard to repeat that same success. When you're so used to winning, and you take some tough losses... it was probably the right time. It allowed them to both be successful in their trial runs. Kevin came pretty close to reaching that final. And who beat him? John Morris with a renewed love of curling, getting the most out of his guys, and ended up a couple shots away from the Olympics with a brand new team.

MIKE HARRIS: It may have been a case of John ducking before he got cut.

KEVIN MARTIN: John did not leave the team. I promise... I just want to say that I was not surprised. And he did not leave the team. I don't think anybody needs to know more.

Kevin alluded that he, again, would reveal more when he writes his book... but also didn't know exactly when that would be. At the time, Martin told the Globe and Mail, "I was surprised a little bit I guess. But you know for our team, it has been seven years. For five of the years it's pretty safe to say we were the best team in curling. But the last year and a half, we haven't been. You get used to a certain level of play and when we haven't been there, change is inevitable. [23]

Speaking of change...

WAYNE MIDDAUGH: I've had to sit down with people and cut them. It's impossible. One of them was Peter Corner... that's family. First cousin. I had to cut him. One of the hardest things I've ever done in my life. I had to tell him it wasn't working out and I had to make a change. For the first 22 years of our lives, we spent every day together. We're first cousins, we grew up a block apart, went to school together. We're six months apart in age. We hung out together and golfed in the summer. A few years later, to say I don't think this is working out... that was really hard to do. It just wasn't the right mix of shotmaking, and seeing the game the same way. And to this day, we're still best friends. At the time it was hard, but you get over it.

The other side of that is... the year that my team with Jon Mead, John Epping and Scott Bailey team broke up, it was because the three of them cut me! I'd never had that happen before. Jon went back to play with Stoughton. Epping wanted to skip, and Bailey wanted to play back end. So they went and did that, and I was left with no team!

RICHARD HART: We had a standing deal. Every year is a one-year deal. If you're looking to make a change, don't let me hold you back. Pick up the phone and call me. Don't call a meeting. Let's not all go out to a restaurant. Just call me and tell me. Then I want the other two guys to call the next day to have a chat. But that's that.

---

[23] John Morris Says Time Was Right to Leave Team Martin -
http://www.theglobeandmail.com/sports/more-sports/john-morris-says-time-was-right-to-lea
ve-kevin-martins-curling-rink/article11575877/

PAUL SAVAGE: I cut a guy... I sent him a fax once. I cut another guy after about 10 Manhattans at the curling rink. This guy had just lost it, he couldn't throw an out-turn to save his life. Everything he threw went sideways. He had no inkling that he was that shitty. Eddie said, "If you don't get rid of him, I'm quitting." We got rid of him in November and replaced him with one of his best friends, which caused them to be at war for 20 years.

I remember stories from my era when five guys would show up for the first practise of the year, because the skip forgot to tell a guy that he wasn't on the team anymore. Stuff like that happened.

JOHN EPPING: Some guys are meant to play together forever... some are only good for a couple of years. I don't know how you change the way we make teams when Canada has so much success.

CRAIG SAVILL: Teams run themselves in Canada. There's no manager making decisions. You're really only accountable to your teammates. Teammates start talking... if it's not playing well, or a team dynamics issue, or something is stale, and needs to change, you're usually the last one to know when it's going to happen. Maybe they try to work on it, if they want to keep you on.

It's kinda tough because the curling community is really close-knit. Teams are always talking to each other. Things happen back door that you might not be aware of, and suddenly you find yourself without a team. They've known about this for a couple of months, but couldn't say anything because of other teams. It's tough, because you become friends with the guys you play with, and against.

We're not making a ton of money out there, we're really playing for the love of the sport with our friends. And when something happens like that, it can rock your world. It changes things completely... you go from knowing what you're doing next year, playing every weekend, to suddenly having no idea, and you're starting from scratch with another team.

HOW I MET CRAIG SAVILL

Craig was playing with John Morris the years we played them in the Ottawa Junior Superspiel, so I suppose I met him when I was 16. The difference with Craig is that he stayed in Ontario, when John moved west to Alberta.

As a result, I got to play against him a few more times with that Glenn Howard guy, and got to know him a little bit more. He's truly one of the nicest guys in the sport.

Craig had a battle with Hodgkin's lymphoma in 2015 and returned to the Brier in Ottawa as a special guest in 2016. Although he was still weak from his treatment, and he hadn't curled in more than a year, he was permitted to throw two rocks as part of Team Ontario - with longtime skip Glenn Howard. There wasn't a dry eye in the place. He went on to recover fully, and was back into competitive curling as soon as his body would allow it.

A year later, I sat next to him in Cornwall, Ontario at the Shorty Jenkins Classic and we chatted. After what he had been through, I was happy just to have him there making jokes, and was very grateful that one of the good guys didn't leave us too soon.

CHAPTER 8:
THE 2010s - ROAD TO SOCHI

While Kevin Martin was in Vancouver winning gold in 2010, the door was open for another Alberta team to make a splash at the Brier. Kevin Koe didn't waste his chance, winning the title in his first Brier appearance, and then going on to win the World championship. In 2011, a re-jigged Jeff Stoughton team won the Brier and the Worlds. In 2012, the reunited Glenn Howard and Wayne Middaugh combo led the way for another Brier and another World championship. Following an Olympic gold, and three consecutive World championships from four different teams, Canada's hopes were high approaching the 2014 Olympics in Sochi.

As the Trials approached in 2013, a new team emerged as a contender. While they'd been around for years, the Northern Ontario foursome skipped by Brad Jacobs found a new gear in 2012-2013 and kept it rolling after that...

BRAD JACOBS: We certainly paid our dues. The driving, paying out of pocket. Hoping to make some money, so we could play the next event. We had a bit of sponsorship to get the year going, but not even close to enough to cover it. But we always worked hard, we were always in the gym... even as teenagers. Certainly being fit helped us win.

CRAIG SAVILL: It's funny. I still remember when they would drive to every 'spiel. It'd be 12 hours in the car because they had no money. And they wouldn't qualify, so they'd get loaded. And then Brad Jacobs would pass out and they'd draw all over him with permanent marker. He'd be driving home with marks all over his face and body.

GERRY GEURTS: The Jacobs team cut their teeth on the OCT. They got in the car and drove. There was no event within six hours of where they lived. But for them, they wanted it. So when anybody complains about not having time, or events to play, or all the bullshit excuses, like not having the money - because they had no money either - look at Team Jacobs.

CRAIG SAVILL: So, good for them for grinding it out, which not a lot of teams want to do anymore. But you have to if you want to get really good. It seemed like Brad figured it out. It's like a lightbulb went off, and they became really good.

BRAD JACOBS: I noticed that there were still a lot of older skips. I wondered what was going to happen when these older guys retire. When these guys who have been around for 20-plus years decide to pack it in, who's going to skip these teams? Because there was a lot of great young talent at all the other positions.

You saw it happening. You knew it was coming. I knew that if we stayed together, and stuck with it, we could be a good team of four young guys coming up. And if we kept plugging away at this thing, we could be a top team.

GERRY GEURTS: You could read it in the online forums. Fans were worried who was going to fill the void when Kevin Martin and Glenn Howard retire. Then a young Mike McEwen breaks through in the Slam in 2006. Brad Gushue wins the Olympics, and was still getting better. Koe and Morris were still pretty young.

EARLE MORRIS: I remember watching Jacobs in some early Briers. You could tell he was really good, and he knew the game. And he assembled a team that really worked, and they've been great. When you hear stories like that, it's amazing that they can continue to make that commitment to high performance for so long. Because sooner or later, you think, "This is kinda fun, but I should move on." For work, or for family, or whatever. That's why there's always a change in champions... life gets in the way.

RICHARD HART: We knew Brad Jacobs. He'd been at Briers since 2007, so we saw him develop. He took his lumps, and developed.

After two Brier appearances with his uncles Al and Eric Harnden, Jacobs formed a team with his cousins E.J. and Ryan Harnden, and Caleb Flaxey in 2008. They won the Northern Ontario title, and made the playoffs at their first Brier in 2010. Scott Seabrook replaced Flaxey for 2010-2012, then Ryan Fry joined the team at third for the 2012-2013 season. Fry had already been to several Briers with Jeff Stoughton and Brad Gushue, but would be looking for his third different provincial jacket with Jacobs.

Not only did they win Northern Ontario in 2013, they went on to win the Tim Hortons Brier in Edmonton.

JOHN EPPING: What a difference it was to add Ryan Fry. The year they won the Brier and the year they won the Olympics, I think Fry was the best curler on the planet.

CRAIG SAVILL: I don't think it's a coincidence that when Fry got on that team, it kind of shifted the team. Brad was always a confident guy, but he turned into a super confident guy who would make absolutely everything.

PAUL WEBSTER: In 2013, when they won the Brier, that surprised a few people. And then they come in second at the world championship. I think the best thing that happened to them in 2013 was not winning the Worlds. They recognized that it's not a given, and that other countries are extremely good at the sport. They came back extremely hungry. They wanted to win a gold medal but also prove to the world that 2013 wasn't a fluke.

Even with a Brier title under their belt, the revamped Olympic Trials system didn't award them a spot. The last few berths were decided by points, and based on the Canadian Team Ranking System. By the end of the 2012-2013 season, the race was very close.

JOHN EPPING: We beat them by a point to get the direct entry in to the Trials. It came down to the semifinal of the Players. We were in a bar and were celebrating because Glenn had beaten Jacobs... that was the difference.

REID CARRUTHERS: We definitely saw the changing of the guard. If you were to rank the top three teams going into the Trials in Winnipeg, Kevin Martin would have been the favourite. We [Stoughton] would have been a close second. Then maybe Howard? Leading into that season, if I were going to bet, I would have bet on one of the veterans to win. Would I have predicted that Jacobs would have his coming-out party? He won the Brier the year before, beat us in the final by the way... then he had to run through the pre-Trials. He wasn't even in the Trials yet.

BRAD JACOBS: I remember going to the pre-Trials and in our first game, we're up big on Greg Balsdon... and we end up losing to him. I think we were up 8-3 or something, playing the seventh, and we lost 10-9.

The game was so lopsided that Balsdon asked Curling Canada's Danny Lamoureux if his team could quit at the fifth-end break instead of playing the required eight ends. I'm sure Jacobs wishes Danny had let them quit.

BRAD JACOBS: That was our first game in the pre-Trials... the start of the Olympic success started with a pretty devastating loss. We were all pretty crushed by it, all in our own way. And me being skip, I really felt responsible. I know everybody missed some shots, but I think being skip, when you lose, you might take it a little harder. I know everybody takes losing hard, but you just feel more responsible. I remember being pretty down on myself when we lost that game, and thinking that maybe this isn't meant to be. Maybe we're not going to get out of the pre-Trials, maybe we're not going to the Olympics. But who cares, it's okay. Because life goes on. We still have some more curling here. If it works out, that's great. If it doesn't, so be it, that's great too. I think that mindset, I know, helped put me at ease a little bit... We were able to go out and play really well after that. It was an eyeopener. It felt like our backs were against the wall, even though it was only our first game. We were a favourite to win the pre-Trials, I would say, and to lose your first game like that was pretty devastating. But we were able to rally, and get things going, and to play well enough to give ourselves the opportunity to play for one of the two [Trials] spots.

We were playing Steve Laycock in the ninth end of the B Final. He missed the shot badly. I hate to bring it up, because if Steve sees it, it might make him mad. On the other side of it, for us... sometimes you just need to get a lucky break. Something that sets you off... you can say, if that didn't happen, none of this would have happened. That was one of those moments where I kinda thought "Wow, if we didn't get that break at that moment, none of this would have happened."

Everyone has stories like that. Where they got a bit of luck, and went on to some success. But when it does happen, it starts to feel like it was meant to be.

JOHN EPPING: To come through that, then win the pre-Trials. They played so well, they made big shots. They had the intensity on their side. That doesn't work for every team.

BRAD JACOBS: We went into the Trials super laid back. We were the last team to qualify, we had zero expectations going into the event. We felt no pressure. We were looking around at everybody wondering why they were so uptight. We were joking around. Apparently we were at the Olympic Trials! It was a big deal. But we just said, "Okay boys, let's see what's going to happen. It's all good, let's try to win some games, maybe go .500" and as a result, we didn't put any pressure on ourselves. We played unbelievable... we made all the big shots when we had to. We barely missed a shot as a team in the Trials. We had some pretty special moments, and as the event went on, and we kept winning and winning, we kept growing more confident.

CRAIG SAVILL: That run they had, Jacobs would just make everything. It's funny... sometimes guys just get it, where you see it in their eyes, this confidence. And he had it that week for sure.

REID CARRUTHERS: Our team started to notice the change mid-event. We played Team Jacobs in the first game. We're in Winnipeg, we've got the home crowd with us. They barely missed. We missed a couple key ones as a team. It was almost like seeing that young fit team really dominate us on home ice. It really burst our bubble. It's hard not to take notice of things going on around you, especially when you've got the best seat in the house for it.

GEORGE KARRYS: I saw a team with a massive amount of self confidence, seemingly coming out of nowhere. That Brier win was absolutely enormous for them. It was huge. They grew confidence the size of their biceps and deltoids. So much of that is needed at the highest level. Everybody throws a million rocks, and everybody has their technique down. So what's left? The ability to laser focus.

GLENN HOWARD: I kind of compare it to Tiger Woods, and how Tiger started that whole fitness thing in golf. There's no question about it. I think guys were getting in shape, only the Jacobs boys probably took it to the next level before anybody.

BRAD JACOBS: When you look at the fitness level... from the Ferbey guys, and Kevin's guys in 2010, then us... it kept getting better. And now you look around and everybody is in good shape, both men and women. It's quite the evolution that we've been a part of. I've said it before, but there's more to go. We're going to raise the bar if we can.

Aside from being the fittest players out there, there was no shortage of confidence on Team Jacobs. As the week went on, their level of swagger increased, and with

221

one dramatic double-runback, they beat Kevin Martin in the last game of the round robin to clinch a spot in the final. The celebration that ensued became the iconic image of Brad Jacobs at the Trials as he rallied the crowd for more noise, with his now-famous "COME ON!" ▶ [24]

They then had to wait nearly two full days for the final

BRAD JACOBS: I'll tell ya, it was the longest 48 hours, waiting to play the final. The only time we didn't feel nervous was when we had practise each day. You'd get out on the ice and feel normal, and we'd throw some rocks, and we knew the ice, and we knew we were playing well, and we'd get some confidence. Then you'd be done practise, and you had so much time to think about everything. That's when you start to feel uneasy or nervous.

I'll never forget, it was the night before the final. We went out to a restaurant and ate supper. We had our wives there. We ran into Carter Rycroft, who was playing with Koe, in the restaurant. He was there with his family. He said, "It's okay to be nervous guys, but we need you to go finish the job, and win this thing, and represent Canada." A couple things he said there lifted a lot of weight off our shoulders. I mean, this is a guy we were competing against that week. Such a nice guy, a classy guy. I remember, I took a deep breath after talking to him, and felt like everything was going to be okay.

I remember seeing them in the arena after the Cotter-Morris (John Morris skipped, but Jim Cotter threw fourth rocks) team beat Kevin Martin in the semifinal. To say they looked pleased with the result would be an understatement. All four of them had huge grins on their faces.

Oddly, the last two teams to qualify for the Trials in the first place would be the last two standing at the end of the week.

---

[24] Brad Jacobs - Runback for win - http://www.youtube.com/watch?v=4lFU6uIkKDg

BRAD JACOBS: We hit the ice the next day, and it was like we were back at home. Feeling good, feeling confident. We made the hit for two in the first end and I thought, "We got this."

REID CARRUTHERS: It's one of those events where you have the perfect combination. You need four guys who are willing to have the spotlight shine on them, and be able to stare back at the light, and go make shots. It's about embracing that pressure, the moment.

A team like Jacobs, when you look back on it... I'm not all that surprised. They're physical beasts, and they're as mentally tough as anybody. I think they changed the recipe for success at an event like that.

BRAD JACOBS: We were pretty fearless. We didn't think we could miss. When you're confident, you just think you can make anything. We definitely did, because everybody was making everything.

When you want to throw a shot, and they set you up for it, you're just licking your chops as it's coming down the ice. There's a good chance you're going to make it.

RICHARD HART: I don't want to say they developed the modern game, but you could say they've perfected it. The big hits... for years, I would have argued that a great draw team would beat a great hitting team every time. And after watching what they did in '13-'14, they changed my mind. A great hitting team will win now, but I never would have said that before.

BRAD GUSHUE: It was certainly a new way of playing... with that level of intensity and the style that they played. They just started running back rocks from everywhere and started making them. They were kind of the first team to really start doing that. Runbacks were big, but they were just calling them on everything. If you got behind something, it was coming back. E.J. and Fry were just making everything, and then if Jacobs had a double for three, it was a foregone conclusion. So they were certainly playing with a lot of confidence and playing the style that I think caught a lot of people by surprise. When they play like that, it's tough.

Just like the rest of the week, Team Jacobs was on fire in the final. They shot 92 percent as a team, while Cotter's team measured in at 82 percent.. Jacobs won 7-4 and earned a trip to Sochi. John Morris had knocked off his old team in the semi and came up just short in the final... as a result, there was no shortage of people asking "What if?"

BEN HEBERT: If we would have had John, if he would have just taken that year off, and just played the Trials - Russ Howard style - honestly I still think we would have won.

JOHN MORRIS: If I could have done it again, not that I like to dwell on regrets, I would have taken a step back and called those guys, and said, "Listen. We're obviously going through some tough times right now. I need a break. I think we all need a break. Let's not even talk to each other until the fall maybe, and maybe start a bit later in the next season. Like really recharge the batteries and just get it together, work on our perspective a bit, and not take what we had for granted."

With that team intact... because we all came back very inspired. If we'd just taken a step back and thought about it, and just had no curling for three or four months, and, you know, no contact at all, I think we could have - and I truly believe this - we could have won the Trials if we had that team intact and if we were able to have the perspective.

I had already booked my own ticket to Sochi. I was set to work with Olympic Broadcast Services as a spotter, which meant I had to watch every game of Olympic curling for the duration of the round robin.

JOHN MORRIS: You really saw Jacobs take the fitness up a notch in 2014. You heard a lot of people saying, "Look at how jacked those Canadian curlers are." They were really looking fit, even moreso than some of the other

Olympic athletes. I was proud to see that, instead of what we used to see… you know, guys with beer bellies, out there hacking darts.

REID CARRUTHERS: When they struggled a bit at the start of the Olympics, it wasn't a big surprise. They were coming off an emotional win at the Trials, they had the experience of losing the final of the men's Worlds the year before. They still had to crack that international barrier of winning the important one representing Canada.

KAITLYN LAWES: We saw them, but we didn't have a ton of interaction with them. We stayed in the same building, on the same floor. We'd kinda see them in passing and say, "Good luck." They got off to a slower start, and I think they wanted to disconnect from us because we were getting a lot of attention for doing so well. I think that really affected their perspective on the Games. So we didn't really interact with them a lot until after.

BRAD JACOBS: We were 1-and-2, and we'd just lost to Sweden. We went to Canada Olympic House in the Olympic Park, we met our families over there. E.J. and I were trailing behind Ryan and Ryan. They'd gone straight from the arena, but E.J. stopped back at our condo first. We hopped on some bicycles that the COC had supplied, and we rode over to Canada House. Standing outside was [Canadian Men's Hockey Head Coach] Mike Babcock. We went up to him and said hi, and Mike shook our hands and we had a bit of chit chat. Then he said, "I know you guys are 1-2 but that doesn't mean a thing. We have a saying in hockey: it's not how you start, it's how you finish." He said, "There's a lot of expectations on you guys. I know you guys, I follow you guys. I know you're worried about winning, and bringing home the gold. Stop worrying about any of that, and start worrying about execution. If you execute constantly, then you'll get what you came here for at the end of the event. Don't worry about any of those distractions or expectations. Focus on execution, and you'll have what you want at the end of the week."

That was a pretty awesome moment. To hear that from Mike Babcock. To hear that he was following us. He knew our record, and that we'd just come off a loss. To meet him at that moment was pretty special, and very motivating. We wanted to hop on the ice immediately and get going again.

It was another one of those moments when you feel like the weight comes off your shoulders. Because you know what? We were distracted. We were worrying about expectations. We were concerned about winning a gold medal. We thought we were going to win before we went there, but there's a lot of other countries and other curlers with their own thoughts on the matter.

JILL OFFICER: Our apartments were right next door to each other. It was hard not to be aware of what was going on. We'd do our best to support them, because it's a tough spot to be in, especially at the Olympics, because it might be your only chance.

BRAD JACOBS: We had to play our game the next day. This is where Curling Canada gets a lot of props from us. Our coaching staff - Rick Lang, Paul Webster, and Tom Coulterman were able to help us right the ship. They had a really good coaching move... We met the next day in our common room, and we had a television. We met when we were 1-2 and we're about to play Russia, in Russia. Even though we should beat Russia, you know they're going to be playing up to a level they're not familiar with, because they're playing Canada in their home country, and they're out to prove something. So you expect that they're going to come out and play well... which they did, by the way.

Before the game, Paul Webster played a video that TSN had put together for us to an Imagine Dragons song. It was a three-and-a-half minute video of our team, and all our highlights from the Olympic Trials. And we were unconscious there. The video is super cool, and motivating. We all watched it, and when it was over, Paul said, "I haven't seen that team here this week. When you bring that team to the ice, I don't want to play against you. In fact, nobody on the planet wants to play you guys when you're that team. Now is the time to bring that team to the ice, and bring it every game going forward."

It was a reminder of the intensity level, the focus, the passion behind every shot. The effort, all that stuff.

Until that point, we were like a deer in the headlights. We didn't feel comfortable out on the ice. There was constant chanting and cheering going on. We couldn't do what we wanted to do, we could barely hear each other.

One of the goals we made against Russia was to be louder than the crowd. We were going to take over the building. We went out and played a great game against Russia. We made a shot for three or four about midway through, and ran away with the game. From that point on, we never looked back.

We played like the team we should have been playing like, like we normally are. We never lost a game after that.

The truth is this: I made that video for Team Jacobs. Paul Webster asked me to make a hype video to show them when they met for their Olympic orientation in Calgary. It was all footage from TSN, set to "Radioactive" by Imagine Dragons. Paul told me later on that they used it during the Olympics as well, but apparently failed to mention to the team exactly where it came from... so I told Brad.

BRAD JACOBS: We loved that video. We *still* love that video. You helped us win the Olympic gold medal. Put that in your book. We watched that video before every game for the rest of the Olympics.

After grinding out six straight wins to finish the round robin with a 7-2 record, the Canadian men had qualified for a semifinal versus China. After their last round-robin game, I ended up going to the Canada versus Finland hockey game with them. As they walked into the lounge where I was waiting for them with our mutual friend Ryan Parker of the NHLPA, I saw something I hadn't seen all week... that swagger from the Winnipeg Trials.

The hard part was behind them, they were now exactly where they needed to be. I remember having one thought: I feel sorry for China tomorrow, because these guys are back.

JOHN EPPING: You couldn't have asked for a better opponent in the semi. Nothing against China, but playing Edin or Murdoch in the other semi would have been more difficult.

BRAD JACOBS: When Great Britain beat Sweden, I was 99.9 percent sure we were winning the Olympics.

REID CARRUTHERS: I think what helped that team was having an opposing coach call them out for their character and their demeanour, what they had worked so hard to build up. He called them out for how they called the game, how they acted on the ice. I think he messed with the wrong people.

Brad took it to heart. He put it up on the wall and used it as motivation. There was no way he was losing that final.

BRAD JACOBS: I was pretty much 100 percent sure we were winning the next morning, before the final game. I read the comments that the Great Britain coach said in that article about our team. That was a terrible decision he made, to make any comments about our team in a negative way. We wanted to murder that team on the ice.

It was something about how he didn't agree with how our team plays the game. He would never tell his team to act like that. "They're aggressive, they're intimidating. They're not good for the sport."

Great Britain's coach Sören Gran told a media scrum, "The aggressive style we have seen from the Canadians here, that's something I don't like about the sport. I don't think it helps anyone. It doesn't help the player and it doesn't help his teammates." The quote ran in papers across Canada. [25]

BRAD JACOBS: We didn't check social media a lot when we were at the Olympics. We were on it a bit, but not a lot, because it's a distraction. The morning before the final, we were feeling confident, so I went on my phone, and somebody had tweeted it at us. I clicked on the link and read the article, and was like, "Okay. Let's go play... like, right now." I felt bad for Murdoch and his team, because that didn't help their chances of winning at all. It was an unwise move. It helped us, and gave us more motivation, and we didn't really need any at that point.

In the final, Canada took two, gave them one, took another three, then stole one to go up 6-1 after only four ends. For Jacobs and the boys, this was more than enough of a cushion to ride out to the end. The final score was 9-3 with Great Britain's Murdoch conceding after eight ends. Jacobs, Fry, and the Harnden brothers were gold medallists. ▶ [26]

BRAD JACOBS: We were like, "Thank God this is over with, and we won!" Everything just seemed to be happening so quickly. You had to do this, then you had to be on this TV program, then you had to go to Canada Olympic House, now you have to do this party, and then the closing ceremonies, and then another closing party, and then you're on the plane going home. Your day is just so scheduled and regimented, and all we wanted to do was have some beers and relax, and soak this in a little bit.

GERRY GEURTS: You can win an Olympic gold medal if you want to. You have to have the talent, but the work is always the most important part. I think there are players as talented as Brad, toiling on the tour. But Team Jacobs put the work in, and put the time in. I don't have a lot of time for people who make excuses, and say this or that is the reason they can't

[25] Uptight British Coach Rips Jacobs
http://torontosun.com/2014/02/20/uptight-british-curling-coach-rips-brad-jacobs/wcm/59623b66-1708-45a9-9725-dbd5d3e763c1

[26] 2014 Olympic Gold Medal- Canada v Great Britain
http://www.youtube.com/watch?v=8xhjLVNaKa0

compete. You make your own life choices. Most people like having a summer vacation, and some time with their family, and a real job and some savings in the bank. I don't fault anybody for choosing that lifestyle, because it's sure as hell more comfortable than becoming a "professional" curler. Those guys who get there put in a ton of sweat equity, they've sacrificed a ton. For them to do all that, it's all on them - it was their choice.

BRAD JACOBS: Pre-Trials, Trials, and Olympics was from November to March. So that's what, five months? It was a really incredible, special stretch of curling that we went through there.

HOW I MET BRAD JACOBS

Brad Jacobs used to drive down from Sault Ste. Marie, Ontario to Oakville to play in the first Ontario Curling Tour event of the year in early September. We saw him every year in Oakville, and at other OCT stops, and played him once, if I recall correctly.

Coming from Toronto, that Oakville bonspiel was a 30-minute drive (depending on traffic) for us. From the Soo, Google says it's seven and a half hours. The Shorty Jenkins Classic in Brockville was 11 hours of driving each way. And there wasn't a lot of sponsorship money for them in the early days, so it often meant paying out of pocket for entry fees, gas, and hotels.

They went on to win the Brier, the Roar, and the Olympics in 2013-2014 which was an incredible run. Along the way, they ruffled some feathers with their intensity, attitude, and on-ice antics. And while I understood what the "traditionalists" were saying, I enjoyed their enthusiasm. It brought some new energy to the sport.

It was sheer will, drive, and commitment that kept them going. It would have been too easy to say that it was too expensive, or too inconvenient, but following a decade of road trips and cramped hotel rooms, I knew where the fire came from.

On the women's side, it appeared that the controversial lineup change three years earlier had paid off. Jennifer Jones, Kaitlyn Lawes, Jill Officer and Dawn McEwen found themselves rolling through the Olympic Trials in their hometown of Winnipeg.

JILL OFFICER: We were really looking forward to the opportunity to play at home. We were obviously hoping that the crowd was going to be loud and supportive, and they were. And that helped. It was almost like having a fifth player, we could feed off the energy and enthusiasm when we were on the ice. I also think that we felt more prepared, and ready, than we ever had in the other Trials. We got off to a good start, and kept it going all week.

KAITLYN LAWES: It was so special to play at home, and have our friends and family come out and watch. I'll never forget looking up and seeing my mom, and all the other moms waving a big Canada flag after we won. That was the moment we became Olympians, and that we got to do it in our home city was the icing on the cake.

SHERRY MIDDAUGH: You have to start peaking so much earlier in an Olympic year. The big stuff comes so much earlier than in a typical Scotties year.

REID CARRUTHERS: The other team that I had a front-row seat for was Team Jones in Winnipeg. We were training at the same gym, we curled at the same club. It seemed like every day leading up to the Trials, they were supporting each other off the ice. They were pushing each other, but they were laughing the whole time. They really enjoyed the experience of being a world-class team, and playing in front of the hometown crowd. And they used that crowd to their advantage.

KAITLYN LAWES: We went in with a plan, and 100 percent believed in that plan. No matter what, we believed that we could accomplish what we wanted to. Our goal was to win an Olympic gold medal, and this was just one of the steps in the process to getting there.

SHERRY MIDDAUGH: We started off 1-3. Things were a little tight at the start of the week. We had to loosen up and tell ourselves that we needed to have fun. And we did. We totally embraced it.

Middaugh was skipping in her fourth Olympic Trials. Her team of Jo-Ann Rizzo, Lee Merklinger, and Leigh Armstrong was the kind of group who seemed like they were always having fun, even when stakes were highest.

SHERRY MIDDAUGH: We had a lot of people cheering for us. They could tell that we were having fun. We were loose and we embraced it. The whole thing. We had routines, but we had to look at it and realize things weren't going so great. We had nothing to lose... and we just got on a roll.

We got into a tiebreaker, won that, and then we played Rachel. And we didn't do anything different. We came together as a team and said, "Let's do this!" We totally loved it. It was amazing. It was a very electric crowd.

EARLE MORRIS: When I was coaching Rachel, and we were getting ready for the Trials in Winnipeg, I think we overprepared. When we got there, we were a little on edge, and we didn't play well. We finished third, which was a disaster. We really thought we were going to win it... or at least come second.

WAYNE MIDDAUGH: Sherry's team was playing great all week, and just came out a bit flat in the final. The team they had probably wasn't as used to that environment like Jen was, and there were a couple mistakes early and Jen jumped on them, like a great team is supposed to.

RACHEL HOMAN: Everything kind of has to come together for someone to win the Trials. I watched Jen for so many years be at the top of her game, and win so much, but still come up short at the Trials twice. For two cycles, that's eight years.

You think that you're at the top and number one, and that you're going to win the Trials...but it can take a long time to win the Trials even if you're the top team because there's so many good teams, and they're all right there. If you make one mistake, a four-year journey is over.

SHERRY MIDDAUGH: We lost the Trials final, but then had to go play down in Ontario regions. We had a long team discussion on how to handle that. We're mentally and physically drained... that was the toughest grind I've ever had, that next event.

RACHEL HOMAN: It's scary because you feel like you put four years into seven days. So not an easy thing to win, and I know it took Jen a few tries to win it. I'm really happy for her, being able to put that feather in her cap on an amazing career.

Jennifer Jones and team moved on to Sochi, Russia wearing the Maple Leaf, and ready to finish off a four-year plan. Starting with a win over China, then a win over Sweden, then another over Great Britain... well, Canada didn't lose a game all week.

KAITLYN LAWES: We embraced everything that was thrown at us. We found a way to make every moment special. Our team dynamics brought us through the games, in every situation we were faced with.

JILL OFFICER: The majority of the time, we did what we needed to do. We stayed focused, and confident, and calm and it worked for us.

Plus, we had a skip who was lights out.

MIKE HARRIS: Jennifer was perfect. She played the best single week of curling that you could hope for as a skip. She played great. She's one of the best clutch players I've ever seen, men or women.

Faced with a draw to the four-foot for the semifinal win vs. Great Britain, an Olympic medal was within their reach.

JILL OFFICER: I was nervous. I can't speak for Jen. I'm sure she felt some nervousness. I know Dawn felt calm, maybe we balanced each other out. I can't imagine you wouldn't have some kind of nerves sitting in the hack, even though you've done it a thousand times. Same with me, I've swept a draw to the four-foot a thousand times... but in that moment it just seems so much harder.

KAITLYN LAWES: I remember holding the broom, thinking that I couldn't imagine anyone else throwing that shot. She had done it for us so many times. I had all the confidence in the world. It was the calmest I'd been that whole game. Draw to the four-foot and we're playing for a gold medal. I'm pretty sure the feelings were a little different at the other end. My job was pretty easy. I just had to hold the broom and say, "line's good" when she let it go. ▶[27]

JILL OFFICER: In the change room afterward, we had a moment to think "Okay, guaranteed medal!" But we came here to go for gold, so we turned our attention to that. We didn't let our guard down. We still went into the gold-medal game like we had unfinished business.

GEORGE KARRYS: For me, nothing encapsulates Jennifer Jones more than the final game at the Olympics against Sweden. If you remember, Kaitlyn didn't have a great game, and Jennifer basically said, "No way. We're winning this thing. Get on my back."

REID CARRUTHERS: No disrespect to any of the other teams, but after watching Jen in the Trials... she wasn't just good in the Olympics, she was incredible the whole way through. Her throwing, through the Trials and Olympics, should go down as one of the best performances by a player under pressure, when they needed it the most. It was incredible.

JILL OFFICER: I felt like it was the closest game we had all week, but I know it wasn't. There were two moments where I was a little nervous about what was going to happen. [Swedish fourth-stone thrower] Maria Prytz had a shot, a really hard shot, where she could have gotten four... but she only got two, so that was a relief.

Same when we stole two in the ninth, they could have taken two instead. I never recalled having a moment all week when I was worried or nervous that it was going to go wrong, until those two moments in the gold-medal game.

---

[27] 2014 Olympic Semi-Final - Canada v Great Britain -
http://www.youtube.com/watch?v=Zi6wAUsOFoA

PAUL WEBSTER: Jennifer Jones... the strategy of going to the Olympics and winning every game is a pretty cool one to watch. It sort of takes away the pressure a little bit. She was unbelievable, on fire all week. And it helps when you have Dawn, Jill, and Kaitlyn playing in front of you. But I think she might have won four or five games with me and you at front end. She wanted that gold medal and I don't think anyone was going to stop her. ▶ [28]

MIKE HARRIS: When Jennifer is playing well, it doesn't matter how the team plays.

AMY NIXON: That was really Jennifer's coming out in terms of the international stuff... the cherry on the top. Because people forget she'd only won one World championship. She had been an incredibly dominant player really in everything except for World championships. I was really happy for that team because they are really professional players, in the sense they are accessible. They care about fans genuinely, but they also obviously had been some of the hardest working players, so you certainly couldn't begrudge them. I was genuinely just really happy for all of them because they deserved it.

---

[28] 2014 Olympic Gold Medal Curling - Canada v Sweden
http://www.youtube.com/watch?v=HM85HfYNVkI&t=219s

HOW I MET KAITLYN LAWES

Like me, Kaitlyn Lawes started at Trillium as a camper. Like me, she joined the staff, and rose through the ranks from Assistant to Coach over the next few years. The only difference is that she won two national junior titles, and won a few World Curling Tour events, before joining one of the best teams in the world, winning a bunch more events, and going undefeated at the 2014 Olympics. Then in 2018, she won another Olympic gold in Mixed Doubles.

But other than that, we're exactly the same... maybe that's why we get along so well.

For a while, she was my only friend from Winnipeg. So I was really excited to call her when I was stranded there following a few botched flights from Rankin Inlet, Nunavut - where I had been teaching Rocks & Rings.

Unfortunately, she was unavailable that night. She was on TSN playing with Jennifer Jones, facing off against Cathy Overton-Clapham at the 2011 Scotties Tournament of Hearts in Charlottetown. So I watched from the hotel bar, incredibly amused by the local commentary I could overhear.

Everybody had an opinion, but nobody had a clue...

CHAPTER 9:
THE 2010s - BROOMGATE

It seemed like every decade or so, there had been some sort of shake up in the accepted landscape of curling. Looking back to the "boycott" years, and the introduction of the Free Guard Zone before that, some sort of controversy would come along and, in the long run, make the sport better.

In that vein, the 2015-2016 season was a fiasco. A few years earlier, Hardline Curling had introduced a new broom, the Ice Pad, to the market. At the time, nobody thought much of the new equipment, but the lightweight brush gained popularity over the course of a few seasons. When Winnipeg's Mike McEwen started using them in 2014-2015 and had a career-year, winning seven events, he showed the curling world that these new brooms were pretty good... but, as it turned out, they might have been too good.

GERRY GEURTS: Mike McEwen ends up using Hardline brooms in 2014. They had the chance to use them during the Trials in 2013, and had they done that, they could have been right there to win it. The next season, they use them full-time. McEwen's team was really good at being a hair tight, and using the brooms to back it up, or keep it straight. They never used them to make it curl. I'm not sure they realized they could do that, but they knew they could keep it straight, and maybe back it up a bit.

MIKE McEWEN: Back then, we were flying by the seat of our pants. We really had no idea what the heck was going on. We had the craziest season that year. We kind of mucked up and didn't make the Brier, so we had that missing, but other than that, we had probably the craziest tour season that the team has ever had.

BRAD JACOBS: McEwen had an unbelievable season with the Hardline brooms, and I think that Reid had a pretty good year too. Everybody else was still using the normal stuff that we'd all been using.

MIKE McEWEN: We didn't realize the weapon we had. There were other teams using it, but not, you know, it wasn't widely accepted. I remember Richard Hart calling them toy brooms, and saying, "What are you guys doing with those things?" It was a new product, the new kid on the block. I mean, they were different.

We weren't the only ones using them, but we were definitely the best top-level team. We had no idea at that point. We didn't realize the advantage we had.

JILL OFFICER: Until then, we didn't really have a great idea of what sweeping with these fabrics was doing. It was more like, "That guy just thought that his out-turn curled."

JEFF STOUGHTON: Thank God I was retired!

REID CARRUTHERS: It really caught on when one manufacturer started to make headway with sales, and more teams started using the product. But I remember sitting in the change room with someone who was sponsored by another manufacturer, and we had a great conversation about fabrics, what needs to happen, and so on. We talked about another team, who I won't mention, who had been using some questionable heads for years... at World Championships, and WCT events. No one really knew what they were doing, and they've never been publicly outed. It was remarkable that things like that could go unnoticed.

KEVIN KOE: It was a bit of a circus all year, and I mean some teams took it personally. But stuff wasn't going to change if it was just the status quo. Some equipment wasn't on a level playing field. I mean, that was pretty evident.

BRAD JACOBS: I remember thinking back to certain shots from that year, when we were playing Mike's team... whether they knew or not, I don't care, especially now... I remember certain shots where they were able to hold the rock so straight, and our sweepers just couldn't do it. I remembered certain shots when I put the broom down, basing the ice on their shot. We'd hit and roll out on the low side, whereas their team would be on-off all the way down and make it perfectly, or even oversweep it a bit. And I thought, "How is that possible? I thought we had the strongest sweepers in the game!"

MIKE McEWEN: I think it was a combination, too. Like we thought we were just in that much better shape. We didn't fully realize what we actually had in our hands.

BRAD JACOBS: When I thought back to certain shots against their team after I'd heard about it, I remembered all these instances where we just couldn't follow, we couldn't do those same things. I just thought maybe they'd been working out like crazy all summer, and they're just that strong now. It came down to a technology.

BRAD GUSHUE: We were at the Brier in 2015 and we were playing Reid Carruthers. In the first end, he made a shot that, out of his hand, he was on the guard. And this rock went backwards. The ice was curling a lot at the Brier. It shouldn't go backwards. He ended up making it for two in the first, and then they went on to beat us, which was the fourth or fifth time they beat us that year. And I looked at Mark and I said, "That's not right." So we went back to the hotel and we ordered four Hardline Ice Pads for us to test when we were done the Brier.

GERRY GEURTS: Gushue's team that summer put in a ton of testing. Whether it was about exposing the brooms or learning to take advantage of them, I'm not sure. They were a Goldline team at the time, and they actually went to Hardline and took less money to start using their brooms.

BRAD GUSHUE: So when we were done the Brier, we went out and did some testing and sent the video off to Gerry Peckham [Director of High Performance] at Curling Canada, to show him some of the results that we were getting. He kind of said there weren't any talks to bring changes or rules or anything like that. So he said, "I suggest you change."

MIKE McEWEN: We'd had little glimpses of what we were seeing, but we just weren't students of sweeping... I don't know if we were embarrassed, but you know, we felt silly that we hadn't put that together sooner. The only reason we finally understood, and started to delve into the intricacies of sweeping was because of what Team Gushue did.

BRAD GUSHUE: We decided to change to the Ice Pad. The next year, we started our year in Korea. We flew over and we played a little event and hopped off the plane with brand new Ice Pads. The first game we lost 17-6 because we were playing with fresh Ice Pads and we didn't know how to use them. So we completely embarrass ourselves against this Korean team. When the event was over we had a few days over there to train and practise, and we started playing around.

We realized that, all of a sudden, we were backing rocks up, when we were sweeping on the inside. And I kind of said to the guys, "What happens if we go on the outside?" And then all of a sudden this rock started to curl. So then we started to play hack weight shots around guards, and we were taking three feet more ice, and so on. And we spent hours out there. We couldn't miss.

What Gushue's team had discovered was that new Ice Pad heads were particularly abrasive, and that the microscopic scratches left in the ice by brushing could actually steer a stone. If a brusher swept against the curl, the rock would back up. If the other brusher swept with the curl, he'd "carve" a path that would make the rock curl even more. Brushing was turned on its head.

MIKE McEWEN: And then, all of a sudden we saw Brad doing these things the following season, and we get "Broomgate." Yes. For whatever reason, things started to click. Like, "Why were we sweeping with two guys all the time?" We were just counteracting our effort. We were basically minimizing the effect, and we didn't even know it.

BRAD GUSHUE: We had the conversation about how to handle this. So that's when we developed the one sweeper method, where we can kind of dictate whether we get it to run straight or make it curl. We had the conversation. We could, kind of, mask it right up until the Brier and then show up and do this, and then we're going to wax everybody. Obviously the morals came in, and we said we couldn't do that.

I felt that the brooms were too aggressive and had too much of an impact, and were taking away from the skill of the game. So our intention was just to do it, and really make it so that everybody was aware and kind of bring attention to it.

BEN HEBERT: We played Brad in the first event that year. It was the final of the Slam in Paradise, Newfoundland. He threw a hack-weighter in the seventh and you could see about two inches of it. He throws it and they're on the guard, halfway down the sheet. Brett backed it up... and before the shot Geoff grabbed a different broom off the boards and I'm like "Why are you guys switching?" We knew nothing at this point. And then Geoff carves it back around the guard, and they nose the rock. After the end I looked at Brad and he goes, "It's impossible to miss."

GLENN HOWARD: I said to my guys, "If we continue with these brooms, I don't need to throw a practise rock ever again." I can just lob it down the sheet. I'd run around looking for hits. You couldn't miss a hit. You could back it up. You could make it curl, you could keep it straight, and do whatever you wanted to. We never actually slowed rocks down, but you could throw the rock heavy, and sweep it hard and slow it down. And it was a disgrace to the game.

BRAD JACOBS: When the next season rolled around... it was the worst stretch we'd ever had as a team. September to December in the '15-'16 season, we were pretty bad, but we were super distracted trying to keep up with everyone and all of the "carving" that was going on. 'Spiels were getting out of control.

BRAD GUSHUE: We started to do it, and the comments were like "That's stupid," or "That doesn't work." We started out the year 25-1. And the only game the lost was to Koe where they just played an incredible game against us. Turns out they had the tinfoil pads [BalancePlus EQ heads with heat-reflecting foil inside] which could drag the rock 20 feet. They had a different weapon than we did, but it brought the attention to it. And obviously things got really ugly for a couple of months because curling teams and broom companies got very territorial. And we took it from a very neutral standpoint. You know, it just wasn't good for the game.

BEN HEBERT: You never faulted Goo [Gushue], he was straight up honest about it. He was doing what was in the rules and he was doing what he had to, to beat Mike and Reid and the teams that were using them. And you know, thankfully Brad came out and said, "You know, we shouldn't be using these," and this and that. Now that's not what ended up kiboshing the whole thing. The thing that ended up kiboshing it all was basically some people going, "Okay, we can just put anything on our brooms. I'll show you guys some shit."

GLENN HOWARD: So Scott Taylor from BalancePlus says, "Okay, I'm in the broom business so I've got to start looking into some more stuff." He does some research and comes up with some material, and ends up coming up with this black stuff. He says, "Guys, give this a go." We take this black stuff to the High Park event in Toronto, and everybody gets wind of it and it was disgusting, like the things you can do. Lo and behold, all the other teams get up in arms. And we're going, "Guys. This is what we have to do to prove a point. We've got a major problem in our sport. Let's get rid of this crap and let's get rid of it now."

GERRY GEURTS: Thanksgiving weekend, it all blew up at High Park. BalancePlus brought out the Blackheads, which essentially ruined the ice. You'd sweep down a path, and the same reaction would be there for a whole end later. There was a players meeting, and a lot of good discussion among the players. They wanted solutions. The Hardline teams too, they wanted it to be fair... the problem was nobody had an equal product. If one was a little better than the other, it made it tough. So the players agreed to go to hair brooms.

GLENN HOWARD: So that's when all hell breaks loose. We have a little pow-wow down in the basement. Everybody sort of makes these agreements. Teams are going to test stuff. We're going to bring it to Curling Canada. We're going to test stuff and go on from there.

MIKE McEWEN: So the pow-wow happened but then nobody lived up to what they said. Whatever gentlemen's agreements were made at that event basically never happened. It was just a mish-mash of an event. But I guess that sprung forward when Nolan [Thiessen] got involved and really tried to get a collection of players on board. At that point, I don't even know if it might have been on Curling Canada's radar. I can't really speak for the associations, but we really had no help at that point.

BRAD JACOBS: We had to go out there and play Glenn in a quarterfinal... They had the Blackhead, and it was unbelievable. If they weren't careful they could flash a shot by putting one or two extra strokes on it. That's when the unsportsmanlike stuff started to come out.

MARK NICHOLS: Honestly, it sucked. Especially with our team kind of bringing it to the forefront. But the next thing you know you've got guys who are calling other guys cheaters, and other guys saying that you're trying to do stuff that isn't allowed, and you get broom companies trying to come out with different pieces of equipment to better the other guys... and not even better, it just made it worse for everyone on the ice. It was a stressful, stressful season.

BRAD JACOBS: I remember playing these teams, and they're sweeping certain ways, and they've got the good fabric, and they're carving... and I'm thinking to myself that this isn't even fun anymore. This is horrible. This is not curling. It doesn't feel like curling.

MIKE McEWEN: We won that event. The most stressful event I've ever played...

Guys tried to put away the Hardline brooms and use hair. But then the other teams wouldn't, and still used the Blackheads. It was very stressful. I remember we played a three-and-a-half-hour, eight-end game in the final, because we had hair brooms, and we swept up and down the sheet on every shot. We were playing Howard, and every time they touched the ice with the super Blackhead, we knew it would damage the ice because we'd seen it. We obviously understood that, and we knew our brooms were doing that to a lesser extent, but we knew what was happening. So we were going up and down the sheet with hair trying to clean out the marks every time they shot swept with it.

I think guys were losing their minds how long it was taking and it was just a crazy event. And I'm just glad we made it through that event without getting in a fight with anybody.

GERRY GEURTS: Mike McEwen called his buddy Brent Laing, because he's playing with Koe, and all the other top teams were in Edmonton for a 'spiel. He said that the players all agreed to go back to hair... and Koe's team basically said, "No. You took a lot of money out of our pockets with those brooms. We're not going back to hair!" That was the beginning of the end for McEwen's dominance, not because they weren't still a great team, but because he took it hard. There was a lot of animosity, and a couple of lost friendships over it.

The year before, they'd spent every day hanging out at the Olympics together in Sochi. They were good buddies. That's why Mike called Brent. That was the connection, they were friends.

MIKE McEWEN: That phone call, and some other comments from other guys, they really thought that we knew that there was a problem or a big advantage that was going on. People, for a time there, thought that we took advantage when we shouldn't have, which isn't the case. But it's hard to defend that. It's hard to defend a thing that you don't know. When you're a top team and you just didn't know... it was hard to believe that we were ignorant to it.

LORI OLSON-JOHNS: It wasn't just one scenario. It seemed like it was changing on a weekly basis, with people trying to come up with different materials and different ways to be most effective out there on the ice. It really took away from the credibility of being a pure, great thrower because I couldn't necessarily look to an opponent and say, "Wow, that was a great shot!" Because you didn't know if it was impacted by the brooms, or if it was truly a shot that was makeable. All of those things happened. They were technically within the rules, but in my opinion, I'm not sure that it really followed the ethics of the game.

REID CARRUTHERS: Sure, no rules were broken because there were no rules. It's unfortunate that it got to where it did, but it almost needed to happen. The one thing I'd like everybody to think about was that the fabric issue wasn't new. For years, there were teams and players who were creating their own broom heads without telling anyone. Or using heads that were more effective than what other people were using. People didn't really catch on.

BRAD JACOBS: We weren't really in the thick of it. We were all joking about it. Even though we weren't getting the results we wanted, and we weren't playing well, we were all kinda like, "For once, our team isn't involved in the controversy! It's everyone else!" We weren't really arguing with anyone.

I remember some pretty big arguments between other teams, and I was just happy it wasn't us.

MIKE McEWEN: We had all this equipment lying around and that we could do these things with, and we had no regulations... which is crazy if you think about it. It was a bit asinine that we had gone so long, and this is in the Olympic era, we didn't have proper equipment regulations at all. We got that wake-up call because it never should have gotten there. It never should have been that long.

BEN HEBERT: We still didn't do the right thing that year. We still didn't get it totally fixed but we got a little bit better as the year went on... with the number of brooms you could use, side sweeping, how many heads you can have, and so on. Because when we went to the [2016] Brier, they had the so-called "approved" fabric that was almost worse than the other stuff... We've never used those brooms, ever, so we said, "Well, we're going to a gunfight with a knife here, boys!"

We're going to go play the Goo, and we're playing Mike, and we're playing Jacobs and they all have this shit. We're going to get fucking steamrolled. So we took a Hardline head, put it in our Balance Plus broom and left the sharp one [with a brand new head] for whenever we needed it. We won the Brier. It was fucking ridiculous.

JEFF STOUGHTON: I thought it was ridiculous. Taking that 180 degree turn was hard to watch. The skill of the thrower should determine most of the outcome of the shot. Maybe the ratio is 70 percent is made on release, and 30 percent can be made perfect by sweepers. It became almost the reverse. It didn't seem to matter how you threw it, the sweeping could make up for it. It just took the skill out of the delivery.

There's no blame. It was just like "Wow... that's not right."

JILL OFFICER: It was exhausting. Every weekend, we didn't know how we were going to be sweeping. It literally changed every weekend we went to play. We either had a new broom head, a new technique, or a new strategy. It was changing so rapidly, it was exhausting. We spent so much time talking about it... it took away from the fun, for sure.

CHELSEA CAREY: I was right with everybody else that they should be banned, but they weren't and so we put in a ton of time figuring out how to do it right. Because while it's in place, that's what teams are going to do to you. So if you don't put in the time, then you're at a disadvantage. Right or wrong, we were like, "Well, we got to figure this out!" And we did, and we spent a lot of time on it that year. We spent a lot less time throwing in practise, and a lot more times sweeping, because that's what mattered at the time.

HOW I MET REID CARRUTHERS

In 2012, Jim Waite invited Reid to work at the Trillium Curling Camp in Guelph, Ontario. Immediately, we became friends... as did most of the camp staff every year.

We kept in touch and caught up at a number of events over the years, usually making time for a drink or some fun. At the Continental Cup in Las Vegas, I recall staying up *way* too late playing blackjack with Reid. We were still sitting in the casino when the ice crew was headed to the rink to prepare ice for the morning draw (Reid wasn't playing that one).

 I don't feel bad about sharing that because most of the players were often out too late in Las Vegas, and Reid also made a thin cross-house double to clinch the title for North America the next day.

Anyway, when Reid started Camp Carruthers in Winnipeg, he asked if I would come be on staff. He had people like Mike McEwen, Selena Kaatz, and Jill Officer lined up to work, but they didn't have much/any camp experience. He also had himself, Kaitlyn Lawes, and me, who had worked a number of camps.

The week at St. Vital went off without a hitch, and in the following two years he was able to expand to a two-week camp at the Winnipeg Granite. I've happily gone back to Winnipeg each year to hang out with Reid and his wife Jodi, and also their fur-baby Jake.

Over the course of the season, various rule changes were implemented. At one point, Hardline heads had to be turned inside out, and the plastic inserts removed. Fabrics deemed too stiff or scratchy were outlawed, and hair brooms became the accepted alternatives.... until curlers figured out that you could create a similar effect with the hair brooms. It was exhausting trying to keep up with the rule changes, and the latest update usually left teams scrambling to find appropriate equipment on short notice.

At the Alberta Provincial Scotties, things came to a head once again...

GERRY GEURTS: Chelsea Carey's team was using these Goldline hair brooms, which had sold out, so they were no longer on the website. But the rule was that they had to be available to the general public. So Sweeting's team is on the website trying to find the brooms, and they couldn't. So they're upset, and they start chirping Carey's team a little bit, and there were some arguments.

LORI OLSON-JOHNS: There was a horse hair-broom that was being used at the time by an opponent that was not labelled with the company's name. And it was really aggressive, like the most aggressive hair that I have seen. It caused some picks on the ice, caused snow to be tracked on the ice. And so there is a meeting about it with officials, Curling Canada was called. We tried our best to negotiate a fair playing environment where it was equal for everyone. We proposed to the other team that we could perhaps use option X, or that they were welcome to use any of our brooms or vice versa, to try to come to an agreement so that we were just playing the game and the best team would win.

CHELSEA CAREY: They accused us of having doctored it. I think they called it a "steel bristle broom." And so a fight ensued from there. That was all just too bad... But then the problem was that Goldline had run out of them, because everyone realized that they were effective. The rule is that it has to be publicly available. So now they've taken them off the website because they're out of stock.

AMY NIXON: We lost that 1-2 playoff game. Members of the Sweeting team celebrated like they'd won the World Cup of soccer... I can't remember if it was Val or Rachelle [Brown] who walked up to me first. I think it was Val, and she said something, and I sort of said, "Okay, whatever." And Rachelle walked up to me and said "Where did you get those steel bristle brooms from?" And I said a few things back with some fairly strong language, probably about eight feet away from some media.

GERRY GEURTS: Amy doesn't put up with that shit. There was a lot of chirping and some name-calling.

AMY NIXON: I was called in by the official that evening and given a warning, to which I replied something along the lines of, "Thank you. Totally warranted and completely worth it." It's just one of those highly competitive situations, with two competitive teams who disagreed. Probably one of my best gifts and worst curses in life is that I definitely have a "Big Little Person" syndrome. I will not back down. I don't think I should and I did not.

GERRY GEURTS: And it all blows up in front of the media. Val's team is basically calling Carey's team a bunch of cheaters, and a lot of it comes from the fact that they can't find the brooms on the website. They're assuming - wrongly - they've created these brooms to cheat.

AMY NIXON: Saturday, we have to play the semifinal. We beat [Jessie] Kaufmann's team without incident, and Sunday morning, I get a phone call from Pat McAdoo, the official, before our game. On a Sunday morning of the finals, to say basically, "Sweeting's team has an issue with the broom and you need to show us that it's legit."

CHELSEA CAREY: They go to the official and say that it's got to be doctored.... I get out of the shower that morning and I could hear Amy on the phone, talking to that official, and he's saying, "You're telling me that it's a Goldline head, but they don't have it on their website."

AMY NIXON: And I said, "You realize it's Sunday morning. We've been using it all week, including yesterday in the semifinal and didn't have any issue with Kaufmann's team." I said, "I'll do what I can." Then lawyer-Amy came out and I said, "I'm going to tell you right now that I object to this bullshit."

CHELSEA CAREY: So I call Erin Flowers at Goldline, and I'm like, "Why isn't this on your website?" She says, "Oh, we ran out of stock, so we took it down." So it's 7 a.m. and we're trying to deal with this before our game.

So Goldline puts it back on the website so that we could prove it was legit. It was a disaster, it was just so much extra noise that was challenging to deal with. Right before you're playing in the semifinal of the provincials. But there was just a lot of that kind of stuff that going on around then.

AMY NIXON: I think it was a terrible mistake on their part. And the reason it was a terrible mistake was because our team also was not the most cohesive... Team Carey. And what they inadvertently did, I feel, is they brought us together. If they left it alone, I think they probably would have beaten us, frankly. But by sort of puffing their chests out and, you know, arguing the whole thing, it brought us together in a way that we would not have come together.

LORI OLSON-JOHNS: So unfortunately, we lost and I'm not saying we were the better team. They did win the game. I think there were a lot of factors. And I think it is a huge distraction for us because we were more focused on the equipment, or maybe perhaps what was happening out there, than our jobs. It was a very difficult situation to.

Carey won the final 8-5, and went on to represent Alberta in the 2016 Scotties. They won that event as well, beating Northern Ontario's Krista McCarville in the final.

LORI OLSON-JOHNS: The week after that, there were stipulations for the Scotties and the Brier that no hair brooms were allowed. So it was allowed to use them to win the provincial championship, but then a week later they weren't allowed in our national championship. So obviously there were some issues with that. But at the end of the day, I do want to play this game just straight up. I want you to commit, I want you to play your best. I want to play my best, and may the best person win.

GERRY GEURTS: Things were heated all year long. There was a lot of this shit going on behind the scenes that was awful for the game. Players yelling at players in the bar. In a public hotel bar, all sorts of non-curlers and fans around, and players are arguing over half-information, and stuff like that. It was ugly.

JILL OFFICER: We were one of those teams who said we won't use them if you don't. We wanted something to be resolved so it would be fair for everybody. We didn't like seeing what the brooms were doing, but there were certainly teams who managed it better than others, and you can't necessarily take that away from them because they weren't necessarily doing anything wrong.

REID CARRUTHERS: The only thing that was hard about it was when it got personal. There were a couple of instances where it got personal, and things were said. The general public has no idea what kind of things were said behind closed doors.

Following the season high-performance curlers from across Canada and around the world met with representatives from Curling Canada, the WCF, and the various broom manufacturers. They tested a number of different products and techniques and eventually agreed on a new set of rules for elite competitions.

Most notably, the fabric on brush heads became standardized. A specific type of mustard yellow nylon that had been previously discarded because it wasn't very effective was now a requirement. The new broom heads greatly reduced the effect of "directional sweeping." All manufacturers now sell "compliant" mustard yellow heads.

KAITLYN LAWES: I'm happy it happened. I think controversy is good. I'm glad that we pushed the limits to see how far we can go, and then we had to take a look and figure out what we actually wanted sweeping to do. It actually brought the curlers closer together after a few heated arguments by some. I think we're now headed in the right direction because of it.

BRAD JACOBS: I'm happy with the way it is now, it's back to normal. I feel like our sweepers have an advantage again, where when all that was going on, I felt we didn't have that advantage that we were used to. I feel like we have our weapons back.

It's nice to see a rock come down the ice naturally, and it curls naturally. Like what your eye is used to, what you've seen your whole life.

GLENN HOWARD: The whole year, I wish we could write it right off. Totally disappointed in the fact that it came to that. But thank God we did. I honestly believe had we not blown the whistle, or the other players didn't bring it up, that we might be in a disastrous situation.

LORI OLSON-JOHNS: It's like those guys who boycotted the Brier. Look at what that did for the sport. So yeah, it was a painful experience. I'm sure it wasn't fun to be sitting on the sidelines, but in the end it did wonders for the sport.

BEN HEBERT: We got it mostly figured out but for curling to never have rules and equipment regulations in 2016 was fucking crazy. I look back and I can't believe this had never happened. Just like, before our time, or anyone's time, how did this not come up? But hey, I'm glad it's dealt with and done and now we can move forward and just play.

BRAD GUSHUE: So it was it was an interesting year. Definitely not something I want to go through again because there was a lot of animosity amongst the teams, a lot of name-calling which was so unnecessary. For the team that used this product for the years before, it was within the rules. Why wouldn't you do that? I'm not sure. Like I said, we had that conversation and we decided to go a different direction but that doesn't mean that what they did was wrong.

In the seasons that followed, rules have been formalized, fences and friendships have been mended, and for the most part, sweeping went back to the old ways (albeit with new fabric). Curling can now look forward to a period of relative calm, as athletes prepare for 2022 and beyond.

HOW I MET CHELSEA CAREY

I have no idea how I met Chelsea Carey. Like most of these interview subjects, our paths have crossed many times.

I recall meeting her at the 2013 Roar of the Rings in Winnipeg, the Sick Kids Charity Bonspiel in Toronto, a few Slams, a bonspiel, a summer camp... and somewhere along the way we became friends on Facebook.

Over the past few years, I've interviewed her a handful of times for Curling Canada articles, and other times, we've had a drink or two, usually with our mutual friend Colin Hodgson. One year, they came with me to the Finals Night party at my home club, the Royals in Toronto, just because they were in town and it seemed like fun.

I ran into Chelsea at Camp Carruthers at the Granite Club in Winnipeg and she agreed to the interview. It didn't happen until months later during the Players' Championship in Toronto. We went to my favourite pub, across the street from the Mattamy Athletic Centre at Maple Leaf Gardens, where the event was being played.

CHAPTER 10:
CLOSING TIME

Just like we needed a place to begin, we need a place to end. These interviews all took place over the 2017-2018 season, some before the Trials and Olympics, and some after. Any curling fan will tell you that Canada didn't get the results we wanted or expected in Korea, but I'll defy anyone who argues that we sent the wrong teams.

As a country with so much depth, the Trials format is the only fair way to decide the honour of wearing the Maple Leaf. The strength of field is always much higher than at the actual Olympics. If you can win the Trials, you certainly deserve to be our representative. And as it stood, the teams we sent to Korea were, without question, among the best in the world and deserved their shots.

We don't have the space to break down the 2018 Olympics. Perhaps I'll start there if I ever decide to write a "Volume II." I know my American friends Matt Hamilton and Tyler George would love to talk about their gold-medal run with John Shuster. Their performance, and ensuing exposure will help boost the profile of the sport in the United States, and that will be great for the game.

What it is safe to say, from a Canadian perspective, is that our four-player teams didn't have their best weeks in Korea, and that other countries are getting really good, too. There are now a lot of countries with amazing athletes, development programs, and fully funded teams. It's getting much harder for the "semi-pro" Canadians to win all the time. There will no doubt be changes to the Canadian model in the years to come. That would likely be another chapter of "Volume II."

As for Mixed Doubles, we didn't really touch on that in this book either. This will be a huge area of growth, especially in international markets where you might have trouble recruiting whole teams. Already the Mixed Doubles World Championships host 40 countries, and that number is growing constantly.

If there is to be a Volume II, I might have to rewind a little bit further. There was the dramatic Pat Simmons draw to the button to win the Brier in 2015. There was Craig Savill's battle with cancer and his emotional return to the ice at his hometown Ottawa Brier in 2016, There was the ridiculous Homan versus. Englot Scotties final in 2017, one of the most entertaining games of curling that I've ever watched. There was the most exciting draw to the eight-foot ever in St. John's as Brad Gushue won his first Brier after a dozen attempts, and then won it again the following year. More than 10 years after his Olympic gold, now they're the best team in the world? Jennifer Jones won another Scotties in 2018, and another World title, and has a team lined up for another four-year run. Teams everywhere have re-tooled for another Olympic cycle.

There is simply too much to include in this volume. All the people interviewed were so gracious with their comments and with their time, that I could have easily filled a hundred more pages. But for now, I think the bulk of this story is told, and we've brought the casual curling fans up to date, and made them familiar enough with the current state of the game.

Of course, for all of the things I chose to leave out, there is almost just as much that I was told to leave out. I heard some incredible stories from almost all my interview subjects about things I'm not at liberty to share. Just rest easy knowing that even though these people are finely-tuned athletes with nerves of steel, they still find some time to unwind.

If you ever find yourself in the company of any of these individuals, they'll likely be happy to share some stories from their life in curling, and maybe even some of the tales they've asked me not to print.

I sincerely thank all of the people involved for their time and contributions, and look forward to crossing paths for many years to come.

Cheers!
And good curling.

Made in the USA
Columbia, SC
11 November 2018